A HOUSE OF ONE'S OWN

A House of One's Own

The Moral Economy of Post-Disaster Aid in El Salvador

ALICIA SLIWINSKI

McGill-Queen's University Press
Montreal & Kingston • London • Chicago

ISBN 978-0-7735-5291-3 (cloth)
ISBN 978-0-7735-5292-0 (paper)
ISBN 978-0-7735-5293-7 (ePDF)
ISBN 978-0-7735-5294-4 (ePUB)

Legal deposit first quarter 2018
Bibliothèque nationale du Québec

Printed in Canada on acid-free paper that is 100% ancient forest free (100% post-consumer recycled), processed chlorine free

This book has been published with the help of a grant from the Canadian Federation for the Humanities and Social Sciences, through the Awards to Scholarly Publications Program, using funds provided by the Social Sciences and Humanities Research Council of Canada.

Funded by the Government of Canada | Financé par le gouvernement du Canada | Canada | Canada Council for the Arts | Conseil des arts du Canada

We acknowledge the support of the Canada Council for the Arts, which last year invested $153 million to bring the arts to Canadians throughout the country.

Nous remercions le Conseil des arts du Canada de son soutien. L'an dernier, le Conseil a investi 153 millions de dollars pour mettre de l'art dans la vie des Canadiennes et des Canadiens de tout le pays.

Library and Archives Canada Cataloguing in Publication

Sliwinski, Alicia, 1969–, author
A house of one's own: the moral economy of post-disaster aid in El Salvador/Alicia Sliwinski.

Includes bibliographical references and index.
Issued in print and electronic formats.
ISBN 978-0-7735-5291-3 (cloth). – ISBN 978-0-7735-5292-0 (paper). – ISBN 978-0-7735-5293-7 (ePDF). – ISBN 978-0-7735-5294-4 (ePUB)

1. El Salvador Earthquakes, El Salvador, 2001. 2. Earthquake relief – Moral and ethical aspects – El Salvador. 3. Humanitarian assistance – Moral and ethical aspects – El Salvador. I. Title.

HV600.2001S65 2018 363.34'95097284 C2017-906174-7
C2017-906175-5

This book was typeset by Marquis Interscript in 10.5/13 Sabon.

Contents

Tables and Figures

TABLES

FIGURES

Acknowledgments

This book is about gestures of giving in post-disaster humanitarian configurations. It is a substantially revised version of my doctoral dissertation, written in French for the Anthropology Department of the Université de Montréal. Although the initial manuscript was completed over a decade ago, the trope of the gift in moral economies of aid continues to resonate and be pertinent in today's world. Since then, a wide group of people whom I wish to thank have encouraged me to pursue this project.

First, I extend special thanks to my doctoral supervisor, Dr Pierre Beaucage, with whom I discovered the joys of anthropological scholarly reflection. His lasting friendship is meaningful to me, and this work is a testimony to the important role he has played in my intellectual trajectory.

Jonathan Crago, editor-in-chief at McGill-Queen's University Press, has trusted in this project ever since I first presented it to him. I thank him for his encouragement and vision. It has been a pleasure to bring this work to completion. I also thank the two anonymous reviewers of the manuscript for their very thoughtful and supportive comments. I am grateful to Robert Lewis for his invaluable attention to detail while copy editing the final version of the manuscript and to Ryan Van Huijstee, Kathleen Fraser, and Pooja Sen for their help at McGill-Queen's University Press. I also thank Anna-Marie Larsen for her work on the index.

I would like to express my heartfelt gratitude to long-time friends who have stood by me through the ups and downs of writing and life. Drs Anne-Marie Colpron, Ersy Contogouris, Isabelle Duplessis, and Tanya Richardson have been unwavering in their conviction about the value of my work. They are amazing, smart, witty, and caring women who pushed me when I was in doubt and who extended their strength when unexpected events stalled me.

Very special thanks go to Dr Ersy Contogouris, who revised the penultimate version of the manuscript with her keen eyes and sharp mind, and to Dr Tanya Richardson and Dr Derek Hall for their judicious comments on a preliminary version of the initial chapters. My gratitude also goes to Drs Patricia Elliot, Alex Latta, and Katherine Roberts, who have continually supported me in this endeavour.

Family is important to me and extends beyond strict parental ties. Pierrette Désy, Gerda Frank, Raymonde Meunier, and Geneviève Rigal are strong and wise women who have given me affection and support over many years. I feel most privileged to have received their love and guidance.

When I moved to Waterloo in 2006 to accept a position in the Global Studies Department at Wilfrid Laurier University, I was propelled into a stimulating milieu. Although it is often a challenge to balance research with increasing administrative duties, I feel fortunate to have colleagues who value the importance of nurturing a collegial environment. I thank them for making Global Studies a great place to be an academic. This research was supported by Wilfrid Laurier University and the Social Sciences and Humanities Research Council.

This book would not exist if not for the families in El Salvador who welcomed me into their lives. I thank them for their ongoing friendship. It carries great significance for me to have kept these ties over the years in ways that extend beyond the customary parameters of ethnographic travel. Seeing how a once dust-laden post-disaster reconstruction site has been taken over by luscious greenery, and how new generations now call this place home, renders my fieldwork experience all the more meaningful.

Finally, I want to thank the love of my life, Juergen Frank. You are my anchor and my home.

A HOUSE OF ONE'S OWN

INTRODUCTION

Disasters in the *Valle de las Hamacas*

"The ground trembled as if a fleet of heavy trailer trucks was passing through." This is how Rosa, a twenty-six-year-old disaster victim, described the earthquake that shook the Salvadoran municipality of Lamaria on the morning of 13 January 2001.[1] In this region traversed by fault lines, the ground moved in all directions, and the sound was deafening. Exactly one month later, on 13 February, a second earthquake struck. Telluric tremors are common in El Salvador, which is sometimes called *el valle de las hamacas* (the valley of the hammocks) to describe the frequency of seismic activity in the region. Rosa was a disaster-stricken *damnificada* (victim). The adobe house she rented on the outskirts of town was severely damaged, and the earthquakes left her with very little. Like many other families who lost their homes, Rosa was also a *beneficiaria*, an official beneficiary of humanitarian aid. Although they were not mega-disasters, the impact of the two seismic events was serious enough for the country to declare a state of emergency and appeal to the international community for humanitarian assistance. And although there is no denying the sense of loss, bewilderment, and tragedy that surrounded this dramatic event, it is also important to realize that the disaster led to new possibilities, especially through the establishment of organized local humanitarian response initiatives. International humanitarian aid comes mostly through multilateral and bilateral channels and through large transnational nongovernmental organizations (NGOs) known for their expertise in emergency response. Most of these organizations are often already present in a given country, where they are undertaking development projects and programs. This was the case in El Salvador, where NGOs such as the Cooperative for Assistance and Relief Everywhere (CARE), World Vision, Oxfam, and Save the Children, to name a few, were already on the ground. After the earthquakes, they shifted their efforts first to emergency response and then to reconstruction initiatives. Prior to the earthquakes, however, no foreign NGO had ever visited Lamaria. The encounters between humanitarian actors, local institutions, and over 3,000 affected people were therefore entirely new.

This book charts the lived experiences of the people who received and gave humanitarian aid in Lamaria after this catastrophic event. It explains what different gestures meant to individuals who were directly involved in humanitarian transactions, focusing on how they engaged with humanitarian activities and moralities, whether on the side that provided aid or on the side that received it. It considers the manner in which three different modalities of aid entailed specific gestures and relationships between donors and receivers: (1) immediate local responses, (2) food aid, and (3) a participatory housing reconstruction project. I call these modalities humanitarian configurations to stress that they were special arrangements of resources, values, and roles. Although they took place at different moments, they were connected to each other and are treated here as related fields of action; each was part of a wider totality of what is commonly called a post-disaster humanitarian response.

The configuration I discuss at greatest length is the post-disaster reconstruction project, for this is where I undertook extended fieldwork between 2001 and 2002. The two configurations that precede it provide important contextual elements required to better appreciate people's prior experiences with humanitarian aid in Lamaria.

An important lens through which to analyze these configurations is that of the gift. In discussions surrounding each configuration, the notion of the *giving* of aid recurred. It informed people's positions and helped to define their relationships as givers or receivers of humanitarian transactions, or even as bystanders. In other words, the category of gift was an important tool with which to frame the various localized humanitarian undertakings. Each configuration included some people and excluded others, and each foregrounded a distinctive logic of giving – or of helping – where expectations of reciprocity and return were either present or absent, as well as accepted, negotiated, or downright contested. Although these events occurred over a decade ago, the humanitarian encounters that are described here are not dissimilar to those that have happened since then, nor to those that will surely unfold again. I hope the story of the people whose lives are at the centre of this book will offer a renewed appreciation of gifting matters in humanitarian contexts, for they continue to give meaning to the everyday moral economy of humanitarianism (Fassin 2011a, 2011b, 2011c).

For many Lamarienses, the experience of humanitarian action was multifaceted. Ramona and Ana, two women with whom I talked regularly, were single mothers who had nowhere to live in the immediate aftermath of the January earthquake. They slept a few nights in the street with their children – as did hundreds of people – fearing potential aftershocks. During those initial days, aid came in localized forms, from concerned individuals, neighbours, and kin members. These gestures were not part of the official humanitarian response, yet they mobilized relationships in which giving gestures were part of pre-existing social networks. This is the first configuration I address.

Ramona and Ana did not stay in the street for long. They took shelter in one of the three temporary encampments for the homeless built by Doctors Without Borders/Médecins Sans Frontières (MSF), where they stayed for four months, receiving food aid from a group of local nuns. The manner in which food aid was organized in Lamaria had its own particular social logic. The nuns' reflections, for instance, on their role and responsibilities in relation to food aid raised the moral and ethical dimensions of their religious calling. This constitutes the second humanitarian configuration.

Five months after the earthquake, a hundred families – including those of Ana, Ramona, and Rosa – were selected by the German Red Cross to participate in a permanent housing reconstruction project called La Hermandad. This project was among the most comprehensive of its kind at the time: it aimed to provide landless "vulnerable" groups with private property while seeking to lay the material basis of a new community, empower women, and distribute financial aid to local institutions that had suffered from the earthquake. According to the tenets of community participation, all beneficiaries were expected to contribute to construction work in order to receive a house. This project is the third humanitarian configuration and the one I address in more detail in chapters 3 to 6. In this case, the notions of participation and community were woven into a discursive "assemblage" (Ong and Collier 2004) that defined the project in terms of a non-monetary exchange. But at times, the project was also described in terms of a gift from strangers, thereby muddying the lines of its conceptual framework and generating conflicting judgments from its "beneficiaries." Ultimately, the earthquake and its aftermath transformed Ana, Rosa, and Ramona from landless disaster victims into new homeowners. The path from one status to the other was marked by different activities, encounters, and expectations in which the gift, participation, and community mixed differently to frame humanitarian activities.

"El desastre nos dio oportunidades" (The disaster gave us opportunities), explained Rosa one day while we were chatting at the housing reconstruction site. She meant that since the fateful day of 13 January, a lot had happened: along with other disaster victims, she had been given shelter for six months by MSF; she had received weekly food rations distributed by a group of local nuns; and in May 2001 she had been selected to participate in the housing reconstruction project, thanks to which she would become a homeowner for the first time in her life. The humanitarian encounter had led her to an unforeseen outcome, namely that of gaining access to a house and a land title, something that local institutional actors and ordinary townsfolk considered a rather sizable humanitarian "gift." Indeed, judgments on the generosity or stinginess of humanitarian aid were not taboo subjects. On the contrary, different modalities of aid were regularly compared and evaluated, receiving contrasting appraisals depending on people's beliefs regarding national and transnational donors.

AFFORDING GENEROSITY

"It's only when a calamity strikes that you can afford to be generous," I was told a few weeks after the February earthquake by Don Rodolfo, an adjunct to the mayor of Lamaria, recently elected in a campaign won by the Frente Farabundo Martí para la Liberación Nacional (FMLN).[2] For over a month, El Salvador's misfortunes had been making international headlines, and the fleet of humanitarian actors was now fully launched. NGOs had identified their respective initiatives in various areas of the country, trying to avoid duplicating their efforts while ensuring "donor visibility" in the most affected locales. By then, most of the debris had been cleared off the streets of Lamaria, and MSF's three temporary shelter camps were fully operational. Don Rodolfo and I were sitting in a *comedor* (diner), sipping instant coffee. He was explaining how his town – like so many other municipalities – had not been prepared to face the impact of the earthquakes. There was barely an emergency plan in place when the new administration had taken office the previous year. For years, the municipality had lacked the funds necessary to train personnel and establish clear guidelines for emergency situations. "This is how we depend on the generosity of foreign countries," complained Don Rodolfo. "They remember us only when calamity strikes."

With a sweeping hand gesture meant to cover the entire district, Don Rodolfo was telling me that the makeshift houses in the countryside had no chance of sustaining the shocks of the earthquakes and that there was rampant poverty in the region, even if national macroeconomic indicators noted steady improvements. He condemned the endemic polarization between the left-wing and right-wing political groups in Lamaria – a situation that also described the national political landscape. To his mind, the mistrust that this polarization engendered prevented any "development gains" from lasting.

Don Rodolfo was adamant: he did not want me to think that he was ungrateful for the arrival of foreign assistance when it was so direly needed; rather, his stance reflected a critique that I also heard from representatives of Salvadoran NGOs, namely that it takes a disaster of some magnitude for solidarity with the Salvadoran people to manifest itself. What Don Rodolfo intimated was that strangers manifest their generosity when a calamity strikes, when innocent lives are lost due to a "natural" (apparently non-political) event. Under "normal" circumstances, the generosity of distant donors – whether institutional or individual – is less profuse. His comments resonate with Luc Boltanski's (1999) critique of the "politics of pity," a politics that is triggered when singular images of distant suffering others or destroyed neighbourhoods prompt concerned citizens to donate from the safety of their homes. For Don Rodolfo, distant donors' humanitarian giving did not amount to *real* solidarity, where he understood "real" as meaning a politically informed and sustained expression of support (of the kind the FMLN had enjoyed during the armed conflict).

Don Rodolfo wished for a more enduring relationship with foreign donors, not one that had been sparked by a disaster and that would then dwindle in its aftermath. Post-disaster humanitarian missions such as the one in Lamaria, however, are generally not mandated to produce long-term social change. This is something that development aid is meant to do. The agreed-upon purpose of humanitarian aid is to alleviate immediate suffering in an emergency by protecting victims and providing basic needs such as shelter, food, and medical assistance. It can extend into rehabilitation and reconstruction initiatives, but the traditional mandate of humanitarian assistance is not to stay lastingly in a given place. Of course, many exceptions come to mind, such as the Palestinian refugee camps established after the 1948 Arab-Israeli conflict and those of Dadaab and Kakuma built in the early 1990s. There are many places in the world where humanitarian operations have been ongoing for decades. This is especially true in the case of population displacements due to war and conflict, a well-studied topic that falls outside the scope of this book. It is worth noting, moreover, that there has been a change in orientation in recent years toward better connecting humanitarian endeavours to sustainable development outcomes.[3]

Although Don Rodolfo lamented that the generosity of humanitarianism is often too short-lived, not all shared his critique. Don Rodolfo was a *político* (politician). His perspective on humanitarian aid differed from Maria Julia's and from that of other institutional actors involved in the humanitarian response, such as the nuns who were entrusted with the logistics of food aid, the representatives of the local Health Clinic and Red Cross who competed with each other over donor funding, or the project managers who supervised the La Hermandad housing reconstruction project. This book explores the ways that local groups and individuals occupying different positions in a changing humanitarian landscape made sense, through their moral frameworks, of their roles within different humanitarian configurations. It traces their involvement in different configurations of humanitarian aid, from emergency to reconstruction. Time and again, Lamarienses from various walks of life with whom I conversed about the disaster, the emergency, and the role of humanitarianism evoked the notion of the gift. But this did not come without its paradoxes, contradictions, and frustrations. This ethnography shows how moral representations of humanitarianism varied and how ideas about giving circulated, crystallized, and were also reified in this post-disaster setting.

It is important to realize that moral frameworks are not monolithic systems; they are neither rigid grids nor static performative scripts that people follow, true to form, once and for all. Furthermore, although gifting may have been a dominant trope for disaster victims in Lamaria, it did not stand alone, because the deployment of humanitarian activities – especially during reconstruction – harnessed other guiding principles, such as those of community building and participation. Together, the gift, community, and participation formed a conceptual apparatus that defined a series of humanitarian gestures and oriented the moral narratives that framed them.

THE 2001 EARTHQUAKES IN THE FIELD OF DISASTER STUDIES

Since the time of my fieldwork, the world has witnessed harrowing disasters that glued people to their television screens. These disasters have names such as Irma, Katrina, Sandy, or Haiyan, or they are referred to by geographical location, as with the Haiti and Nepal earthquakes and the South-Asian tsunami. These spectacular events overshadow the dozens of smaller-scale disasters that shatter people's lives every year. In those instances, whether the caravan of transnational humanitarian experts arrives on site depends on a series of factors. In many parts of the now-called Global South, national governments have yet to fully build their capacity to respond to such emergencies. This was the case in El Salvador in 2001. The humanitarian response that ensued was of a particular kind, in the sense that the disaster was a "natural" one and that national authorities welcomed international aid. The crisis was not a "complex emergency," a term that describes a combination of natural and manmade causes where violence and warfare, massive population displacements, and famine or epidemics create a difficult political and security environment. This is not to say that natural disasters are devoid of politics or manmade catalyzing forces.

On the contrary, over the past decades, considerable research on disasters has enriched our understanding of their multifaceted and multiscalar dimensions. Moreover, saying that a disaster is solely a *natural* event is somewhat misleading unless it occurs in a remote and uninhabited locale affecting no one – but then it would not be seen as a disaster since the notion of disaster implies a human component (which is quite an anthropocentric point of view). A disaster is about the human failure to adequately manage risks. Undoubtedly, disasters are complex systems, now compounded by the effects of climate change, and they cannot be understood without taking into account the development models that countries adopt and pursue. The United Nations International Strategy for Disaster Reduction (UNISDR n.d.) defines a disaster as "a serious disruption of the functioning of a community or a society involving widespread human, material, economic or environmental losses and impacts, which exceeds the ability of the affected community or society to cope using its own resources." It continues, "disasters are often described as a result of the combination of: the exposure to a hazard; the conditions of vulnerability that are present; and insufficient capacity or measures to reduce or cope with the potential negative consequences."

After the two earthquakes in 2001, El Salvador found itself in a state of emergency, with 1,159 people dead, 8,200 people injured, more than 150,000 houses destroyed, and another 185,000 damaged to various degrees, as were 32 hospitals, 121 health centres, and 1,556 schools. This represented 40 per cent of the health sector and 30 per cent of the education sector (Romano and Acevedo 2001). The total economic losses amounted to US$1.604 billion. Could the scenario have been different? The losses fewer? These questions were not difficult to answer for the forty NGO representatives I met or for the journalists and academics who commented on the earthquakes at the time. For all, it was an unequivocal yes.

Although science explains natural phenomena, understanding disasters comprehensively requires a broader approach, one that includes the social sciences. In 2001 this integrative perspective was becoming increasingly prominent, and the rallying cry that characterized disaster studies became "los desastres no son naturales" (disasters are not natural). To be fair, social studies of disasters had begun in the 1940s with the work of geographer Gilbert White (1974), as well as further developed in the 1960s with the research of Russell Dynes, Enrico Quarantelli, and Gary Kreps (1972) on the sociology of disasters. Although their work was central, it did not have as much of an impact in Central America as the contributions of Frederick Cuny (1983) or Ian Davis (1981), which were translated into Spanish.[4] The writings of Kenneth Hewitt (1983) and Ben Wisner and colleagues (1977) also had a significant influence in Central America, as elsewhere. The earthquakes in Peru (1970), Nicaragua (1972), Guatemala (1976), Colombia (1983), Mexico (1985), and El Salvador (1986), as well as the effects of El Niño, which were particularly challenging in 1982–83, prompted researchers to consider anew the social aspects of disasters. It is ironic that it was during the 1980s, "lost decade of development," that Latin American research on disasters gained momentum.

By 2001, when the earthquakes hit El Salvador, experts agreed on the importance of understanding the relationship between disasters and development in order to better prevent and mitigate the devastating effects of disasters.[5] El Salvador's development history created various political, economic, environmental, and social conditions of risk. The political economy of the nation had forced endemically poor and marginalized people to migrate to urban centres, where they had established themselves on steep volcanic slopes in shanty and unsafe dwellings (called *quebradas* in the capital region), thus incurring a greater risk of loss when a hazard of some magnitude occurred. An underlying theme that resurfaced during my talks with Salvadoran NGO officials was that the disaster's victims had been the "collateral damage" of the macro-economic model of development that the government was implementing – the neoliberal agenda of privatization, liberalization, and deregulation. Writing about the poor, Alan Lavell (1999) states, "the vulnerability they suffer ends up being the 'necessary' and supposedly 'non-structural' result of someone else's adequate growth and development policy."

Today, the field of disaster risk reduction, which includes capacity building to strengthen the resilience of communities, is well established. But in 2001 there was a tendency to foreground technical considerations over social ones when working on disaster reduction or response. Mainstream focus was on infrastructure – an approach to disaster response that Hewitt (1983) described as "physicalist" and technocratic[6] – and the emphasis was less on resilience and more on vulnerability.[7] Understanding a society's vulnerability to disaster was a key issue being addressed by researchers and practitioners in the field. The lesson they put forth was that so-called natural disasters are outcomes of social and historical processes; in other words, they have manmade origins linked to the development trajectory of societies and communities.

The earthquakes came on the heels of the devastation wrought by Hurricane Mitch a mere three years earlier, where the losses amounted to at least US$6 billion for the region. Insofar as it was a highly mediatized event, it showed the world the extent to which Central American countries such as Honduras and Nicaragua (the two most affected ones) were unprepared. Three years after Mitch, El Salvador still did not have a sufficient disaster response, neither at the national level nor at the municipal one. It could be argued that in such a limited amount of time the Salvadoran government could not have fully developed and implemented such measures. But scholars such as Ben Wisner (2001) have argued that the Salvadoran government failed to apply the "lessons learned" from Mitch and that its commitment to implementing programs of disaster risk reduction proved to be nothing more than lip service since no real measures were taken.

Since then, various international protocols regarding disaster risk reduction have been developed. The 2005 Hyogo Framework of Action, endorsed by 168 countries at the World Conference on Disaster Reduction held in Kobe, Japan, aimed to guide nations to better reduce losses and impacts caused by disasters. In one way, the Hyogo Framework of Action achieved its aim, and in another way, it did not. Alan Lavell and Andrew Maskrey (2013) explain the paradox in a report to the United Nations highlighting the key challenges of disaster risk reduction, saying that mortality due to hydrometeorological events like cyclones and hurricanes has decreased but that livelihood and economic losses due to geological hazards like earthquakes and tsunamis have increased.

The issue of vulnerability also received continued critical analysis in the wake of the various disasters that marked the past decade (Esnard and Sapat 2014; Phillips and Fordham 2010), especially in light of growing mega-urban settlements and the impacts of climate change (Tanner and Horn-Phathanothai 2014). One important issue is finding ways of curbing the creation of new risks, beyond the mitigation of identified ones. Experts have called on policymakers and governments to adopt an adaptive, forward-thinking approach that is inclusive of different local cultures of risk reduction (Dekens 2007; Mercer et al. 2010; Shaw, Sharma, and Takeuchi 2009). Hewitt, Lavell, Maskrey, Wisner, and many others advocated decades ago that a change of paradigm was needed – one that fully acknowledged the fact that disasters were not foreign or exogenous events that disturbed the working of "normal" economies and societies. Although this message was far from novel even then, they argued that it had still not made sufficient headway in the national and international governance structures that deal with disasters – a situation that continues today. What this entails, then, is that socially constructed disasters will continue to dramatically affect the lives of people and mobilize the humanitarian response industry. Explaining how Salvadoran risks were compounded over time through the production of vulnerability is what the next section addresses.

VULNERABILITY IN THE *LONGUE DURÉE*: ELEMENTS OF SALVADORAN HISTORY

As is the case with all other disasters, the Salvadoran crisis lay at the nexus of two converging forces: processes generating vulnerability and a natural hazard. In their book *At Risk: Natural Hazards, People's Vulnerability, and Disasters*, Piers Blaikie and colleagues (1994) stress that vulnerability should be understood in the *longue durée* and analyzed according to the spatial and temporal distance between a given process and a group of people. Here, vulnerability refers to the characteristics of a person or a group and to the manner in which one's situation influences one's capacity to anticipate, cope with, and recover from the impact of a natural hazard. Vulnerability can be decomposed into different causally related temporal configurations that lead to a disaster.[8]

In anthropology the seminal work of Anthony Oliver-Smith and Suzanna Hoffman (1999, 2001) has used the lens of political ecology to explain that disasters, whether natural or technological, cannot be understood without taking into account the constitutive mutuality between society and environment. Disasters do not occur on their own but over time, born out of a given socio-cultural context in a biophysical milieu. Thus vulnerability is also an unfolding process at the crossroads of society, culture, and environment that reveals the exploitative structures that predate the event.[9] In this perspective, vulnerability is a political concept, but it is always mediated by culture. Oliver-Smith (2004, 10) describes vulnerability as "the conceptual nexus that links the relationship that people have with their environment to social forces and institutions and the cultural values that sustain or contest them."

Vulnerability in El Salvador can be traced back to colonial times. At the beginning of the colony in the early sixteenth century, the Salvadoran population – the Pipil and the Lencas – numbered approximately 116,000 to 130,000 inhabitants, according to conservative estimates (Martínez 1996, 49).[10] The Pipil were closer to the Aztecs and spoke Nahuatl. The Lencas resided west of the Lempa

River, which divides northern and southern El Salvador, and had descended from the Mayas. The Pipil named their land Cuscatlán, which means "land of the jewel" or "land of precious jewels." Today, one of the country's departments is called Cuscatlán, and Salvadorans frequently use the term to evoke their native land, calling themselves *cuscatlecos*.

The Indigenous populations were rapidly vanquished (like elsewhere in Mesoamerica) in the colonial enterprise initiated in 1524 by Pedro de Alvaro and his brother Diego, both under the orders of Hernan Cortés. By 1539 El Salvador had become part of the Spanish-run Captaincy General of Guatemala.[11] The spoils of war were not gold but land – a very rich and arable land. The pre-Hispanic populations generally lived in valleys nestled in volcanic mountain chains. These *tierras de humedad* (humid lands), which remain fertile due to the volcanic ash of lava deposits, were highly prized, especially for agriculture. The colonial regime imposed itself quickly and limited Indigenous collective ownership of land to the immediate vicinity of villages. Spaniards created *haciendas*, large privately held estates, designed for grazing and for the cultivation of indigo. The transformed relationship to land tenure and the impact of export agriculture on the ecosystem in the form of increased deforestation constitute important factors that explain Salvadoran vulnerability to disasters. The gradual settlement of colonists had changed people's vulnerability to risks.

Central America is prone to volcanic eruptions because it rests along the volcanic "ring of fire."[12] Geologists have identified four major systems, each made up of numerous fault lines, that crisscross El Salvador.[13] Indigenous societies were relatively well adapted to seismic activity. The majority lived in wooden houses, with walls made of dried cornstalks and roofs made of straw or palm leaves. But this changed with colonization. Some studies suggest that the adaptability of Indigenous Mesoamerican societies was a function of their "degree of complexity." Payson Sheets (1999) undertook a comparative analysis between small egalitarian and stratified societies' respective vulnerability and resistance to risk of volcanic eruption. He explained that the more a society is hierarchical, centralized, demographically significant, and dependent on an integrated agricultural economy, the less it is able to withstand the negative impacts of eruptions. Conversely, smaller, less dense, and more egalitarian societies can more readily relocate themselves and cultivate crops anew when such events occur. However, studies on pre-Hispanic Andean people nuance this conclusion. Indeed, the Inca Empire was located in a highly seismic zone. To better mitigate the risk of earthquakes, the Inca developed various strategies: they built granaries and warehouses throughout their territory so that scattered communities could access foodstuff, and they used straw as roofing material for their adobe and stone houses, as well as developing special masonry techniques to better withstand the impact of telluric shocks (Oliver-Smith 1995; Oliver-Smith and Hoffman 1999). According to Luís Ernesto Martínez (1996), Andean people were better prepared to face risks of natural origin than were Cuscatlán's Indigenous populations.

As a general rule, the Spaniards established themselves on the outskirts of Indigenous towns. They arrived not only with their exploitative ambitions but also with their own building techniques. By introducing brick and stone masonry in order to erect monasteries, churches, and administrative offices, the colonists were making themselves more vulnerable to earthquakes. Settlements in El Salvador were similar to other colonial towns of the Americas: narrow streets reproduced a grid-like pattern around a central plaza, and tiled instead of thatched roofs were preferred, thus increasing the risk of disaster. As Oliver-Smith (1995) has discussed for the case of Peru, Spaniards were generally ignorant of adaptive measures that allowed Indigenous societies to curtail environmental risks.

During the earthquakes of 1575, 1581, 1593, 1594, 1625, 1648, 1650, 1656, and 1671, to name only some of the major ones – at times accompanied by volcanic eruptions – colonial buildings regularly collapsed (Lardé y Larín 1978). San Salvador, which was located in the epicentre of the *valle de las hamacas*, was particularly vulnerable. In the seventeenth century, Spanish colonists began to integrate adobe into their constructions, even for more opulent buildings in the capital, which explains why there were fewer losses during the 1798 quake (Martínez 1996). Since then, adobe has become a customary building material in El Salvador.

In the nineteenth century, national authorities began to think about preventative measures. After the 1868 earthquake, President Francisco Dueñas decided to move the capital to Soyapango, and then to Cojutepeque. He laid the foundations of a new agglomeration named Santa Tecla, 12 kilometres west of San Salvador. After the 1873 earthquake, President Santiago González decreed that all new buildings should use lighter material than adobe, such as wood or corrugated iron. Gonzalez also agreed to widen the channels of Lake Ilopango, located east of San Salvador, based on the erroneous belief that elevated water planes could provoke earthquakes (Barón Castro 1942, 36). This undertaking caused massive inundations in the neighbouring area instead.

Two significant factors impacting El Salvador's vulnerability to disasters are agriculture and urban migration. Over three centuries of colonial rule, the Spanish consolidated commercial and export agriculture, completely altering the environment and the modalities of land tenure.[14] Resistance from Indigenous and Ladino communities led to the Nonualco Revolt of 1833, which was crushed by government forces (White 1973). Around this time, immigrants from Europe introduced new agricultural and commercialization techniques, which facilitated crop diversification away from indigo and sugarcane. The introduction of coffee cultivation in 1846 by Eugenio Aguilar marks a turning point in El Salvador's political-economic history and in its vulnerability to environmental disasters. The indigo market was declining due to the introduction of artificial dyes, whereas the cultivation of coffee projected important economic gains. But it radically transformed land occupancy since it led to the establishment of large private estates of arable land, called *fincas*. Contrary to indigo, which can grow almost anywhere, coffee grows best in high altitudes ranging from 450 to 600 metres on mountain slopes. This is where villages would have kept their communal form of land ownership.[15] Furthermore, tending a coffee *finca* requires a large contingent of seasonal manpower and substantial start-up capital. Neither peasants nor small farmers could afford the initial investment to participate in this new capitalist venture. Thus the cultivation of coffee became the prerogative of the rich. It also became the motor of economic development.

From the oligarchy's perspective, the greatest impediment to coffee exports was the continuation of an "archaic and obsolete" mode of land ownership. The best way to ensure productivity and profits was to have private property all over the country. With the 1881 decrees, which applied the most drastic land reforms in Central America, dozens of municipalities and thousands of Indigenous and Ladina families were dispossessed of their communal landholdings.[16] The decrees allowed a coffee-growing elite to consolidate its power, leading to the irreversible polarization of Salvadoran society.

During the golden age of coffee production from 1880 to the Great Depression, large landholding families secured their power. They became the agro-industrial elite of the twentieth century, diversifying their investments through ventures in banking, finance, commerce, tourism, and real estate. These are some of the ancestors of what have come to be known as the fourteen ruling families of El Salvador (Paige 1993), who supported the military dictatorships from 1931 to 1979 in order to protect their assets.

The loss of communal lands, the adverse working conditions, and tensions between landowners and peasants, as well as between Indigenous and Ladinos, led to the dramatic revolt of 1932, in which thousands of peasants and Indigenous groups took up arms. Also named La Matanza (the Killing), it was actively supported by communist partisans, with Farabundo Martí as their leader. Twenty thousand died in La Matanza.[17] The country remained politically unstable: between 1931 and 1979, there were ten military dictatorships and five military-instigated coup d'états. However, it is important to underscore that the political culture of El Salvador was based on longstanding patron-client networks extending from the national level to the municipalities, which operated as a "body of unwritten rules" (Ching 2014, 337) regarding the petitioning of all sorts of political favours. Thus, despite the apparent political instability, successive governments and the military had established patronage relationships with the middle classes of rural municipalities (Ching 2004). What is called *clientelismo* (clientelism) still looms large in local affairs, even during disasters (Barrios 2014).

Nevertheless, El Salvador was on a path toward modernization. After the Second World War, large infrastructure projects such as highways, hydroelectric plants, and ports were undertaken. Workers organized into trade unions. New legislation fixed a minimum wage and established social security. There were some legislative attempts aimed at fostering social justice, but effective reforms never materialized (Grenier 1999, 39).

In the 1960s El Salvador underwent a cotton boom,[18] and what little forest remained was cut down, especially along the coastal lowlands. The socio-environmental impacts of the cotton industry increased vulnerability through the use of chemical products – pesticides, insecticides, and fertilizers – that contaminated ground water. The cotton boom also led to the migration of workers toward the Pacific region, a process that increased the number of landless peasants from 12 per cent of the population in 1960 to 40 per cent in 1970 (Álvarez and Chávez 2001, 30).

The years preceding the civil war of 1979–92 were characterized by an authoritarian political regime. The number of unions and grassroots associations was growing, but military authorities regularly repressed popular social movements. Elite social groups were organizing under various banners, notably the Asociación Nacional de la Empresa Privada (ANEP). The government established free trade zones but prohibited unions within them. It was also at this time that the infamous Organización Democrática Nacionalista (ORDEN) appeared, the paramilitary group known for its "anti-subversive" missions: executions, torture, disappearances, and intimidation of union leaders and other "leftist" groups.[19]

A social upheaval seemed imminent. The disparity of wealth, evidenced by the distribution of land, was flagrant: the richest 20 per cent of the population earned 65 per cent of the income, whereas the poorest 20 per cent controlled 2 per cent of the national income (Silber 2011, 36). Popular and community-based organizations of intellectuals, students, and workers were demanding their rights. Dozens of oppositional organizations, committees, and leagues appeared, many of which came together to form the five main branches of the FMLN.[20] And in nearby Nicaragua, the 1979 Sandinista revolution was victorious. The Salvadoran revolution did not originate in the countryside but was due to the combined efforts of three institutions: the Communist Party, the universities, and the Catholic Church. The latter proposed an ideological interpretation (Marxist-Leninist) and logistical advantages, the universities allowed for middle-class individuals to mobilize, and the Church, through the teachings of liberation theology, acted as a bridge between the revolutionary intelligentsia and the popular masses in both cities and rural areas.

The history of the ensuing armed conflict is complex and falls beyond the scope of this book. Suffice it to say that after twelve years of a bloody and very violent civil war, with close to 75,000 killed, a peace accord was signed in January 1992 after lengthy deliberations and with the help of various international parties.[21] The nation embarked on a national reconstruction plan and "entered the path of 'transition' to electoral democracy" (Lauria-Santiago and Binford 2004, 1). Researchers specializing in peace processes declared at the time that the event had been a textbook success (Juhn 1998; Macías

1993; Montgomery 1995), but a few years later, the outcome was judged more ambivalently (Artiga-González 2002; Cañas and Dada 1999). Without suggesting that the circumstances in the 1980s were more enviable, there is no doubt that many Salvadorans I met also felt half-hearted, disillusioned, or bitter about the aftermath.

NOTES ON THE CONTEMPORARY SITUATION

The day I set foot in El Salvador, I met Don Manuel. He was a forty-year-old man with a heavy build and was a great fan of *pupusas*, thick handmade corn tortillas filled with beans, cheese, and chopped pork. We spent many hours in his little car driving around town while talking about my work, my country, and my "vision of God" and about his work, his country, and his vision of God! There is no doubt that religion was a recurring theme in my conversations with many individuals, although I do not delve into that subject in this book. Don Manuel was among those who found the political and economic situation worse in 2001 than during the war. Yanira, the receptionist of a small hotel where I stayed in San Salvador, shared the same opinion. So did Don Augusto, the older gentleman with whom I lived in Lamaria, and Maxwell, the coordinator of the beneficiaries of the La Hermandad housing reconstruction project. These individuals did not come from the same socio-economic background, yet they shared a similar opinion regarding the state of their nation. Don Manuel was a small entrepreneur, Yanira was a salaried worker, Don Augusto had retired from a good career as an agronomist for a tobacco company, and Maxwell was a daily worker who was often unemployed. That they all found the situation after the peace accord worse than before surprised me, but it was also telling. Of course, they did not prefer living under the threat of bombs; their statements pointed to a shared sense of disillusionment after the promises of the peace accord – a rather generalized sentiment at the time in El Salvador.

In 2002 the country commemorated the ten-year anniversary of the signing of the peace accord. The event was hardly celebrated and was instead criticized by the intelligentsia. Two large earthquakes had rocked the country the previous year, revealing the extent to which poverty persisted in the villages and municipalities of the countryside.

Today, development and economic growth depend less on agro-export and more on foreign direct investment. They also rely a lot on remittances, which are the main source of foreign currency and therefore economically significant. In 2001 El Salvador's population was 6.3 million people, and 2 million Salvadorans were living abroad. Today, it is estimated that 3 million Salvadorans live abroad. This migrant population has a significant influence on the nation's political, economic, and social life. From 1995 to 1999, remittances represented 11.9 per cent of gross domestic product. In 2000 they represented 13.3 per cent of gross domestic product. This number rose to 16 per cent in 2004 (Maldonado et al. 2009), and in 2011 it was estimated at 15.7 per cent, representing a total of US$3.6 billion (World Bank 2011).

Some say that El Salvador is "addicted" to remittances (Coutin 2007, 122). However, this source of income has not lifted Salvadorans out of poverty. In 2013 the United Nations Development Programme for El Salvador calculated that 40.7 per cent of the population still lived in poverty (PNUD 2013, 105). Inequality and inequity are still major problems, and people's overall quality of life actually seems to have decreased over recent years. This is especially true for relative poverty, which has increased in both rural and urban areas since 1980 (ibid.). If poverty remains a serious matter in El Salvador, a pressing issue is also the question of insecurity.

Violence due to organized crime has steadily increased in El Salvador since 1992. Gangs have acquired new levels of professionalism, in part due to the expulsion of gang members from Los Angeles. Mexican drug cartels have expanded into El Salvador, causing even more violence and insecurity for ordinary citizens.[22] Corruption can be found at all levels of government, so it is not an easy task for the current administration to "clean up" the streets and national institutions. In 2015 El Salvador was described as the "most violent country in the Western hemisphere," with 6,640 murders occurring in that year (Daugherty 2016). The general political and economic landscape offers few substantive remedies for those who have to cope with enduring levels of poverty and insecurity, which explains why migration to El Norte (the North) remains an attractive option for many Salvadorans, especially youth who want to escape the tentacles of the *narcos*.

Explaining vulnerability warrants considering the development history of a country. At the very least, it needs to take into account the accumulated effects of economic, political, and social factors that influence people's livelihoods and their environments. These pages present a partial review of some key events and issues that contributed to the making of Salvadoran risks and vulnerability. With this backdrop, we can better appreciate the disaster that hit Lamaria in 2001 and the ensuing humanitarian response.

LOOKING BACK: REFLEXIVE COMMENTS ON FIELDWORK

Transnational humanitarian professionals are not the only people who arrive in the wake of a disaster. The desire to help also rallies ordinary individuals wanting to provide assistance. People can engage in humanitarian giving through religious orders, for instance, which can become important players through their networks. Some may knit, weave, or make objects to be sent to faraway places – a rather discounted way in which people enact subtle yet meaningful ties between domestic "arts and crafts" and distant sufferings (Malkki 2015). Yet most choose to send a cheque to well-known NGOs that appeal to the public's generosity in times of calamity. This is by far the easiest way to help, one encouraged by many NGOs because in-kind relief is often less effective. But aside from these prevalent channels, and certainly in a less conventional manner, some people may decide to organize from the ground up and bring the aid themselves. It is an entrepreneurial kind of humanitarianism, the logistics of which are harder to set up.

The urge "to do something" was certainly strong within the Montreal Salvadoran community upon witnessing the catastrophe that hit their homeland. After the January quake, many felt extremely concerned, and some joined ad-hoc associations to provide relief to their compatriots, bypassing official aid avenues. It was with one of these associations, the committee Avec Toi Salvador Contigo, that my ethnographic journey with the people of Lamaria began. The following observations are meant not only to clarify my role as an anthropologist but also to highlight how ties were created that facilitated this particular undertaking. I had planned to conduct doctoral studies on post-Mitch reconstruction, but the Salvadoran earthquakes and my involvement with Avec Toi Salvador Contigo steered me toward a different trajectory.

In late January 2001, I attended a gathering held in an interior-decorating store on Saint-Laurent Boulevard in Montreal. Around a dozen Salvadorans were there. The intent was to discuss how aid could be given directly to the disaster victims of El Salvador. France, our energetic hostess, had gone to Honduras in 1998 after Mitch to deliver humanitarian aid firsthand. Inspired by this previous experience, she had contacted a Salvadoran church to convey her desire to help. The outcome was this first meeting. Walking on Saint-Laurent one afternoon, I had seen a poster announcing the gathering on her storefront window and had decided that this sounded like an interesting opportunity I should not miss.

Over the following weeks, and mainly due to France's connections and strong organizational skills, we registered the committee as a not-for-profit association, collected money door to door, and stockpiled all kinds of goods, primarily food, clothing, and medicine. In collaboration with the Montreal YMCA and the Centre d'Études et de Coopération Internationale (CECI), we organized a fundraising concert at Club Soda, a well-known Montreal music venue.

The choice of many Salvadorans to support or get involved in grassroots initiatives such as Avec Toi Salvador Contigo reflects their mistrust of government – that is, the Salvadoran government. Obviously, the latter was an unavoidable player with which official humanitarian agencies had to cooperate. Therefore, aid collected by NGOs (and all bilateral aid, of course) passed through Salvadoran governmental structures. For the Salvadoran migrants I met, many of whom were political refugees who had fled to Canada during the civil war, the government represented an untrustworthy entity. They wanted to make sure that *all* the aid they gathered would reach those who really needed it and not end up in the pockets of bureaucrats – hence their desire to oversee all the steps of their initiative: collecting goods and money, finding a secure means of transportation, and witnessing successful delivery. If the first step was fairly easy, the question of transportation was trickier. The Canadian Red Cross could not accept our boxes, and the cost of financing a private freight was much too high. Luckily, one of the committee members worked as a long-distance trucker. He held all the necessary papers to cross the American, Mexican, and Guatemalan borders. So he took time off and volunteered to drive the cargo down to El Salvador.

One decision we had to make was where to deliver our collected goods and money. Committee members came from various municipalities affected by the earthquake, and there was so much need that committee members thought it best to select just two areas where our modest efforts could be put to use. We drew their names out of a hat. The truck unloaded its cargo in Lamaria, one of the selected towns, in mid-February. A week later, I was there myself.

Salvadoran committee members did not necessarily want a foreigner (me) to represent them at the truck's arrival in Lamaria; in fact, someone else volunteered to go. But since I was scheduled to be in Guatemala shortly before for an academic conference, it was easy for me to take a bus to Lamaria. Once there, I could observe first-hand how a humanitarian emergency unfolds. I stayed almost a month in Lamaria, living with a family related to one of the committee members. During this time, I explored the surroundings, met various institutional actors, and helped the group of local nuns in charge of food aid deliveries in the municipality.

Following this stay, I decided to conduct extended fieldwork in Lamaria, and I returned there in October 2001 for a period of ten months. What strikes me now is that I had a unique opportunity that has not often been replicated. There are few full-length ethnographic works that squarely address the interwoven dynamics between the gift and community participation in the context of an unfolding series of humanitarian configurations from emergency to reconstruction. Michele Ruth Gamburd's (2014) rich ethnography on Sri Lanka following the tsunami of 2004 comes to mind as one example. Part of the reason for this book is precisely to bridge the gap in a way that may prove useful for educators, practitioners, and students interested in these matters. Anthropological studies on disasters and humanitarianism have become their own subfields, so research tends to fall within the literature either on disasters or on humanitarianism, and there are few studies that converse with both (Hyndman 2011). That is precisely what this book seeks to do.

In the chapters that follow, I address three humanitarian configurations that marked the main forms of humanitarian deployments in post-earthquake Lamaria. I should specify that my objective is not to pen another "ethnography about suffering" (Robbins 2013a, 454) by explaining how dominant salvational ideologies exerted forms of violence and power over individuals and groups. I could easily decry the plight of poor and vulnerable subjects in the wake of disaster, inviting the reader to empathize with them, but this would downplay the important ways in which the Lamarienses I met were actively, and sometimes quite cunningly, coping with their situation. Sure, the people whose experiences are at the centre of this book are still mostly poor, certainly compared with middle-class citizens of Canada, and they did suffer; but I do not want to reduce their lived trajectories to a structural position that says too little about the way in which they engaged in humanitarian activities and, more importantly, about their aspirations and hopes for a better future.

OVERVIEW OF CHAPTERS

Providing the theoretical grounding for this book, the first chapter considers three concepts that frame the moral economy of humanitarian aid in Lamaria from emergency to reconstruction. Each has its own *problématique* referring to a set of relations around a practice, or an object of knowledge, that needs to be scrutinized, unpacked, and explained – which, in this case, concerns humanitarianism. The key issues are those of the gift and morality. I am not the first to discuss humanitarian action through these conceptual lenses, but throughout this book I do so in a manner that exposes the multifaceted ways that they combine in a given social context as different humanitarian activities follow one another over time. One of my objectives in this chapter is to offer the reader a concise understanding of the rich anthropological literature framing these concepts, for they continue to inform the moral grammars with which groups of donors and receivers of aid interpret assigned roles and positions. As humanitarian frameworks go, it is a durable one. However, the experiential always exceeds the scripted, so categories can get blurred, which is what transpired in Lamaria.

Indeed, the tendency in the literature is to tackle the conundrums related either to gifting or to community participation but not to treat the two together. Yet people who find themselves at the receiving end of a humanitarian response cope with these matters simultaneously. The gift is not an abstract category with which to make sense of humanitarian conduct in the face of disaster. It is a lived dimension fraught with contradictions, perhaps even more so when different actors perform humanitarian roles. The gift is also relevant to the rhetoric of community participation when the latter is the preferred methodology for conducting housing reconstruction projects financed by foreign donors.

Certainly, these conceptual frameworks reflect personal choices, and other analytical ones could very well have been added to the mix. I am thinking here of Foucauldian analyses that flesh out the many ramifications of power ("bio-" and otherwise) and governmentality. These studies have been extremely effective in deciphering the ways that many brands of salvational endeavour reproduce forms of domination and population control. That biopower and governmentality were at work in La Hermandad is doubtless, but saying this is insufficient, for these forces require particular mediums and techniques through which to be operationalized. And by that I mean a set of claims, present in overarching discourses, defining concrete practices such as those I name "humanitarian configurations." "Gift," "community," and "participation" were regulatory keywords that defined both the representation of humanitarian gestures and their embodied actualization. They created affective responses as well. Indeed, people of different backgrounds talked a lot – sometimes happily and at other times acrimoniously – about shifting experiences of humanitarian giving, about the challenges of creating a new community, and about the tensions that emerged from the labour conditions of building houses.

Chapter 2 begins the ethnography. After introducing the municipality of Lamaria and reviewing the impact of the January 2001 earthquake, I discuss the first forms of assistance that took place, including the establishment of a local humanitarian response structure. I focus on the dynamics of non-official forms of aid, where gifting gestures mobilized pre-existing social networks, to then discuss the humanitarian configuration of food aid, which was led by a group of four nuns who were well known in the municipality. This chapter draws on the discussion of gifting theories covered in chapter 1.

Chapter 3 discusses overarching issues about reconstruction in Lamaria, with a particular emphasis on questions pertaining to community participation. Indeed, participatory methodologies were the preferred option for post-disaster housing projects in El Salvador. Reconstruction projects that seek to nurture relocated people's appreciation for their new collective future generally incorporate community participation as their execution methodology when building houses. An ample literature, including my work, analyzes important milestones on the multidisciplinary critique of community participation as it applies to development and humanitarian endeavours (Barenstein 2005, 2008; Cleaver 2001; Cooke and Kothari 2001; Cornwall 2008; Mosse 2003; Sliwinski 2010). Taking the case of a reconstruction initiative in Los Mangos, a settlement not far from the town centre where residents did not have to relocate, the chapter illustrates how challenges emerge when the framework of community participation is imposed on people who do not really care for it and see it as suspicious. It reveals how local expectations around reconstruction create tensions in the receiving groups targeted, especially when dealing with property rights and building methodologies. This chapter also introduces the main protagonists who represented the German Red Cross in La Hermandad and explains how their respective responsibilities mirrored conceptual orderings regarding the "social" and "physical" dimensions of reconstruction. In all, this chapter exposes how decisions are made, beneficiaries selected, projects assembled, and projections of better futures enacted through reconstruction endeavours.

Chapter 4 is an account of the daily life of the fifty families living in La Hermandad. More descriptive than analytical, it offers the reader a feeling for the place, illustrating in broad strokes how people interacted, what kind of micro-groups developed, and how work was the central activity shaping social dynamics between them. I pay particular attention to gender relations, for they proved to be significant. I also explain the concrete steps to build a house. After all, constructing houses was the principal reason the collective existed, and it was arduous work. Most social science research on post-disaster reconstruction tends to omit more technical accounts of reconstruction processes, but I wish to redress this tendency because a more phenomenological appreciation of what it takes to do to this kind of physical labour can enrich the critiques of community participation in reconstruction.

In chapter 5 I analyze what participatory work entailed in La Hermandad. In doing so, I emphasize its gendered dimension, which was a significant facet of the human relationships in the small collective. I also examine a series of conflicts arising around work activities and between the "physical" and "social" aspects of reconstruction that intensified as the project fell behind schedule. Problems were also linked to the monthly food distributions. All these issues reveal the extent to which the project's framework – anchored in a participatory execution methodology and in narratives based on giving and non-monetary exchange – did not achieve the desired result of creating a "community spirit," at least not during the time-space of reconstruction. In other words, this chapter outlines fundamental components of the moral economy of the reconstruction project and how they oscillated between figures of gift-like gestures and regimented, efficiency-driven concerns.

In the final chapter, I relate two crises that reveal what were, for some individuals, extreme challenges of everyday life in La Hermandad. I also tie together the conceptual threads that made up the economy of aid in this post-disaster humanitarian configuration. I end with my final day there, but my relationship with some of the families is enduring. I owe an immense debt of gratitude to all the people who took me into their lives for close to a year. These ongoing ties are a testimony to the joy and uniqueness of fieldwork and to the human connection we can experience in the most trying circumstances.

1

Theoretical Underpinnings: The Gift in the Moral Grammar of Humanitarianism

The reader will have noticed that I sometimes use the term "gifting" instead of "giving." Since my mother tongue is French, I probably cringe less at the sound of it than a native English speaker who may feel "utter" aversion toward its "mouth-feel" (Garber 2014) or may dislike contorting a perfectly good word for another. The term "gifting" has crept up in social media parlance, gaining increased acceptability as a go-to word in corporate marketing-speak. In this case, "gifting" implies a transactional quality that corrupts the "delight of the just-because present" and turns it into "something that is given just-because-you-have-to" (ibid.). Even the Canada Revenue Agency (n.d.) refers to "gifting and receipting" when outlining what is recognized as a gift under the law.

My reasons for using this word have less to do with its current trendiness than with my desire to emphasize the transactional qualities of humanitarian gestures over the traits that are customarily associated with the idea of making a gift – such as those of generosity, liberty, or spontaneity – without resorting to the concepts of transfer or exchange. Distributing food and building temporary tarp shelters for homeless families are not presents, nor are they the opening gestures of an exchange cycle. We can ask whether they are unrequired. In today's world, humanitarian aid is expected to materialize after a "natural" disaster; to argue the contrary would be fallacious and go against international norms. If we concur that humanitarian aid is a required transfer, can it be considered a gift? Most contemporary critiques of humanitarian action do not support this view and describe it as a one-way transaction. Yet, when we listen to the way individuals talk about their own roles and relationships in immediate humanitarian gestures, there is something occurring that exceeds the notion of one-way transactions. The gestures certainly express codified transfers from donors to receivers, but the way that people ascribe meaning to them incorporates elements – many symbolic – that the notion of transfer or exchange does not convey, including questions about gratitude, about generosity and selflessness, about recognition and appropriateness, and about expected returns or not. I refer to "gifting" because the term, although semantically related to "giving," is less forceful and thus conveys transactional characteristics more suitably.

CHARTING HUMANITARIANISM

The idea of humanitarian giving – or gifting – is pervasive in society, not only in everyday mediascapes but also in social research. Scholars have discussed the politics that shape it, the motivations that uphold it, and its effects on the ground. The "humanitarian gift" has proved a lasting trope (how many times are people invited to "give the gift of hope" by a humanitarian organization?), not least for the paradoxes it carries, which revolve around the "goodness" of aid. This does not imply equivalence, however, between the gift and institutional humanitarianism. The goal in this book is rather to tease out from people's discourses and judgments about a "fluid" situation called a "humanitarian emergency" what they mean when they refer to the notion of the gift – or to the idea of gifting.

The concepts of humanitarianism and giving are neither synonymous nor coextensive, yet they share rich philosophical traditions extending back into various religious histories. For Christians, the most outstanding exemplar of the gift is Christ's sacrifice of his own life to save humanity. Following this foundational gesture, Christian morality came to interpret life on earth as a gift from God, whose love for humankind is the source of the gift. This tradition leads to the cardinal notion of charity, which still informs much of today's humanitarian action. Christianity is not the only religious system that instructs its members to give to those in need. Similar moral teachings are found in the Islamic *zakat*, Jewish *tzedakah*, and Buddhist *dān* (Bornstein and Redfield 2007). Although each tradition holds its own cultural specificities, which are expressed in unique ethnographic contexts, we can generalize and say that a humanitarian gesture has moral undertones in that it aims to ease the pain of others. At the same time, it is important to understand that the making of modern institutional humanitarian action originated in the West and cannot be divorced from its distinctive cultural roots.

The creation of the International Committee of the Red Cross (ICRC) in 1863 and the signing of the Geneva Conventions in 1949 established the parameters of international humanitarian law. This law led to a secular form of institutionalized humanitarianism that was grounded in core principles meant to ensure the legitimacy of humanitarian actors and their independence, as well as their protection, from warring parties.[1] The ICRC, the world's flagship humanitarian organization, continues to abide by its founding principles. This is not, however, the case for all humanitarian players. The principle of neutrality has received extensive critique and reconsideration (Redfield 2011; Rieff 2002; Slim 1997, 2015; Terry 2002, 2011), notably from Doctors Without Borders/Médecins Sans Frontières (MSF), which is well known for speaking out against atrocities and human rights abuses (it describes its role as that of *témoignage*, of bearing witness) and for sometimes even shaming governments – a course of action with which not all humanitarian organizations agree (DeChaine 2005).

Around the late 1990s, after the debacles of high-profile crises such as Rwanda, Somalia, and the Balkans, a large collective of humanitarian NGOs began a process of deep self-reflection and sought to better align their missions and mandates with (at least minimum) human rights standards. One outcome was the drafting of the *Humanitarian Charter* (Sphere Project 1997) and the *Sphere Handbook* (Sphere Project 2011).[2] Although many organizations now ascribe to a rights-based humanitarianism, and there is a rich literature on the subject (Darcy 2004; Klose 2016; Orbinski 2009; Slim 1997), there are points of resistance from both within and without the humanitarian field (Bricmont 2006; Donini 2012; Forsythe 2013).[3] Many would nonetheless agree that humanitarian action now reflects a dominant worldview that Richard Rorty (1993, 112) has called "the human rights culture" – a culture that strives toward social justice while producing the ethical horizon for things we "should" and "ought to" do.

Many writings in the social sciences have challenged the virtuousness and effectiveness of the humanitarian aid "business" (Weiss 2013) by assessing the global assemblage of institutions, practices, and discourses specialized in alleviating the suffering of populations (Cahill 2003; Eade and Vaux 2007). Some have shown how contemporary humanitarian interventions, particularly those of the military humanitarianism kind, are akin to "migrant sovereignties" (Pandolfi 2003, 327) that fail to help people or defend their human rights (Chomsky 1999; Fassin and Pandolfi 2010; Weiss 2012). Others have exposed how images of suffering bodies (epitomized in the figure of a famished black orphan) are reified and how they normalize the racial politics of humanitarian operations (Razack 2007). A critique has crystallized around the multifaceted forms of violence that come from imperial charity and the universalistic stance that permeates the salvational rhetoric of humanitarian governmentality in different political and social arenas (Aaltola 2009; Forte 2014).

In the field of anthropology, studies on these matters have unsurprisingly been prolific. Anthropologists are usually guarded about grand narratives – and the interventions they uphold – that subsume the plurality of human experiences (of suffering or other states) under normative precepts. They prefer the situated space of a given ethnographic context and have found in humanitarianism a fertile field of study. In her review of the history of anthropological studies of humanitarianism since the 1980s, Miriam Ticktin (2014) outlines three periods that express different engagements between anthropological scholarship and "transnational humanitarianism." She defines the first moment as characterized by research in legal and medical anthropology. Legal anthropologists looked at the way that refugee populations and the category of the refugee itself were subjects of international law and humanitarian regimes of governance (Harrell-Bond 1986), whereas medical anthropologists focused on the figure of the suffering body. Universal suffering became an operative category that reflected the growing presence of a "global humanity" entitled to care and protection (Scheper-Hughes 2000). Near the turn of the twenty-first century, Ticktin (2014) argues, the discourse shifted toward a sharper critique that addressed the moral and political conundrums of humanitarian endeavours. It focused on the consequences of humanitarianism in three areas: spaces such as camps and detention centres (Agier 2002; Feldman 2011; Malkki 1996); people and organizations such as MSF, the International Committee of the Red Cross, and World Vision (Bornstein 2005; Redfield 2013); and events, whether disasters, epidemics, or conflicts (Petryna 2002; Vasquez Lezama 2010). Many works produced since the early 2000s have found inspiration in Michel Foucault's (1978, 1991) seminal writings on governmentality and biopower and in Giorgio Agamben's (1998) theses on states of exception and bare life. Moreover, these writings show that the very notion of "humanity" that morally grounds humanitarian action evokes contradictory claims: it appears "as both sentiment and threat – an object of care and a source of anxiety" – which leads to a hierarchization of interventions (Feldman and Ticktin 2010, 6). They point out that there is always a "hierarchy of humanity" at play, with political processes that determine the ethical and biological features of the humanity to be saved (Asad 2003). This rich scholarly production has given a new impetus to studies on morality and ethics in anthropology, particularly on the moral economy of humanitarianism (Fassin 2011a, 2011b). The third moment Ticktin (2014) defines is the current one, which encompasses the newer studies that tend to blur the neat contours of humanitarianism as a circumscribed field of practice. They address issues concerning the intersectionality of race and gender (Abu-Lughod 2013), the role of faith in today's humanitarian landscapes (Barnett and Stein 2012), or humanitarianism's linkages to development regimes (Gabiam 2012; ICRC 2015).

The present book similarly engages with overlapping logics of aid, for the politics and ethics of post-disaster reconstruction in Lamaria were not strictly about saving lives. Nor did they define a blueprint for long-term social change. Rather, they revealed a particular assemblage of rationalities that drew on both arenas, where ideas about humanitarian gifting were projected onto scenarios for a better future. In the anthropological literature on humanitarianism, post-disaster reconstruction has not figured prominently compared with other iconic spaces such as the refugee camp. Ticktin's (2014) review, for instance, does not pay much attention to reconstruction as a hybrid form of humanitarian practice. Other works, however, have engaged with such matters. For example, Vincanne Adams's (2013) ethnography *Markets of Sorrow, Labors of Faith* on New Orleans following Hurricane Katrina in 2005 presents a critical account of market-led recovery programs, including profit-driven housing initiatives that left thousands of returning residents in a state of "chronic disaster syndrome." Katrina's racialized politics have been well documented, showing how hierarchies of humanity operate in technologies of salvation (Levitt 2009; Marable and Clarke 2008). Gamburd's (2014) *The Golden Wave* examines the localized experiences of emergency and reconstruction aid in Sri Lanka after the 2004 tsunami, showing how the circulation of humanitarian gifts impacted the social status of different recipients and reshaped identities. Aid engendered ambivalence and ambiguities reflecting pre-existing socio-economic and cultural hierarchies expressed according to structures of class and gender. Gamburd relates the vernacular moral conundrums people struggled with, noting that humanitarian gifts were constantly the object of valuation in terms of whether they were appropriate or sufficient and whether people deserved them or had tried to manipulate the system. Similar issues transpired in Lamaria. People who move through consecutive interventionist regimes of "doing good" experience complementary and competing claims framing the provision of aid, yet the boundaries between them are not clear-cut, especially when both resort to specific tropes such as that of the gift.

It is not surprising, in light of this extensive critique, that the notion of the gift has been treated with circumspection. The emerging consensus is that global humanitarianism is far from a gifting system. With the exception of a few authors (Bornstein 2005, 2012; Bornstein and Redfield 2011; Hollenbach 2013; Korf et al. 2010), the stance of addressing humanitarian action through the lens of the gift is often regarded as apolitical and as running against the flow of the powerful critique that uncovers the ways humanitarian activities, politics, and moralities reproduce – or introduce – highly questionable techniques and regimes of power, including in post-disaster contexts (Adams 2013; Adams, Van Hattum, and English 2009; Gunewardena 2008a; Klein 2007; Schuller 2015). Here are cautionary tales about disaster capitalism's propensity to find economic opportunity where others suffer. Reference to the gift is then viewed as a smokescreen that cannot hide or assuage inherent systems of patronage, dependency, and domination – a well-based line of argumentation applied to both humanitarianism and development (Barnett 2005; Latouche 2000). The purpose is rather to expose the shortcomings of dominant organizations that channel funds and goods, experts and volunteers, policies and directives to populations in need. As a result, there is a tendency to restrict the validity of the gift's explanatory scope to the ways in which humanitarian action expresses a failed, biased, or deceitful "gift." For example, a well-known analysis is provided by Roderick L. Stirrat and Heiko Henkel (1997), who chart the "biography" (Kopytoff 1986) of a humanitarian donation. The authors trace its trajectory – from the free and disinterested gift of anonymous individuals given to institutional actors such as NGOs and other aid brokers – to show how an initial gift is transformed by the aid chain into something that produces lasting indebtedness and power imbalances because the system forecloses any possibility of reciprocity (see also Silk 2004). Such studies seek to expose the ways in which what may begin as an altruistic gesture morphs into an instrumentalized and oftentimes humiliating gift – not only when recipients cannot reciprocate but also when they have to perform scripted displays of gratefulness to foreign donors, as authors have examined in different locations affected by the 2004 tsunami (Hollenbach 2013; Korf 2007; Korf et al. 2010). These analyses lead to complex discussions – on virtue ethics, for instance – that fall outside the scope of this book.

Despite the soundness of these narratives, the gift remains resilient in the humanitarian moral horizon. It resurfaces time and again, urging concerned citizens to alleviate the plight of a distant humanity through their donations. In its non-immediate (i.e., there is no direct encounter between donor and receiver) and secular form, it is akin to what Jacques Godbout (1998, 65) has called the "modern gift to strangers."[4] It is true that certain events trigger more significant gifting than others, as was particularly obvious after the 2004 tsunami, indicating that generosity tends to be more substantial when a disaster affects "innocent victims" than when people are the victims of war (Gamburd 2014; Hyndman 2011). It is also true that the salvational impulse of humanitarianism in the context of natural disasters remains ancillary to donor priorities and funding opportunities, even if the geopolitics can appear less "complex" compared with situations of armed conflict. Nevertheless, when disasters occur, humanitarian actors make public funding appeals in which the rhetoric of giving is widely broadcast. It seeks to rouse emotional responses and summon altruistic values. And people do give; they do it to feel good about themselves (Godbout 1998), out of a sense of solidarity (Chouliaraki 2013), or for ethical reasons (Singer 2009).[5] Whatever their personal motivations, we cannot deny that the gift is a leitmotiv, and sometimes a call to action, even if it is instrumentalized.

The point I want to make is simple: although there is no doubt that the humanitarian field is traversed by regimes of power, I think the gift remains useful as a lens through which to analyze how power operates. In making this statement, I am surely simplifying a complex field of practice; yet I do not think scholarly reflection on humanitarian affairs through the gift has run its course. Not only is there a timelessness to these matters, there is still much to learn from the ways that local populations make sense of the humanitarian activities in which they are involved precisely through changing appreciations of gifting gestures.

As they move through the aid chain, initial gifts undergo a series of transformations before reaching their intended recipients. Money becomes food and shelter, anonymity makes way for social relations, and a new regime of value is created – a situated humanitarian regime. At this final junction, very specific humanitarian gestures, narratives, and practices arise, reflecting plural logics of gifting. When we engage in the analysis of humanitarianism's situated deployment in a given ethnographic context, not all is symbolic violence, patronage, or simulacrum. Here, the gift can signal a relational value that bridges the distance between those "in need" and others who want to "help." In other words, the gift remains an important dimension of what Didier Fassin (2011a, 2011b, 2011c) has called the moral economy of care that permeates contemporary humanitarianism.

THE VALUE OF THE GIFT IN EVERYDAY HUMANITARIANISM

The notion of moral economy has recently made headway in anthropology, and under this rubric fall many different areas of inquiry that engage with the moral and ethical dimensions of life. For some, moral economy provides a new way to talk about classical concerns in the social sciences – from Émile Durkheim (1895) onward – namely how to make sense of the moral dimension(s) of society and culture. Is morality best understood from a macro-perspective emphasizing societal norms, constraints, and questions of obligation? Or should we focus our analytical gaze on agents' subjectivity or on the intersubjective relationships between individuals who engage in moral reasoning and make ethical claims and choices?

Modern secular societies have tended to locate morality in religion. The "moral narrative of Modernity" has favoured a separation wherein religion inculcates moral teachings, whereas different precepts are assigned to other institutions such as the marketplace or the education system (Keane 2010, 79). Yet ideas and beliefs about what is desirable, about what is right and wrong, are also social (and not strictly religious) insofar as they speak to the values that are upheld in a given society, or in a given context, which can change over time. As a result, they are conventions rather than fixed and rigid entities. Morality is always a cultural construction.

My fieldwork experience certainly motivated my choices, and I focus on the everyday discourses and practices of humanitarian moralities, drawing on a particular definition of "moral economy" that has made headway in anthropological studies of humanitarianism. In *Moral Anthropology*, Fassin (2014, 158) writes that a moral economy is "the production, distribution, circulation and the use of affects and values in the social space."[6] The following chapters look at moral values that are expressed in concrete gestures and tied to humanitarian resources, which engender affects, assign roles, and define identities; when one is labelled a disaster victim and becomes entitled to receive humanitarian aid, there is a new identity apposed to this person, that of "beneficiary" – although there is less and less approval of this term (Global Humanitarian Assistance 2013). The reception of humanitarian goods participates in the production and circulation of values (e.g., we have to help and assist those in need because it is *good* to do so, or *natural*, or the *right* thing). These values circulate in the social space of the disaster-affected municipality.

The common acceptation of "morality" defines it as a particular domain of social life and thought made up of values, codes of conduct, and agreed-upon principles that circumscribe what is right and wrong, good and bad. It seeks to establish what should be done. Morality is often defined in opposition to what it is not, such as when morality is contrasted with economics, non-market systems with market systems (Polanyi 1944), and the gift with commodities (Gregory 1982). Various works have sought to bridge such dichotomies (Browne and Milgram 2009; Parry and Bloch 1989), showing the fluidity and continuity at play. There are many hybrid moral spaces, and humanitarianism is one of them.

No doubt, contemporary humanitarian action is the subject of many moral evaluations and conundrums. However, my aim is not to discuss the moral legitimacy of humanitarianism but to address the latter as a field of practice that generates vernacular moral judgments. It is about how people like Don Rodolfo, Ana, and the nuns made such judgments, ascribing meaning to specific gestures.

The concepts of the gift and morality are loaded, and in what follows I select particular texts and positions that are most relevant to my purposes. Indeed, there is an ongoing debate about the way that these categories are used in order to make sense of social phenomena – a debate that originated with Marcel Mauss's (1925) seminal text "Essai sur le don" (Essay on the gift), whose thesis is developed in his subsequent book *The Gift* (1954). Today, Mauss's ideas still have a grounding effect, even if they remain subject to critique.

When Mauss published *The Gift*, he was running against the tide of anthropological theories of his time that aimed to explain how exchange operated in "primitive" societies. In proper evolutionistic style, these theories slotted economic transactions on an ascending arrow of development between barter and monetary exchange. Through a detailed examination of ethnographic works available to him, Mauss (1954) suggested that there was something else going on, a form of gift-like transaction anchored in what he called "total social facts." The gift systems Mauss analyzed were complex networks of reciprocal exchanges involving entire societies. Following the Durkheimian tradition, he considered them "total social facts" in that they mobilized all dimensions of social life (religious, economic, political, symbolic, etc.), exemplifying a canonical holistic view. In the Maussian conception, the gift is structured around the triple obligations of giving, receiving, and giving back, and it incorporates opposite characteristics; it is at once free and obligatory, unbound and constrained, (self-)interested and disinterested, giving it a paradoxical nature. Many publications have assessed whether Mauss was right to use the concept of the gift in order to explain various Indigenous practices involving the exchange of things, although this was not limited to material objects.[7] One important critique comes from Alain Testart (2013), who explains that ever since Mauss wrote about gift exchange, anthropologists who have followed in his footsteps have erred, tremendously so. The gist of his argument is that a gift should refer only to a free one-way transfer that does not entail an obligation to repay; although a return may ensue, it is never required. The notion of exchange, in contrast, implies a required counter-transfer (also called a counterpart). The cycles of gift exchange (rather than gifts) that Mauss described – or those that we find in contemporary gift-giving practices during birthdays, for instance – hold a particular quality that the notion of exchange does not. For me, this is crucial. Testart's reasoning is sound, but since there is a surplus of meaning in the notion of the "gift" that is absent in "exchange," we find circumstances that lend themselves better to the infelicitous expression of "gift exchange."

Mauss's (1954) analysis led to two major interpretations regarding reciprocal practices of giving: in one, the gift is a model of solidarity (as in the case of the Melanesian Kula ring),[8] and in the other, it is a model of social hierarchy (as seen through the potlatch of the North American west coast).[9] In the ethnographic cases examined in Mauss's book, the point is to acknowledge that the exchange of gifts was not merely an economic practice because it also participated in other value-making processes, moral ones. Talking about the gift as only an economic matter reduced its meaning, flattening it into something it was not.

What I retain from this seminal work is that the Maussian gift is indicative of morality in the Durkheimian sense.[10] Mauss sees gifting in "archaic societies" as the bedrock of their morality. For him, the gift becomes *the* core value that defined these societies as essentially moral ones.

The Maussian conception of the gift describes forms of exchange that extend beyond strict economic valuations between groups. The exchanges maintain and reproduce social ties, which implies that people know each other. With respect to humanitarian action, this model can be useful when we consider how localized enactments mobilize identifiable groups of donors and receivers. In the case of the first humanitarian configuration in Lamaria, people who entertained mutual aid networks performed helping gestures toward one another, drawing on these pre-existing systems of reciprocity. In the post-disaster housing reconstruction project, however, the model is less applicable because the different entities involved in La Hermandad were not groups that knew each other. Here, a non-monetary exchange framework, coupled with talk about a "gift from strangers," defined the entire endeavour.

The way I address humanitarian activities through the category of the gift requires that we not see it as a fixed dominant value structuring an unchanging field of practice, unlike the way that commentators discuss the macro-scale of humanitarian action, for this curtails the scope of its explanatory reach. There are two main positions: one that draws from the Maussian model, in which the gift is dismissed because humanitarian giving forecloses the possibility of a return, and one that relies on the idea of a unilateral, generous, and free gift, which is equally dismissed in light of all the contradictions humanitarianism produces. This book takes a different approach. I do not seek to tag an exact logic of giving to a particular humanitarian configuration in a cookie-cutter manner. It is more interesting to show how vernacular understandings of the gift get reworked through different localized humanitarian activities involving gift-like gestures that also produce ambivalence and uncertainty.

VALUES, MORALITY, AND ETHICS

With respect to an appreciation of the place of morality in society – and in anthropological reasoning – there has been a renewed interest in questions related to moralities, values, and ethics, not least because our contemporary world affairs are increasingly traversed by moral conundrums, humanitarianism being a good case in point. Anthropology has been rather hesitant to discuss these things in the past, preferring to avoid the murky waters of moralizing judgments. But lately this has changed, and there is now a solid body of literature on the anthropology of moralities and ethics. The problem is that there is no agreement on the scope and content of these analytical categories. The field is burdened with conflicting views and variable usages of key concepts. I will not attempt to resolve the matter. Rather, I illustrate these challenges by tracing how the gift, taken as a value in the moral economy of humanitarianism, assumes a different explanatory scope depending on the framework adopted.

There are at least three major tendencies in the anthropological literature on these questions. The first squarely engages with the concept of morality and discusses the ways in which values structure moral orders, or moral spheres, as they are also sometimes named. The second approach favours the concept of ethics and argues that the latter is better suited to discussing the ordinary ways that people engage in moral reasoning. The third approach seeks to bridge moral orders and ethical action; such bridging projects partake in the longstanding use of the social sciences to articulate structure and agency. Each of these three approaches brings into play different philosophical legacies, to which I cannot do justice in these pages, and I must underscore that this division is a heuristic device and by no means a definite categorization on the matter.

When approaching morality as a specific domain, authors have rethought Durkheim's (1895) legacy of morality as an all-encompassing sphere of life and have preferred to speak of "moral value spheres" that determine one's capacity for action and moral reasoning. For example, drawing on the work of Louis Dumont, Joel Robbins (2007, 297) explains that a moral sphere is structured by a set of core values, where "values are those elements of culture that structure the relations between other elements." Here, core values determine what is important and arrange other cultural elements according to logics of encompassment and hierarchy. To be fair, Robbins does not promote a single formalist model to explain how people, everywhere, engage in moral reasoning and behaviours. In a more recent work, he explains how values relate to one another differently – in a structural sense – according to monist and pluralist versions of value theory, where, for the first, one supervalue dominates and, for the second, plural values enter into conflict with one another (Robbins 2013b).

From this standpoint, we could say that charity is a core value of Christianity. It guides action since it teaches the faithful what is right. This perspective on morality is useful when explaining the second humanitarian configuration I address. Notably, when the nuns became responsible for the food aid in Lamaria, they did so partly as a result of their ongoing engagement with a particular moral way of being in the world, one that values charitable action. I am not saying that food aid amounted to a charity but that service to others was something the nuns valued. In other words, one could argue that it was a core value that defined their moral horizon. The nuns would say that they were giving their time and energy to help those affected by the disaster. And this "gift of self" was also a disposition they valued and hoped would be recognized by others.

One aspect that has challenged authors is how to explain change. Although values do structure cultural elements and delineate moral spheres, they are not all equal, nor are they always stable. When conflicts arise between key values – for instance, as new values are introduced or as their hierarchical arrangement changes – certain "value-complexes" or moral spheres are reworked. This is where, according to Robbins (2007, 300), "a morality of freedom and choice comes into play and people become consciously aware of choosing their own fate." In other words, we need to distinguish between normative moralities of reproduction and more reflexive moralities of conflict or change, which are open to choice and transformation. But his model rests on core values being introduced that cause friction with a pre-existing moral assemblage.

Referring again to the case of food aid can illustrate this process. When the nuns took over the distribution of food, the overarching value-complex at play was that emergency aid was the right thing to do, and the gifting of food reaffirmed this. For the receivers, however, the distribution of food did not necessarily entail a gifting relationship, especially once it became routine. And when issues arose concerning the logistics of distribution or the quantity and quality of rations, people started proclaiming their right to aid. This is referred to as a rights-based approach to humanitarian action, a value-complex that is rather distinct from the Christian one entertained by the nuns. The two are not incompatible, but the change in the receivers' attitudes triggered a reflexive process in the nuns, who began to voice that receivers were "no longer behaving as they should!" Behaviours, expectations, and feelings of gratitude or ambivalence are the very things that give body to the moral dimensions of life. They make values visible. The many ways that people engage with one another, negotiating their day-to-day lives, exceed strict interpretative models anchored in value-driven moral spheres.

Some commentators similarly argue that instead of seeing one or a few primordial values structuring a moral sphere, it is more productive to envision moralities – in the plural – as embodied dispositions, which the notion of ethics more appropriately conveys. Here, ethics is less about the way people enact or embody moral values and more about the mundane way people question or make judgments in their everyday lives about a plurality of themes, such as freedom, truth, dignity, character, care, empathy, and responsibility (Lambek 2010, 6). The manner in which I approach humanitarian configurations of gifting in post-disaster Lamaria is closer to this perspective.

There are, however, differing points of view. For example, Jarrett Zigon (2009) does not abandon the concept of morality altogether. He argues that there are three different interrelated aspects of morality that are themselves pluralistic: institutional morality, which derives from, and is disseminated by, institutions in power (e.g., legal precepts); morality located in public discourse, which can include a wide range of beliefs, conceptions, and hopes that circulate outside of formal institutions (e.g., witchcraft, or for that matter, humanitarianism); and embodied dispositions, which comprise people's fundamental ability to be "non-consciously moral" in their day-to-day lives (ibid., 258). This latter aspect of morality is an incarnated disposition of being-in-the-world (Zigon 2008, 2009), akin to a habitus acquired over years of "socialization" and "enculturation." It is a non-conscious embodied morality performed by people on an ordinary basis, which is acceptable and naturally recognized by those around them. This aspect comes closest to Robbins's (2007) morality of reproduction. However, in order to explain tension or transformation, Zigon (2009) does not refer to collisions between spherical models of morality; instead, he calls them moments of "moral breakdown," when tensions arise that disturb the "business-as-usual" way of being moral and cause the person to consciously experience a moral questioning either alone or with others. Zigon (ibid., 261) terms this moral questioning an ethical moment: "Ethics is what is done in those occasional moments when one calls into question any of the three aspects of morality. Ethics is a kind of stepping-away [when] a person becomes reflective and reflexive about her moral world and moral personhood and what she must do, say or think in order to appropriately return to her non-conscious moral mode of being."

The ethical moment is therefore one of creativity, and it becomes a regular activity in people's lives. Zigon's phenomenological approach foregrounds the plasticity between forms of morality and ethics, as well as between the elements that may constitute them – although I do wonder how he would distinguish "embodied unconscious dispositions" from the concept of culture, a task I will not venture to undertake.

This approach can elucidate the way that humanitarian configurations on the ground evolve and cause people to question them. As will become clear throughout this book, the humanitarian response to the earthquakes in Lamaria in 2001 set in motion a series of gestures that created new groups of donors and receivers of aid, even if they were just temporary. There was a shared understanding that emergency assistance, food aid, and post-disaster reconstruction were all exceptional measures framed by a public discourse on the importance of assisting those in need – one that could be found in newspaper articles, in the mayor's speeches, on the radio, and on television. People accepted that it was the right (i.e., moral) thing to do. Ideas of gifting certainly permeated the humanitarian moral sphere – if one accepts this phrasing. But things get complicated on the ground. What the present ethnography exposes is precisely how participants became attuned to arising contradictions that could delegitimize a given humanitarian moral representation promoted by others. The La Hermandad reconstruction site is a case in point: after months of labour for no pay – building houses manually from scratch – people began to wonder whether they would really receive a new house. They felt they were being treated like cheap manpower, and what was initially defined as a humanitarian endeavour came to be perceived as an exploitative relationship, one akin to those found in the labour market. They now doubted the purpose of the project and became suspicious of the motives of those in charge. In Zigon's (2009) terminology, the families who were the official beneficiaries of the Red Cross's initiative entered a "moral breakdown," halting the "business-as-usual" social relationships of the project. Within this dynamic, then, the project could no longer be defined as a non-monetary exchange thanks to the gift of strangers. It came to be perceived as an exploitative scheme, resembling the "master-worker" relationships many knew all too well.

Although Zigon's model has merit, I do not completely endorse his characterization of a moral breakdown, for people may question a given state of affairs on a more ongoing basis than what he argues. Is a breakdown necessary to reveal the workings of moralities in everyday life? Of course, singular moments of realization do occur when something that had previously been taken for granted reveals itself to be problematic. Nevertheless, ethical reasoning becomes circumscribed as an event – an event of a reflexive kind.

A third anthropological stance that also emphasizes the mundane character of ethical reflexivity invites us to abandon the concept of morality altogether in order to consider more thoroughly how ethics infuses our ordinary existence. Michael Lambek (2010) believes that ethical modes of thinking and being do not need an event to materialize, that ethics is a distinct domain of thought, and that the emphasis should not be placed on values either – a category he leaves aside. Instead, Lambek focuses on the notion of virtue. He argues that ethics is a tacit "property of speech and action" meaning that it reveals itself through ordinary language when people make judgments about a wide range of phenomena around them. He sees ethics as "a modality of social action or of being in the world, rather than a modular component of society or mind" (ibid., 10). In this sense, ethics is neither normative (it is not about what is right or good) nor a distinct realm characterized by values that structure or shape moral spheres, orders, or dimensions. Thinking this way is a category mistake, according to Lambek. So we should refrain from locating ethics as something discrete, separate from daily life, and defined by rules. For him, ethics is intrinsically linked to practice as a feature, a quality, or an entailment of action – the latter covering acts and speech – and particularly linked to the way that people make judgments about situations and people around them, including themselves.

Lambek (2010) thus defines "ethics" as a fundamental and dynamic capacity constantly in the making as people reflect on acts through the judgments they make about them. There is a mutually reinforcing quality to this dialectic since performed acts create criteria about which judgments are made, thereby giving rise to new actions. The criteria help to establish a judgment, but they are usually implicit in the actions we perform. They are part of the social makeup, in a way, since in a given cultural context, people will agree on criteria that are not outwardly enunciated. We can appeal to them when we need them, such as when a disjunction arises between the actual and the expected.

This line of thinking is clearly at odds with the Durkheimian legacy and brings us closer to practice theory. For instance, when turning to the gift, Lambek (2010, 18) argues that the Maussian exemplars of giving and counter-giving are performative ritual acts that "initiate or cancel particular ethical criteria, conditions, or states, minimally of living under a promise, obligation or debt but usually also connected to the production and circulation of value and to transformations in social status, relationship, honour and the like." We can see how aspects of Pierre Bourdieu's (1977) critique of Mauss's conclusion about the gift are reintroduced. Indeed, Bourdieu's famous essay on giving in Kabylia, Algeria, shows how the rule of reciprocity masked hidden structures that were internalized by agents – the habitus – and how ultimately the to-and-fro of gift exchanges was an individual and collective misrecognition regarding the accumulation of symbolic capital. Here, symbolic capital partakes in the movement of exchange, but it is never openly stated; doing so would kill the system. For Bourdieu, people are socialized to talk about gifts as free and disinterested gestures, but this is a strategy. When we dig a little deeper and peel off the discursive veils, we inevitably find calculation and interest at play in cycles of exchange.[11]

Bourdieu (1977) does not discuss ethics; he is more interested in the strategies people employ to advance their chances of accessing what they seek – in the case of Kabylia, honour, prestige, and fame. In Lambek's (2010) view on ethics, practice theory is important. Because people are generally invested in what they do, culturally speaking, ethics reveals the qualities of acts and utterances that compose practices. It is here that the notion of virtue appears, not as a rule or floating value to be cognitively uncovered in the way that Bourdieu approaches the matter but as a feature always embedded in practice, manifesting both continuity and change.

Through the lens of ordinary ethics, questions regarding the nature, place, and scope of the "gift" in a changing humanitarian response become easily apprehensible. Gifting gestures (i.e., concrete acts and the narratives that accompany aid transactions) populate humanitarian practices, but this does not mean that they go unchallenged. They are not automatic exchanges between static groups of donors and receivers. My point is to underscore that gifting is an attribution of gestures that are performed in a contingent situation. It is one among other attributions but an important one. Hence, when I speak of humanitarian configurations, I seek to mark a discontinuity within a larger undertaking but not an abrupt hermetic break between them. When I state that the gift can be discussed as a humanitarian value, I adopt a stance that puts to the fore a generalizable feature of humanitarian action, one that precisely causes so much debate in the literature. But for the families of Lamaria whose trajectory led them to experience a series of humanitarian activities, as well as for the institutional representatives who initiated and managed them, gifting was not a reified value structuring the morality of humanitarianism taken as an abstract domain of thought. People had so much to say about aid, how it was delivered, whether it was sufficient, whether they deserved it, whether receivers were thankful, and whether promises of a new house could be believed. This is what ordinary ethics looks like in a humanitarian context. Each configuration engendered judgments and reactive attitudes, many revolving around questions of gratitude and resentment, which became the object of intense talk in La Hermandad. These configurations rested not only on certain criteria depending on the position of actors as official beneficiaries or providers of aid but also on other parameters that framed the modalities of each configuration.

So although I draw on personal accounts to explain judgments about humanitarian gifting, we must keep in mind that it is not only individual subjects who can be ethical agents. Various kinds of groups (based on kin, caste, or religion) can form ethical agents (Laidlaw 2014); some scholars even argue that the "composite" of an anthropologist and his or her informants can make up such a group when they share intense moments (Faubion 2011). Ethical agents are indeed not confined to culturally bounded entities.

The families whose route along the aid chain I recount can be viewed as a group, for they underwent comparable experiences leading to similar appraisals, which allowed me, at a methodological level, to draw general characteristics. Moral judgments and ethical reflection are always situated and relational. But I would not want to push too far the idea that the La Hermandad residents engaged in homogeneous moral self-fashioning; as will become clear, this collective was prone to internal division, in part exacerbated by the parameters of the housing project itself. So although shared moral conundrums did emerge, not everyone thought alike about humanitarian affairs.

When morality and ethics are juxtaposed, the first appears to be more ideational and the second more immanent to practice, and the gist of much recent anthropological reflection is how best to analytically bridge the two in a way that reveals the richness of people's being in the world. I find the notion of value very useful for unpacking the discourses surrounding humanitarian action, particularly those that harness ideas about gifting. But I also believe that ethnography should convey the inconsistencies and shifts in situations that either imperceptibly or precipitously push people to re-evaluate their circumstances through the lens of ordinary ethical reflexivity.

2

Chronicles of an Earthquake

When I arrived in Lamaria, my initial reaction was that the town looked better than I had anticipated. I had been expecting more devastation perhaps or palpable misery. My imagination had conjured images without comparing them to reality, in part because real-time data did not stream on social media in 2001, as it does today. Now we can witness events at the antipodes of the globe almost as they happen. It makes for a qualitatively different experience of events – and a different role for the imaginary.

I knew that the municipality had been more severely hit by the January earthquake than by the second one in February, so when I arrived in late February, the roads had been cleared and people had already been organizing for a month. In the immediate aftermath of the first earthquake, there was chaos and trauma, yet it was also at this particular juncture that initial helping responses arose. They came first in the shape of spontaneous gestures from kin and friends and then in collective efforts to establish formal channels of humanitarian aid delivery. Chief among them was the distribution of food, which is the first formal humanitarian gifting configuration I address. But I begin this chapter by introducing some general information about Lamaria, weaving older descriptions from my field notes into more recent impressions of the town when I visited again in May 2014.

A TOWN PERCHED ON A HILLTOP

Lamaria is one of the 262 municipalities of El Salvador. Located 40 kilometres west of the capital, in the department of Sonsonate,

Lamaria sits on a volcanic promontory overlooking the fertile Zapotitán Valley to the north. Its total surface area is 65 square kilometres, and in 2001 its total population numbered 23,813 inhabitants, 56 per cent of whom lived in the rural zones. Lamaria does not offer any picturesque tourist attractions; I still have not seen it mentioned in English-language tourist guides. However, many inhabitants were proud to consider themselves Lamarienses.

One enters the town up a steep road, Avenida Principal, that leads directly to the central park. The height of the buildings does not exceed two or three storeys, and the tallest structure is the Catholic church, which is painted white and yellow. Lamaria lost much of its colonial cachet in an earthquake in 1917. The church overlooks the central park, which is by far one of the most vibrant areas of the municipality, along with the market. On the other side of the park stands City Hall. All around the park, various shop owners sit outside, chatting with would-be customers. At the corner of Avenida Principal and Secunda Calle Poniente, a newspaper vendor sets up shop every morning. Just a little farther, at the corner of Secunda Avenida and Secunda Calle Poniente, a half-dozen men regularly meet during weekday afternoons to play cards. I was pleased to find them still at their habitual spot twelve years later! One can also find many small *comedores* there, which are modest eateries and hash houses. Before the civil war of 1980–92, orchestras played in the park on Sunday evenings, offering young men a venue to invite girls to dance. The new rotunda in the park still welcomes musicians, and when I went in 2014, I saw a band playing there for an evangelical baptism. During religious celebrations, processions circulate around the park, especially during Semana Santa (Easter Holy Week). The streets are then covered with petals and other colourful materials that are arranged to depict episodes of Christian history. Funerary processions also amble around the park. Apart from being a meeting place, the park is sometimes also a drinking spot, a fact the new mayor abhorred and began to remedy when he had the park rebuilt after the earthquake.

Four hundred metres southeast of the park stands the central market, a bustling place on Saturdays, but deemed unsanitary because the drainage system was defective. The mayor wanted to modernize it, but with the impact of the earthquake, the project had been delayed. The delay seems to be long-lasting, as the market had not changed much by my last visit. The market stalls sell everything from

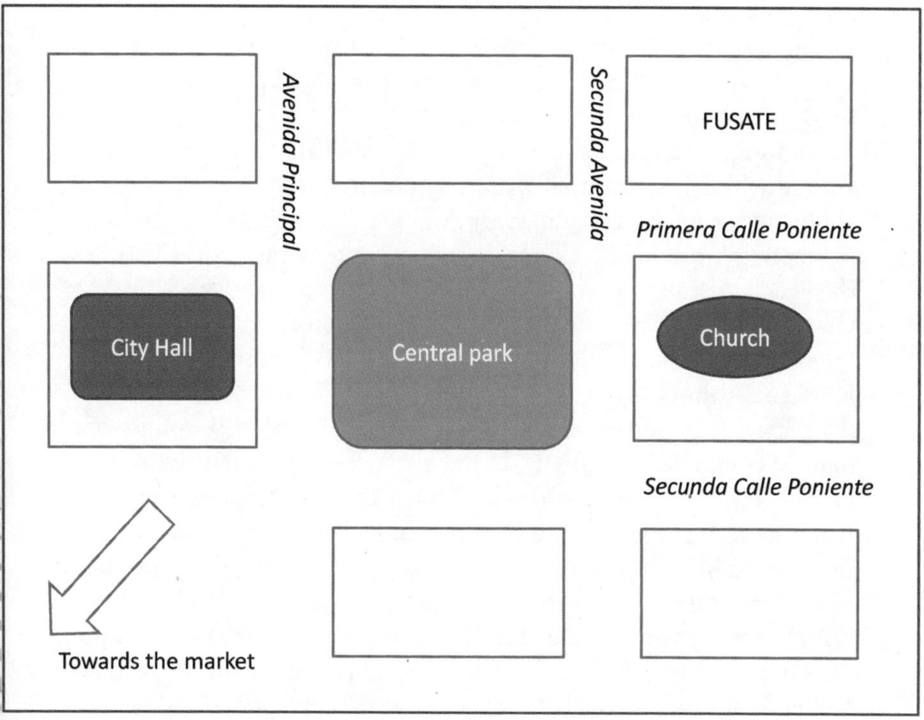

2.1 Lamaria town centre.

meats, poultry, vegetables, and fruits of all sorts to clothing and small household items. In the heart of the market is a well-known *pupusería*, selling handmade corn tortillas filled with beans, cheese, and pork, "the best in town" according to many residents. Bordering the market is the red-light district (red-light *block* would be more accurate), whose most famous house of ill repute collapsed during the earthquake. North of town is the main bus station; local mini-buses are yellow, whereas larger buses are typical for travel throughout Central America, with colourful designs that sometimes mix religious and erotic imagery. The decrepit station was another item on the mayor's list of infrastructure to modernize, and it did look better in 2014. Close by is the soccer field, a rather large open sports ground without bleachers. Now there is a new walled-up sports complex with a pool, the *polideportivo*. East of the central park is the Fundación Salvadoreña de la Tercera Edad (FUSATE), a national institution assisting the needy that was locally headed by Sister Elena, a very well-known nun in Lamaria. In February 2001 the building was converted into a warehouse for stockpiling emergency food aid. Many disaster victims converged there in the early days. Continuing east, and on higher ground, stands the cemetery, with its flaking white and turquoise painted gravestones and plastic flowers rolling in the wind. At night, stray dogs make it their private domain. When one looks at the city from this vantage point, a detail strikes the eye: a well-kept patch of greenery. It is the private garden of the Claretian monks, who financed a housing reconstruction project not far from town. Extending our gaze to the south is the *colonia* San Damian. Although the label *colonia* generally refers to an urban district with better built structures, the San Damian borough was mainly comprised of cob and adobe houses that collapsed on the fateful day. Looking north, one can see a large building detached from the rest, the high school, where students take their *bachilerato*, the last qualifying year before entering a professional institute or university. Whereas the central park is animated in the morning, all is quiet during the torrid afternoon hours. Most stores close during the siesta. In the early evening, the buzz starts up again. There are a few bars but no discos. There is no movie theatre, fast-food restaurant, supermarket, or shopping mall; and in 2001 there was only one gas station.

Historically, the economic base of the city was agriculture, especially the production of cereals and, to a lesser extent, coffee, vegetables, and citrus fruit. In the late 1990s, Lamaria was one of the few municipalities developing commercial and manufacturing activities. Today, it is known for its traditional open brickyards, visible from the highway, which in 2001 numbered twenty-one. These small factories are no competition for the large cement companies that benefited from the many reconstruction initiatives throughout the country. Concrete blocks are faster than bricks to assemble, and there was some debate in Lamaria over what kind of material to use for housing reconstruction projects.

In 2001 the town had one public health centre, always full, where six doctors and seven nurses and auxiliaries conducted more than a hundred daily consultations. And there was a small Red Cross clinic, whose ambulance was out of service due to lack of operating funds. Citizens are better served now by two fully operational ambulances.

Apart from the town centre, which is divided into *barrios* (neighbourhoods), the municipality of Lamaria is made up of *colonias* and *cantones*. The more urban *colonias* are adjacent to the town centre, and the *cantones* are rural districts located a few kilometres from town. Small *cantones* – around twenty families or less – are called *caseríos*. At the time of my research, Lamaria comprised 10 *cantones*, 33 *caseríos*, and 28 *barrios* and *colonias*. In 2001 the majority of the houses in *cantones* were built using adobe and corrugated iron, and a few were made of bricks.[1] These generally older and often unsteady constructions were not very safe when the earth started to shake.

Electricity was available in seven *cantones* and in the town centre and *colonias*. The price of the connection was the equivalent of US$70, so not all households could afford it. At least 25 per cent of the entire population did not have electricity. Water was even harder to access, even in the centre of town. Close to 55 per cent of the population did not have household access to drinkable water, and 72 per cent of households were not connected to the sewage system. In the countryside, people walked to public faucets and wells located near the larger roads. The situation may have seemed better in the town centre, but this was not always the case, for water often ran only for a couple of hours a day, sometimes only at nighttime. It was important to ensure that the faucets of the *pilas* (large concrete basins) were open to collect water. But even that system did not always work and had not been fixed by 2014. Those who could afford the expense paid young men for water deliveries. The situation was worse for people living in rural areas, particularly for women, who walked with pails and buckets to wells or public taps, as water collecting was a gender-specific task. During winter, the wells often dried up. There were eleven streams in the area that people used for different tasks, which increased their level of pollution. The paradox is that Lamaria rests above an important aquiferous zone; although the resource exists, the infrastructure was sorely lacking.

The local government was headed by a municipal council consisting of the mayor, eight town councillors, and four deputy councillors. The 2001 government was a coalition of three left-wing parties: the Frente Farabundo Martí para la Liberación Nacional (FMLN), the Partido Demócrata Cristiano, and the Unión Social Demócrata. Before that, City Hall had represented the interests of large landowners affiliated with the Alianza Republicana Nacionalista (ARENA).

The mayor, Don Moisés, was not a professional politician but the owner of a large ironworks shop. In small towns, the mayor is not a distant person; Don Moisés was quite approachable, and he regularly received small delegations from *caseríos*. A short rotund man with a warm smile, he explained to me how difficult the political campaign had been in a municipality that had voted for the ARENA party for the past twelve years. Alas, when the progressive forces were envisioning a series of social development initiatives, the earthquake struck. "No estábamos preparados" (We were not ready), he said. How many times did I hear these words? Countless individuals I met during my stay in El Salvador expressed this idea, whether they were promoters of local grassroots initiatives or directors of large NGOs. All talked about the need to be ready, prepared, organized, and coordinated in case another calamity struck the country. These words also conveyed a feeling of letdown, as for Don Moisés. He wanted to do more for the Lamarienses, but he lacked the financial resources and the means to do so.

Nevertheless, in terms of local organizing, the earthquake had a boosting effect. Indeed, residents of *caseríos*, *cantones*, and *barrios* had to gather and elect delegates who would carry out necessary discussions with local authorities and "humanitarian" representatives.[2] A delegation was called a *directiva*, and although the more important *cantones*, such as Las Crucitas and Los Mangos, had established *directivas* prior to the earthquake, this was not the case for many others. The wish to form a political entity (a *directiva* is a legally registered body) did not always emanate from the residents themselves. The accelerated formation of *directivas* shortly after the January earthquake reflected logistical imperatives. Deciding where and how to distribute food and first aid required detailed information from the affected rural areas that only local residents could provide. The organizing that came with setting up the *directivas* is one of the positive consequences of the earthquake. It also illustrates the extent to which poorer segments of the population lacked direct political representation at the municipal level in Lamaria – contrary to other areas of El Salvador, such as the well-organized communities of the Lempa River region in Usulután.

EMERGENCY AND SOLIDARITY

On Saturday, 13 January 2001, at 11:34 AM, the earth started to shake. The magnitude of the earthquake was 7.6 on the Richter scale. It made a deafening sound, not only because buildings were falling but also because, as Maria Julia described it, a horrible noise was emanating from the depths of the earth.

That day, thirty-two seconds is all it took for the face of Lamaria to change dramatically. Yanira – the wife of a doctor with whom I stayed in February – described how people ran out of their homes panic-stricken, how children were crying while covering their ears, how walls were rattling and falling to the ground in great clouds of suffocating dust. The earth felt like an agitated sea moving in all directions. While I was in Lamaria, I experienced some aftershocks, one in particular that registered 5.2 on the Richter scale; this was on 28 February, the same day that a 6.8 earthquake shook Seattle with little damaging effect. You wonder whether the house facing you will crumble, whether the earth will collapse under your feet, and how long these telluric tremors will go on. As frightening as these sometimes were, the Lamarienses told me they were *más suaves* (softer) than the earthquakes. In the following months, I asked people how they had reacted to the earthquakes, and their responses were often quite emotional, especially among the La Hermandad residents. For those who lost the little they had, recalling the disaster was not easy.[3] Their first reflex, they all said, was to "save your skin and that of your children."

After the initial shock, there came the realization of destruction, of all that was now gone – or not, depending on one's location. Most of the houses that fell were near the centre of town. Among those were *mesones*, large rental units for low-income families who found themselves homeless in a town half-destroyed. This was the case for the family of Rosa, who rented a room with her seven-year-old daughter, her husband, her sister, and her sister's partner in a *mesón* not far from where I later stayed. The building was completely shattered, and they had to sleep outside under a plastic tarp by a tamarind tree for weeks. They were not alone. Even people whose houses had not been damaged chose to spend their nights outdoors on the sidewalk in fear of another "big one." Candles lit the streets, some people listened to the radio, those who could boil water distributed coffee, and all feared that another earthquake would happen while they slept.

The number of damaged and destroyed houses became the criterion for the distribution of emergency food aid and later for the selection of beneficiaries for permanent housing reconstruction projects (Vargas 2001).

Table 2.1 Houses damaged and destroyed by the earthquake of 13 January 2001

Houses	*Urban sector*	*Rural sector*	*Total*
Destroyed	1,888	1,198	3,086
Damaged	1,342	297	1,639
Subtotal	3,230	1,495	4,725
Intact	1,604	1,191	2,795
Total	4,834	2,686	7,520

These numbers are conservative; according to a census undertaken by the mayor's office and the Health Unit, the damages in rural sectors ran to 1,722 houses destroyed and 746 damaged, for a subtotal of 2,468. There was also extensive damage to schools, roads, churches, and businesses. In all, 13,440 people were affected by the earthquake. Twenty-three people died. Without wanting to minimize the impact of the earthquake, these numbers are far less dramatic than those of other Salvadoran municipalities. For example, in the departments of Usulután and San Vicente, the second earthquake registered 6.6 on the Richter scale and caused the complete destruction of various small villages. Of the hundred or so municipalities affected by one or both earthquakes, Lamaria occupied the sixty-second position according to the Fondo de Inversión Social para el Desarollo Local, a government agency supporting local development.

The first modalities of aid came from Lamaria itself, not in the form of official humanitarian assistance per se but through spontaneous helping gestures. A friend, a neighbour, a family member, anyone who could do something to assist those in need would extend a hand.[4] However, in many cases, these gestures were not entirely unstructured but followed patterns of reciprocity found in mutual aid networks.

Anthropologists have documented at length the ways that mutual aid obligations are mobilized in times of crisis. These obligations are organized according to different regulations expressed in terms of kinship, residency, modes of production, and distribution of goods and services, as well as according to rules of reciprocity that vary depending on the cultural context. In Lamaria structured relations of reciprocity exist between people, even though they are neither of the same nature and intensity nor as systematic and institutionalized as in the canonical examples of the Trobriand Islanders or "closed corporate communities" (Malinowski 1922; Wolf 1957).

In this respect, two significant modalities of reciprocal help materialized in the aftermath of the disaster. The first concerns *compadrazgo* (godparenting), and the second involves religious affiliation. From the onset, let me be clear that, contrary to the reciprocal gifting cycles studied by Mauss (1925, 1954), I do not talk about *obligatory* relations of reciprocity, for the notion of obligation conveys a sense of enforcement or of necessity that is too rigid in this case. The term "preferential reciprocity" is more appropriate, because here the notion of sanction is not as manifest when reciprocity fails. I refer to moral relations that may express a sense of duty but whose failure does not automatically engender a sanction. That is why the idea of a looser preferential reciprocity is more adequate in this context.

One example of a loose bond is the relationship between *compadres* or *comadres* (godfather or godmother to one's child) and their *ahijados* (godchildren). This relationship is formalized through baptism, and becoming a *comadre* or *compadre* usually entails preparatory catechesis and Bible studies led by a priest before the ceremony. However, in practice, the bond of *compadrazgo* does not always require official recognition by religious authorities, Catholic or otherwise. Becoming a *comadre* when one is not kin means becoming a symbolic member of the family. The incumbent responsibility toward the child is important, but so are the ties with the parents. Although it is customary for kin members to become *compadres* or *comadres*, the relation can also develop in a less formal manner, extending beyond strict kinship ties. It then designates a mark of affection and friendship.

Many services are rendered to *ahijados* by *compadres* and *comadres*, and one expects the relationship to last, for it establishes a channel of mutual help that widens other kinship ties. The logic that governs *compadrazgo* "transactions" has nothing to do with the market logic. In a Maussian perspective, these exchanges express regular giving and counter-giving transfers that reinforce the social bonds between people. Personal interest is not completely absent since there is not a unidirectional logic of gifting without expectation of return. But it is not to be conflated with the type of calculated economic self-interest that seeks to maximize the value of what is received in exchange for what is given. In the case of *compadrazgo*, the one who asks another to become a *compadre* or *comadre* bestows an honour upon that person, which will be acknowledged by a favour in return, usually something for the child. Later, one partner becomes indebted – or "obliged" – to the other. Refusing to reciprocate would risk hurting the relationship.

These are important networks of mutual help; severing them means depriving oneself of significant sources of assistance when in need. For poorer people, doing so can leave them in great difficulty, which is what happened in La Hermandad, where only members of the nuclear family were allowed on the reconstruction site. The dimension of interestedness is better explained when taking into account the socio-economic and cultural situation of Lamaria's *campesinos* (peasants). In 2001 their living conditions were already precarious, and many faced ongoing job insecurity, scarcity, and vulnerability. In addition, a general climate of *desconfianza* (mistrust) characterized many aspects of the social life of small rural Salvadoran communities (as was also common elsewhere in Mesoamerican populations). This mistrust was compounded by a general feeling of insecurity due to gang-related troubles in the country, which have only worsened since then. *Compadrazgo* relations could counteract this climate of uncertainty by providing a trustful bond between people. Sure, there is an *expectation* to "give" in the Maussian sense of the term, but it is also a way to say that one trusts the other, that one can count on one's *comadre* or *compadre*. In this context, refusing to sustain this preferential reciprocity means more than rejecting a mere gift; it could also jeopardize a significant social relationship.

After the earthquake, kinship ties, including the bonds of *compadrazgo*, were mobilized to provide assistance to people one knew. This is a common-sense procedure, for in a culturally determined context, it is expected that one will first help those one knows, all the more so when calamity strikes. The norms of Salvadoran society foreground biological and ritual kinship ties – something that became manifest during my initial stay.

The second significant modality of reciprocal help involved religious affiliation. The church remains a strong institution in El Salvador. The official religion is Catholicism, but Protestant and evangelical churches have gained a lot of ground.[5] The core message of these religions promotes personal salvation through faith in Jesus. Salvation, however, comes in the afterlife, not here below. A lawyer working for a human rights organization told me that born-again Christians, for instance, are meant to "accept their terrestrial sufferings and patiently wait for their redemption" in the afterlife – an attitude he bemoaned. Tensions existed between evangelical churches and the Catholic Church, and the competition for souls sometimes became a matter of public display. In Lamaria, during Semana Santa, the priest asked practitioners to sing wholeheartedly during the processions so as to show the *evangélicos* the vigour and strength of Catholicism in the municipality.

Throughout the four months of the emergency period, that being the timeline given to me by City Hall, religious affiliation played a significant role in the way that aid was organized. This aid does not fall under the rubric of professional institutional humanitarianism.[6] It is, rather, a form of assistance between members of a given group – in this case, a religious group. There was a difference between the immediate forms of aid that came from the evangelical churches and those that came from the Catholic Church. The former had a tendency to help their own members, whereas representatives of the Catholic Church said they distributed aid to whoever was in need, regardless of creed. The Mormon church in Lamaria best illustrated this distinction, with the American ministers who were officiating in town receiving funds from Salt Lake City, which they distributed to their converts, not without causing envy in other smaller, less prosperous evangelical parishes. As for the Catholic Church, it gained a prominent role in the distribution of food aid, thereby greatly increasing its social and symbolic capital. A humanitarian emergency necessarily entails various political stakes. Who will distribute the goods? Who will receive them? Where, how, when, and how much? In a municipality such as Lamaria, all these dimensions of the aid process caused friction and competition between local institutions and community groups, not only religious ones, especially at the very beginning of the crisis, when a humanitarian response structure was being consolidated.

Because humanitarian emergencies allow religious institutions to put into practice the moral principles at the core of their teachings, such as charity and benevolence, we can ask whether these principles produce acts of giving. Within the Christian universe, the gift is believed to be free – and therefore without return – a disinterested, unilateral act of generosity and altruism. Perhaps the idea of no return should be nuanced: the faithful believe that the return of their good deed will come in the afterlife. It would then be like reparation after Judgment Day. In Christian exegesis, therefore, the donor does not expect any terrestrial return. The Christian gift is caritas and should suffice unto itself. Could we then consider the gestures performed by those religious orders in Lamaria that gave during the initial moments of crisis to be acts of solicitude akin to a form of gift? My discussions with representatives of various religious orders suggest that charity and compassion guided their motivation to act. They were recognized values that helped to define the initial humanitarian gestures of aid performed by churches.

As for the receivers, the arrival of aid made them feel lucky and grateful: "Las monjitas vinieron a darnos las primeras ayudas. Que buena gente" (The nuns gave us the first forms of aid. What good people). Many individuals recalled with emotion that a group of nuns had arrived in their *caserío* shortly after the earthquake with a pickup truck full of food. The memory of these first days remained vivid when I discussed them months later with the people at La Hermandad. For many, these gestures expressed a recognizable disinterested gifting logic. In general, "donors" would not expect a return in the form of exchange or debt. The situation was one of those unique social circumstances in which we witness gestures that correspond very closely to spontaneous, free, unilateral gifts devoid of calculation or interestedness. The "gift to strangers" that Godbout (1998, 65) describes comes to mind.

Interest and utilitarianism do not necessarily explain the motivations or reasoning behind people's humanitarian actions. In Lamaria individuals of diverse backgrounds, whether they were poor or middle-class, disaster victims or not, institutional players or not, concurred on this matter. The food, clothing, and even shelter whose distribution the religious orders ensured at the beginning of the emergency were often received as expressions of compassion and solicitude. Hence, at a first level of analysis, the religious congregations' helping gestures were often interpreted as unilateral "free gifts" without the expectation of any counterpart or reciprocity, thus reproducing the well-set belief ascribed to Christian religious entities that they are supposed to be there for those in need, like the Good Samaritan. Nevertheless, other aspects were equally at play.

People may have initially perceived these giving gestures as disinterested, but does it necessarily follow that they were indeed so? Here, nuance is required when comparing evangelical churches with the Catholic Church in Lamaria. The first, no doubt, tended to aid their own because of financial constraints, but they also had an interest in doing so, mainly that of ensuring that their followers would not seek the help of "competitors." Issues of leverage and influence were not entirely absent from the evangelical ministers' moral reasoning. This became obvious with the advent of housing reconstruction projects. The Catholic Church appeared less partisan because through the local chapter of the Missionary Sisters of Saint Peter Claver, it took charge of food aid distributions, which were done regardless of religious affiliation. By giving food to all those who qualified for it, the Catholic Church could appear benevolent. The opinion of disaster victims on these subtleties depended on one's religious allegiance and was not always clearly expressed. However, those middle-class families who were of Catholic obedience were not shy to criticize the "sectarian" attitude of the *evangélicos*.

As time passed, people began to question whether it was truly charity and solidarity that were driving the religious orders' acts of giving. Conflicting views about the recognition or non-recognition of gifting gestures arose, gestures that were dependent on the circumstances and configurations of activities designated as humanitarian.

One last point, before we delve into the organization of the humanitarian aid, concerns relations between neighbours. These were also important in shaping initial experiences of gifting. In a given neighbourhood, households were not uniformly affected: one house may have been almost completely demolished, whereas the one next to it remained standing with only superficial cracks. One person may have lost almost everything, whereas a neighbour felt lucky to still have a roof overhead. There were instances of neighbourly help in the disaster's wake, but people did not behave with equal empathy. Individuals' reactions depended on their own life trajectories, and although I do not dwell on these aspects here, *barrio* residents did not easily forget who was generous and who was not. For example, at the street corner where Rosa stayed before her rental unit fell down lived a well-to-do elderly lady whose house hardly fissured. "She barricaded herself inside for weeks," said Rosa, "impassive to the plight of her immediate neighbours like me." In any case, for many Lamarienses, the first forms of help were more spontaneous than the organized aid that arrived a few days later with humanitarian organizations.

To summarize, in the immediate aftermath of the earthquake, various gestures occurred between strangers, neighbours, and kin. In light of the chaos and destruction, many reacted in spontaneous ways that expressed a form of gifting; but we can also speak of solidarity and caring. In this extraordinary social context, special modalities of engagement were enacted, namely through customary mutual help networks and religious affiliation. Under the lens of the gift, two logics are at play: one of disinterested, free, and unilateral gifts couched in a language of compassion and one that corresponds to a Maussian understanding wherein these gestures articulate preceding forms of social relations. Yet, in this case, if the obligatory and interested dimensions of the Maussian gift are precisely those that confirm the "spirit" of these social ties (Godbout 1998; Godelier 2002), and given the unique circumstances, the expectation of a return was indefinitely postponed or dismissed. The various gestures that occurred in the immediate aftermath of the disaster were part of a moral economy that was not the sole purview of humanitarian action, for they expressed and affirmed pre-existing social ties and cannot be characterized as formal humanitarian configurations. When the NGOs arrived in town, the case was different: their goal was to establish a local response structure in order to distribute aid to all victims.

ORGANIZATION OF A LOCAL HUMANITARIAN STRUCTURE

Before the earthquake, Lamaria had not been visited by foreign development NGOs, contrary to other municipalities in El Salvador. At the time of the events, there were just a handful of national NGOs working there – such as the Unidad Ecológica Salvadoreña (UNES), OIKOS (linked to the World Lutheran Federation), and the Organización de Mujeres Salvadoreñas (ORMUSA).[7] UNES and OIKOS worked together on a project aimed at protecting the environment of the San Andres Valley, which had become very polluted because of the industrial free-trade zones nearby. ORMUSA was involved in a decontamination project for Lamaria's rural water wells. ORMUSA and OIKOS were partly financed by the Italian Cooperation, which injected more funds after the January 2001 earthquake. Some NGO employees arrived in town the day after the earthquake and others a little later.

It was imperative to get organized in order to help the victims, count them, take stock of the damage done, and clear the debris blocking access to the main road. City Hall became the gathering point for representatives of various institutions and NGOs. Among the organizations that joined the municipality's attempts to establish a coordinating structure were the Health Unit, the local Red Cross, FUSATE, the local police force, the order of the Claretian Brothers, and the aforementioned NGOs that had been working in the area.

No local institutional representative had any previous experience in responding to a post-disaster crisis. Yet that was precisely what awaited them. One might expect the personnel of the local Red Cross clinic to have had some knowhow in these matters, but that was not so. Lamaria's Red Cross office did not have a working ambulance, depended heavily on student volunteers, and was barely financially afloat despite its annual fundraising among local landowners and businessmen. Open all night, the Red Cross welcomed anyone in distress, but if people had the money to pay for a medical consultation, they preferred going to the Health Unit, where they had a better chance of seeing a doctor and getting medication. In fact, the earthquake was a "buena suerte" (good opportunity) for the Red Cross, said the young doctor who volunteered there, because it led to the organization receiving substantial help from the German Red Cross later on. In terms of emergency management and response, the local Red Cross did not have the expertise or the manpower to take on a leadership role. Given this leadership vacuum, the various local institutions decided to form a Municipal Emergency Committee, which was comprised of representatives of City Hall, the Health Unit, the police, the Red Cross clinic, FUSATE, and national NGOs present in the municipality at the time. In theory, all municipalities were meant to already have such an administrative body in place because of the frequency of earthquakes in the region, but it did not exist in Lamaria. Don Rodolfo, the city councillor from the FMLN, told me at length about his desire to form a Municipal Emergency Committee prior to the events, but other priorities had been deemed more pressing.

The Municipal Emergency Committee did not function smoothly. Aside from the lack of expertise and the suddenness of the events, an important impediment was the lack of trust between the different players. For example, the local Red Cross clinic and the Health Unit did not like collaborating with each other. The young director of the Red Cross thought that the doctors from the Health Unit were *egoistas* (selfish) and did not truly care about people's well-being! That the police were involved in the committee also engendered mistrust. The left-leaning city councillors were not inclined to coordinate their activities with the local police force, which was historically associated with the right, and although it was not as close to the right by 2001, the mistrust remained.[8] There was also *desconfianza* between the Red Cross and the mayor's office. I had not expected to hear individuals involved in the committee be so suspicious of one another's motives, but this mistrust should be understood as the lingering effect of years of civil war, which had pitted communities against each other all across the country.

According to Don Rodolfo, the divisions between left and right in Lamaria were exacerbated by the humanitarian emergency. This political polarization, which he called "ideological fanaticism," had a negative impact on coordination within the Municipal Emergency Committee. The situation was not unique to Lamaria but could be found in other municipalities and even at the national level. Don Rodolfo's comments echoed what the national press was publishing regarding the central government's management of international aid.

Although local representatives of the Municipal Emergency Committee agreed that their priority was to focus on the needs of the affected communities, they dissented as to the approach that should be adopted, which caused blockages. "Too many chiefs, not enough Indians," complained Don Rodolfo. The issue of coordination is a thorny one in any humanitarian emergency, and this was also true at the national level. In Lamaria the Municipal Emergency Committee still had not been established a week after the January earthquake. According to Blanca, a young woman working for OIKOS, the committee's discourse was circumscribed; when interacting with outsiders who had come to help, city councillors tended to express their party's line. They felt that even admitting that Lamaria did not have a functioning committee reflected badly on the municipality. As a result, the committee was not a functioning body. In fact, the words "emergency committee" were rarely expressed. When I was in Lamaria at the end of February distributing food with the nuns, no one ever mentioned the committee – even though the main players were regularly meeting at the mayor's headquarters. A month later, there was still very little evidence of a committee structure, and whatever it amounted to was dissolved as soon as the emergency period ended, after four months.

During the first weeks following the January earthquake, organizations from nearby townships, the army, and officials from Doctors Without Borders/Médecins Sans Frontières (MSF) helped Lamaria's institutional representatives to establish the Municipal Emergency Committee. The armed forces arrived shortly after the February earthquake, as did a representative of the Ministry of the Interior, who sought to place an army major and a police captain in charge of the management of humanitarian aid in Lamaria – even though the aid did not come from the central government. For a left-wing municipal office and like-minded NGOs, this was objectionable, all the more so considering that the majority of aid that had arrived since the first earthquake originated with foreign governments and with international organizations, namely the United Nations, the World Food Programme, international NGOs, the Salvadoran, Italian, and German Red Crosses, and different religious entities. The aid came in the form of food, drinkable water, medication, blankets, mattresses, plastic sheeting, tents, and so on. The mistrust toward the central government and its military took over, as Lamaria's City Hall and the NGOs did not want to see the army "usurp" control of the operations. Questions of power and control over relief efforts created tensions between institutional actors. In Lamaria the greatest mobilizing forces were no doubt the NGOs. Within three months of the earthquakes, close to ten NGOs had consolidated their presence in Lamaria and were playing an active role. People running the local Red Cross clinic were uneasy about the arrival of these sometimes very left-leaning and politically engaged NGO volunteers, for they were weary of the potential politicization of aid.

Conversely, many inhabitants appreciated the soldiers' presence in the municipality, especially because they could be seen packaging food items for distribution or lending a helping hand in the construction of temporary shelters. The army's contribution was particularly noteworthy in Lamaria, and many disaster victims approved of its help. Various individuals on the La Hermandad reconstruction site told me in retrospect that their opinion of the army had changed, for it had acquired a *mala fama* (bad reputation) as a result of the civil war. In a way, the army restored its standing during the humanitarian emergency, either leading or integrating itself into humanitarian relief efforts across the nation.

The Municipal Emergency Committee's first task was to identify sectors of intervention: food distribution, medical and psychological assistance, and the erection of temporary shelters. Such division of labour is of the utmost importance in any humanitarian crisis. In emergency interventions today, it is still not uncommon to hear representatives of humanitarian and national organizations lamenting the lack of coordination between agencies that leads to the duplication of aid in one locality to the detriment of another. This was not the case in Lamaria, where there was no duplication of aid and little overall critique regarding the amount of emergency assistance. Many organizations offered help in various forms, from emergency to reconstruction. Needs were so great that all the aid received was put to good use – an opinion shared by many people I met.

The next task was to tally the damages, especially regarding the number of houses that had collapsed or become structurally unsafe. NGO representatives and city councillors visited all the *cantones* and asked residents to count how many houses were damaged or destroyed in their area. A damaged house became the criterion according to which the distribution of food aid and construction materials, especially corrugated iron sheeting called *lamina*, was decided. The need for information pushed various rural communities to elect delegates to form a *directiva* that would act as their official representative body. Ultimately, this was a positive experience for the smaller settlements of Lamaria, allowing them to gain access to municipal deliberations, but it took many weeks to compile the definitive lists of disaster victims.

The Health Unit and MSF were put in charge of all health-related issues. The mayor's office was in charge of the distribution of *lamina* coming from the national government. And food aid was entrusted to the group of Catholic nuns running FUSATE. The question of food aid constituted an important element of the humanitarian response in Lamaria, one that expressed a particular moral configuration.

FOOD AID IN LAMARIA

The order of the Missionary Sisters of Saint Peter Claver was headed by Sister Elena, who was born in one of Lamaria's *cantones*. A short and dynamic woman with a sparkling gaze, Sister Elena was and remains an important figure in the municipality. She was the *comadre* of Doña Leonora, with whom I lived during my extended stay. During our last conversation, Sister Elena confided that she had always wanted to be a saint. She had started to pray, confess, and do penance when she was eight, and when she was thirteen, her mother allowed to enter the convent. Before the earthquake, Sister Elena had been fundraising in order to build a retirement home. No such institution had ever existed in Lamaria. The situation of elderly people could be quite dismal when they did not have any family, were poor, and received very few old-age pension provisions. Sister Elena's project had been six years in the making and was built just a few hundred metres away from what would become the La Hermandad reconstruction site. The *casa de retiro* (retirement home) is now a quasi-self-sustaining establishment with farmed tilapia pools, an orchard, and regular volunteers attending the elderly who live in two adjacent buildings, one for women and one for men (Sliwinski 2016).

Before the earthquake, the nuns had been running FUSATE, a community centre where single mothers were offered support and where a few elderly people lived on a permanent basis. During the emergency, it became the gathering point for food distribution for the entire municipality. It was there that the Montreal committee with which I was originally involved – Avec Toi Salvador Contigo – delivered its cargo.

Four nuns, Elena from Lamaria, Luz Miriam from Columbia, and two others from Nicaragua and Costa Rica, as well as a Spanish volunteer who had worked in development in Honduras, were put in charge of food aid at the request of City Hall. FUSATE was converted into a stockpiling area for hundreds of boxes and bags of corn, beans, oil, salt, rice, baby food, and clothing that needed to be sorted, divided into family portions, and distributed to the different *cantones* and *colonias*. All these goods arrived by truck from San Salvador, sometimes directly from the central government, but most food items came from the World Food Programme. The members of the *directivas* had to present the list of disaster *damnificados* (victims) in their area to FUSATE and schedule a distribution date.

Local truck drivers were hired for a nominal fee to help distribute the rations. I visited different *cantones*, driving along muddy and sinuous roads, to give out food rations to disaster-stricken families. Sister Elena thought it was good for a foreigner to be present, feeling perhaps that it conferred a more "international" air to the enterprise. A few soldiers helped with the packaging at FUSATE, but they did not participate in the distribution. They did not talk much, and I thought they seemed somewhat peeved at being under the command of a nun! When a pickup truck arrived at a distribution site, a small crowd would assemble at the rear of the truck, and each "beneficiary" would wait for his or her name to be called before receiving a ration. There would sometimes be confusion due to errors on the lists.

2.2 Stockpiling food aid at FUSATE, 2001. Boxes of food aid received from the World Food Programme and family rations await distribution to disaster victims.

2.3 Emergency food distribution, 2001. A local pickup truck arrives with family rations to be distributed in one of Lamaria's *colonia*. Only those whose names were on the lists of disaster victims were entitled to food aid.

The perceptions of local "aid givers" about the receivers and vice versa over time reveal changing moral configurations depending on donor identity. At the very beginning of the emergency, expressions of compassion, solidarity, and mutual help seemed to predominate, at least in the nuns' accounts, even though the logistics of official aid distribution did not leave much room for sentiment. In fact, gestures from official donors such as the mayor's office were often looked upon with distrust or even dismissed. "It is only 'normal' that the government assist its citizens in time of need," was one opinion I often heard. Some were much more skeptical of the municipal authorities' intentions, associating the distribution with a kind of bribe (e.g., one gets *lamina* in exchange for one's vote), which would not have been an unheard-of practice in national political life. The Catholic Church escaped this suspicion but only in part. Relations with official institutions are so often marked by mistrust that for some people, it was unthinkable that the aid came freely; they believed instead that it hid some kind of scheme. Foreigners, however, escaped the stigma to a certain degree; the thinking was that since foreigners were rich, they could afford to be generous.

These comments underscore the prevalence of political clientelism, which is as well entrenched in Lamaria as anywhere else in the country, or in Central America for that matter. As I previously mentioned, historically rival patronage networks linking peasants and landed elites were routine in municipal and national electoral processes. These networks were based not just on political party lines but also on familial and ethnic relationships – including that of *compadrazgo* (Montes 1979). After the civil war, they continued to be mobilized along ARENA and FMLN ideological cleavages. Yet it would be wrong to regard rural populations as completely subservient, for they have long had a bargaining power (Montoya 2015). In Lamaria ARENA had always ruled until the 2000 elections, which the FMLN won. Don Moisés called upon the nuns to manage food aid in the municipality partly to avoid potential accusations of partisanship and clientelism, which are easily exacerbated in the context of humanitarian emergencies. Indeed, disasters occur in "politically and epistemologically charged" circumstances because the political culture of a locality inflects the manner in which the relationships between government, aid agencies, and disaster-affected populations unravel (Barrios 2014, 330).

Because the management of aid requires a minimum of ordering and security, the soldiers' presence was appreciated at FUSATE, as there had been a few burglary attempts. But most importantly, as the months went by, a phenomenon of dependency emerged. "A poor community affected by an earthquake that receives food aid twice a week for four months gets used to it," said Sister Elena. In retrospect, the nuns felt that the people "had not responded as they should have." The attitude of the *damnificados*, confided Sister Elena, had become, "Que todo me lo den, traiga, hagan!" (Give, do, and go get me everything!). Her opinion of the disaster victims had changed over time, and she blamed this change on the dependency that food aid generated in people who "lacked education" and who did not "have the same capacity for compassion" as she did. In spite of this dependency, and although the nuns found the experience exhausting and often frustrating, it also rekindled their faith on a personal level. We may appreciate how the notion of the "gift of self" oriented the way that they interiorized their humanitarian work in Lamaria.

Delivering food rations to thousands of people scattered around Lamaria's *cantones* for four months, even with the help of many volunteers, was a tremendous task for four nuns without prior experience in humanitarian operations. In fact, at a purely organizational and logistical level, they managed rather well.

Can we call this a gifting gesture? What was being offered were staples distributed to victims whose houses had been seriously damaged or destroyed. The nuns acted as intermediaries between international and national donor institutions, on the one hand, and disaster-affected families, on the other. They were the penultimate step in the food aid chain. Although this "gift" of food itself did not result from their own labour, what they gave (time, leadership, logistics, etc.) was significant and represented a service to the community. We could ask what motivated their decision to perform it. The moral dimension is important here. The nuns did share a cause: that of helping vulnerable people, whether earthquakes or other disasters had hit the municipality or not. However, they were not obligated to take on the responsibility of managing food aid. Their motivation can be partially explained by their sense of moral duty stemming from their religious belief. To assist the poor is a core feature of their religious mandate. "We should give the example to the community of Christians and strengthen its faith," said Sister Elena. This symbolic dimension is significant, and the nuns did not dismiss it when they reflected on their action in conversation with me. But there is more.

The nuns' involvement within the local humanitarian structure put them in contact with various donor organizations, both national and foreign, such as the German Red Cross. We could say that these collaborations and the nuns' acceptance of responsibility for the distribution of food aid increased their "social capital" and can therefore be seen as serving more utilitarian and interested motives. In turn, this social capital would facilitate their access to economic capital later on, when reconstruction funds became available, which not only reinforced the position of the Catholic Church in the municipality but also boosted the nuns' project of building a retirement home. The disbursement of money a few months later from the German Red Cross to the retirement home initiative confirms this rationale. As time passed, the nuns' reputation and prestige grew, especially among institutional actors such as international humanitarian organizations and local delegates from Lamaria.

I conversed many times with the nuns, and although there is no denying the calculating dimension of their involvement, I do not abide by Bourdieu's (1977) thesis of misrecognition to describe their social practice. The nuns did not disavow or conceal the strategic possibilities of their humanitarian work, but they did keep them secondary to an embodied "logic of compassion." This moral reasoning draws from two different spheres of value: an altruistic one and a utilitarian one. My contention is that a one-dimensional reading of the nuns' gifting gestures fails to acknowledge the complexity of their social practice. For the nuns, interest and utilitarianism were compatible with the Christian conception of caritas.

On the side of the receivers of food aid (i.e., the hundreds of disaster victims), utilitarian reasoning was more clearly evident. Having been labelled "victims" of the earthquake, they acquired a special identity – that of "beneficiary" – and benefited from the advantages that came with it. I am not inferring that their fate was enviable, far from it. But a poor family whose home fell down was on the humanitarians' lists and received emergency food aid, whereas another family just as impoverished whose house was still standing did not. We should not underestimate the strains that arose in neighbourhoods between those who were entitled to receive food aid and those who were not. This scenario is far from unique and speaks to the complexities that arise from the superimposition of "foreign" humanitarian logics of inclusion and exclusion onto those that people mobilize in their daily lives, including prevailing patron-client networks. This situation extends well beyond the Salvadorian context; for example, Gamburd (2014) shows in detail how the introduction of emergency food aid and shelters in Sri Lanka after the 2004 tsunami was increasingly viewed as "unfair," brewing tremendous distrust among the population of the area where she worked because new normative criteria of belonging and entitlement were defining who had a right to aid.[9] Gamburd (ibid., 173) describes a tense humanitarian context where people's "moral logic has been warped by greed, jealousy and an expanding sense of entitlement." This tension is exacerbated when the intermediaries in the aid chain are individuals known to a given locality, like in the case of Sister Elena, who complained that beneficiaries were "not behaving as they ought to."

Food aid lasted four months in Lamaria. At the start, some perceived these gestures as gift-like – at least that is what families from La Hermandad later confided to me when they were recollecting their impressions of those first months. But with the institutionalization of food aid, a form of habit or dependency developed: what was given came to be seen as an entitlement, as a right to aid. "Somos damnificados, tienen que ayudarnos, tenemos derecho" (We are disaster victims, they have to help us, we have rights) are comments I heard during my tours in the pickup trucks. The gratitude that the nuns received in recognition of their efforts (as an immediate form of return) was diminishing. Indeed, recognition is an important dimension of gifting dynamics. For Mauss (1925, 1954), reciprocity is the key concept that underscores the significance of sociality. The notion of recognition, however, derives from the Hegelian tradition, and it enriches our understanding of processes of mutuality. Both theories are framed by a tripartite structure.[10] Different authors "have recently argued that it would be fruitful to read Mauss's ideas as a contribution to a more general theory of the role of mutual recognition in human life" (Robbins 2009, 47). Marcel Hénaff (2010, 114), for instance, seeks to deepen our understanding of these questions by insisting that gifting "relationships of recognition" must not be conflated with the "struggle for recognition" expounded by Hegel. He explains that ceremonial gift exchanges (the forms of gifting relationships about which Mauss writes) are not a moral form of gift giving; in fact, they should not be called gift exchanges but "sumptuous offerings" (ibid.). They are not moral because they seek first and foremost to establish *social* ties, not *moral* ties. Hénaff concedes that they exist in our contemporary societies in the guise of wedding invitations, birthday presents, and so forth, but these gestures are distinct from the ethnographic cases studied by Mauss.

They are also quite distinct from the modality of gifting that the nuns were performing through food aid. This latter gesture was moral and drew on two complementary traditions because of the agents enacting it (i.e., Catholic nuns): that of Christian charity and that of secular humanitarianism. Both rest on moral bedrocks. Both seek to help the other not through networks of reciprocity but on the basis of compassionate, generous behaviour and concern for fellow human beings. Moreover, and this is important, the givers and the givers alone decided upon the gifting gestures to be performed. Indeed, disaster victims had little to say about the content of the "gift" of food aid they received. But the point I want to make regards the centrality of recognition in this specific humanitarian configuration.

In theory, charity and humanitarian assistance do not require a return of any kind. But things were more complicated for the nuns, especially for Sister Elena, who came from Lamaria. First, the nuns were well-known public figures in the municipality. Sister Elena was the *comadre* of various middle-class individuals I met. She had privileged access to the mayor's office, regardless of who occupied it. And her reputation was a central part of the decision to assign food aid distribution to her organization. In other words, food aid in Lamaria was enacted not by anonymous donors but by identifiable and reputable local public figures. Conversely, this situation meant that the receivers were not anonymous either, so the notion of the "gift to strangers" analyzed by Godbout (1998, 65) does not fully apply in this case. Second, although the nuns did not expect any form of reciprocity, they did appreciate the recognition from the people they were helping. It validated their efforts, their "gift of self." This phrase is no mere figure of speech; the nuns had risen up to face a huge challenge for which they had no prior experience, and they needed to build alliances with different groups, such as the army, local truck drivers, and a vast array of institutions like the World Food Programme and NGOs, in order to "deliver the goods." And they spent hours at FUSATE stockpiling food, managing accounts, organizing logistics, and dealing with unforeseen problems, all the while tending to their equally pressing "normal" duties. In February they were tired; after fourth months of "emergency," they were exhausted. To name their involvement a "gift of self" is not to overstate the matter; it speaks to the Christian teachings of selflessness through charitable gestures that the nuns had interiorized.

Being recognized as performing a valued service to the community was one important aspect of the nuns' involvement. Another was the more phenomenological experience of recognition – or gratefulness – as something addressed to them, personally, by the families they visited on a biweekly basis. When the receivers did not feel obligated to the donors anymore because aid had become routine, when they did not participate in the logic of mutual recognition but behaved according to a much more individualistic logic, the "spirit" of the gift withered, and another strategy was revealed, a strategy of survival. One thing is clear: contrary to the gifting cycles studied by Mauss, donors and receivers of food aid are not established social groups transacting with each other based on interpersonal ties of reciprocity. Although such relationships did exist between the residents themselves, as in the case of *compadrazgo*, in the context of the distribution of humanitarian food aid, the "exchanging parties" were not as familiar with one another, and the form of return that was perhaps there at the beginning, marked by the gratitude the nuns recognized, faded for various reasons.

On the side of the receivers, we are referring to a social group that had been marginalized economically, socially, and politically for decades and that generally did not trust political authorities, whether they were from the left or the right. They may have had more respect for religious representatives, such as the nuns, but their main worry in the post-disaster context was to ensure their survival. The residents of the *cantones* and *caseríos* entered into the humanitarian system and in a way "capitalized" on a new identity that was assigned to them: that of "disaster victim" and "beneficiary." This identity designated them as entitled receivers of aid. In these conditions, why enact for months on end the rhetoric of a gifting match? And why express anything in return since one has the right to food aid?

As Roberto Barrios (2014, 344) underscores, aid configurations do not arise out of a vacuum but emerge from "epistemically ideologically charged" environments and relationships. His work on post-disaster reconstruction in Choluteca, a province in the southern part of Honduras severely hit by Hurricane Mitch in 1998, shows that entwined clientelist relationships between rural populations, municipal governments, and aid organizations had an effect on reconstruction initiatives and on communities' vulnerability and disaster resilience. Lamarienses share a similar political culture to that of Cholutecans, having participated for decades in patron-client relationships with local governments. And these relationships have long been part of important strategies of survival; they are "not just a set of calculative practices through which ordinary people receive goods and favours" but are "problem-solving networks through which people deal with survival-related needs" (Montoya 2015, 113). Disaster-affected populations in Lamaria's *cantones* and *caseríos* receiving food aid from a non-customary political actor – the nuns – engaged with this humanitarian configuration through prior ideological lenses informing local political culture.

A humanitarian crisis is a context of exception. In Lamaria the victims of the earthquake were predominantly poor families in a traditionally marginal position. When a sudden event alters, even just slightly, the customary social hierarchy, putting the poor at the forefront of a humanitarian response, and even if this change endures only for the period of the emergency, a strategy of survival may mean having to take advantage of it as much as one can. However, in Lamaria not all actors agreed with the shift from a compassionate gifting logic to a more utilitarian one. Some donors sought to remain aligned with the former logic, although it became clear that the receivers had withdrawn from it. This outcome explains the difference between the nuns and the people to whom they were distributing food. For a long time prior to the disaster, the nuns had interiorized the logic of compassion; it was part of their identity as the Missionary Sisters of Saint Peter Claver. For the "beneficiaries," the logic of compassion was perhaps sustainable for a while but not interminably. People knew very well that this food aid was temporary, that it was a time of exception and thus an opportunity, so why not make the most out of it? Why not use their new identity as beneficiaries to ask for more? There is nothing surprising about this stance.

Various middle-class families to whom I spoke shared the nuns' opinion regarding poor people's dependency on food aid. A few words on how people perceived me may be informative here. At the beginning of my fieldwork, I was associated with the donors. I was a foreigner after all, helping the nuns distribute food in the rural areas of the town. It was therefore logical to associate me with those individuals and institutions that provided aid. Later, when I returned for ten months to study how the politics and dynamics of aid evolved on a housing reconstruction site, I was associated with the poor families of La Hermandad. But with time, people from the town centre, such as the doctor with whom I had stayed in February and Don Augusto, with whom I lived in Lamaria, as well as vendors in my *barrio*, felt more at ease telling me what they thought about the entire humanitarian enterprise. And the general feeling was that although it was laudable to help the poor, they did not appreciate it and simply got used to receiving things from others. The point is not to confirm or deny the truth-value of this statement but to highlight that under a humanitarian regime, distinctions and tensions are produced between people due to the creation of new social categories: the "most vulnerable" people become the prime "beneficiaries" of humanitarian assistance, whereas other groups deemed "less vulnerable," such as people who own a small business or who have not suffered injury or lost property, are excluded. These categories express new criteria by which persons come to be defined and by which further judgments about humanitarian gestures are made. These are precisely the kinds of narratives that enable ordinary ethics to take shape. What I have called the middle-class families were not the main targets of the humanitarians, but we should not imagine them as a well-to-do group. Aside from the large land and industry owners, no one was ostensibly rich in Lamaria. Well-off people resided in the newer (sometimes gated) suburbs of San Salvador. Hence, when referring to Lamaria's middle class, I mean a socioeconomic group of individuals who were employed and who generally owned a house. They would remind me that although ruled out as receivers of humanitarian aid, they *too* had suffered.

THE ROLE OF NGOs IN AN EMERGENCY

The mission of the few Salvadoran NGOs present in Lamaria before the events was different from that of the nuns, as were their discourses. Their objective was to promote social development by raising "the awareness of communities," especially rural communities, in a Freirean way through a series of educational, agricultural, and environmental projects. They tried to kindle "community solidarity" – a theme that was very much promoted on the La Hermandad reconstruction site. The Salvadoran NGOs did not participate in food distribution and were only marginally involved in the construction of temporary shelter, but after a few months, they participated in various reconstruction activities.

These initiatives ranged from housing to school and public infrastructure reconstruction projects (e.g., wells, rural roads, and latrines) but only in a few *cantones*. The NGOs' perception of disaster victims (who were also their "beneficiaries"), and of aid dependency more specifically, was different from that of the nuns. According to various NGO field representatives I met, the needs of the poor were so great that there was no real risk of dependency. The humanitarian emergency allowed the NGOs to develop a range of projects, extending from construction to training. Once the height of the emergency had passed, they offered courses to communities, targeting especially the *directivas*, on topics such as risk reduction, environmental sanitation, and vulnerability assessment. This education was rendered possible partly through the backing of international NGOs, better financed by foreign donors who defined the larger programmatic orientations of relief efforts. In this respect, the majority of the funds were allocated to the rebuilding of infrastructure: first, temporary shelters and, second, permanent houses. In the chronology of events, the priority of international donors was to build shelters and houses, and although some international and national NGOs were integrating more "developmental" components into their "bricks and mortar" initiatives, what Hewitt (1983) calls the "physicalist" approach to disasters and reconstruction predominated.

The NGOs working in Lamaria were part of the Foro de la Sociedad Civil, a group of Salvadoran civil society organizations that shared a critical stance toward the macro-economic neoliberal model that the ARENA government was pursuing at the time. Some of them, such as UNES and OIKOS, clearly connected their critique of the dominant neoliberal economic model to the discourse on the social causes of disasters.

In light of this affiliation, one can better understand why the perception of the Salvadoran NGO workers stationed in Lamaria was different from that of local institutional representatives who did not work in the field of development. Furthermore, these NGOs were not emergency respondents (i.e., specialized in immediate response to humanitarian crises) in the way that MSF and the Red Cross were. As members of organizations committed to achieving longer-term social change, NGO fieldworkers would discuss the plight of disaster victims in light of a critical development model. Their interpretative framework was neither that of charitable morality nor that of a stereotyped paternalistic discourse where the poor are viewed as "lazy and unappreciative." Rather, they saw the Salvadoran poor as the historically marginalized and exploited underclass dominated by rich capitalist elites.

As for the presence of emergency organizations, there were only two: MSF and the Salvadoran Red Cross. MSF took the lead in establishing temporary encampments and was helped by the army and the Red Cross. Together, they put in place three campsites for a few hundred homeless families. Almost all the families who were sheltered there qualified for permanent housing projects beginning in May 2001, something these families did not necessarily foresee. However, MSF did not get involved in the building of permanent houses. Its members left the municipality in May 2001, and responsibility for transitioning from temporary shelters to permanent housing was transferred to the German chapter of the Red Cross.

What came across very clearly from my talks with the La Hermandad residents who had been sheltered by MSF was this organization's generosity. Indeed, everyone I spoke to insisted that MSF had been a great donor and had given them shelter, food, and hope at a most dire time in their lives. The feeling that they were *fortunados* (lucky) to have been selected as beneficiaries, thanks to an earthquake and to MSF, was a recurring theme in my discussions with the families. The NGO had "given without counting," it had distributed *lamina*, and it had sheltered them in the encampments where the nuns made their rounds, with the end result of increasing their chances of becoming new homeowners. In terms of the moral economy of humanitarianism, MSF was judged as a most generous donor. It received important symbolic capital in return, a point of view widely shared by local institutional players. MSF had been efficient in assisting homeless disaster-affected families. And the latter found themselves in the position of receiving unidirectional gifting gestures, a stance they later contrasted with their experience on the reconstruction site.

For the 2,500 families who did not have to live in the temporary encampments, questions regarding shelter and home repairs came under the responsibility of the mayor's office. In the entire country, it was estimated that there was a deficit of 400,000 homes before the earthquake. Afterward, this number increased to 600,000. In Lamaria hundreds of families did not have a decent and safe roof over their heads. Providing families with building materials to fix their homes before the rainy season began in May was a priority. During my stay in February, many were worried, hoping that the government would remedy the situation in a timely manner. Materials such as corrugated iron sheets, wooden beams, and waterproof plastic were being distributed via government channels, such as the Fondo de Inversión Social para el Desarrollo Local, to the many affected municipalities in the country. Although essential, the problem with this particular type of aid is that structures that are meant to be temporary can be rendered permanent.

The mayor's office had stockpiled sheets of *lamina*, and city officials began distribution at the end of February and throughout March and April. Military personnel sometimes assisted families in the assemblage. A lot of gossip circulated about the distribution of *lamina*, notably the idea that the mayor and councillors were keeping some for themselves, that only FMLN sympathizers would receive *lamina*, or that there was not enough to cover everybody's needs. People were suspicious, and as far as I could tell, the distribution of *lamina* was not viewed by anyone as part of a special humanitarian benevolence. Instead, it was seen as an impersonal transaction. The mayor's office was mandated to provide construction material to the affected citizens, and this gesture was squarely distinguished from the gifting gestures of MSF and the nuns.

CONCLUSION

Overall, the establishment of a humanitarian structure in Lamaria was done with the direct help of the Catholic Church through an order of nuns and the support of a few Salvadoran NGOs that had been working in Lamaria. The local institutions that became involved in this process collaborated during the four months of the emergency period. Afterward, all returned to their usual operations, although they did perform some activities during reconstruction. Despite the lack of preparation, the magnitude of people's needs, and the customary mistrust toward official institutions, the local humanitarian structure succeeded in answering people's needs in a rather transparent manner when we consider the political polarization that characterized El Salvador. The post-disaster emergency was a catalyst for many NGOs. It gave them the opportunity to boost community organizing and to participate in local reconstruction initiatives. However, these projects did not always endorse their progressive vision of reconstruction: the process of reconstruction would reveal contrasting interpretations of what it meant to build a *casa digna* (decent house).

3

The Time of Reconstruction: Actors, Challenges, and Ideals

Post-disaster reconstruction gave rise to much debate throughout El Salvador, including in Lamaria, about how to reconstruct the municipality, how to help the hundreds of homeless families, and how to rebuild half a dozen schools. These issues were on the minds of all who took part in the municipal humanitarian response effort. This chapter addresses the challenges posed by reconstruction in Lamaria and introduces the La Hermandad reconstruction project, where I undertook extended fieldwork in 2001–02.

It begins with a general presentation of the reconstruction activities in Lamaria. I then discuss the way in which reconstruction integrates community participation as a guiding principle. Here, I recall a few central points regarding the rise of community participation as a preferred policy in development interventions aimed at social change. The third section discusses a reconstruction project that took place in Los Mangos in 2001, which illustrates how community participation can be misconstrued and challenged by project participants. The fourth section introduces the La Hermandad site, explaining the antecedents of the project, the choice of location, and the main rules and regulations. Finally, the last section unpacks the project logic from which many paradoxes ensued.

MAPPING RECONSTRUCTION IN LAMARIA

There were different permanent housing reconstruction projects in Lamaria. The largest one by far, headed by the German Red Cross, included one hundred families located on two sites in the Los Almendros area, fifty in La Hermandad and fifty in La Fraternidad.

Even though this project was also the lengthiest, lasting from May 2001 to June 2002, it was completed quickly if we compare it with other post-disaster initiatives; for instance, in various areas affected by the 2004 South-Asian tsunami, some projects took five to eight years to complete. Similar issues arose after Hurricane Katrina in 2005 and after the Haitian earthquake in 2010. The projects I discuss below did not, however, cover the housing needs of all the people affected by the earthquake. They targeted only the "most vulnerable population," namely the families who had been living in the temporary encampments set up by Doctors Without Borders/ Médecins Sans Frontières (MSF) since the earthquakes in January and February 2001.

Aside from the German Red Cross projects, the other main projects included an initiative to build fifty houses led by an Italian NGO called the Comitato Internazionale por lo Sviluppo dei Popoli (International Committee for the Development of Peoples) and by its Salvadoran counterpart the Organización de Mujeres Salvadoreñas, as well as a project to build another fifty houses led by the Marist Brothers. These initiatives were also located in La Fraternidad. La Hermandad was a few hundred metres to the south. Both La Fraternidad and La Hermandad were envisioned as examples of new "model urbanization" strategies, serviced with drinkable water and electricity.

Aside from these projects, there were others but smaller in scale. For example, the Costa Rica government financed the building of ten houses in the *colonia* San Antonio, not far from the town centre. A Japanese NGO subsidized the reconstruction of a large primary school, located on the other side of the highway. OIKOS (linked to the World Lutheran Federation) was also involved in reconstruction in various *cantones*, but the difference between these projects and the ones in Los Almendros is that the latter involved the resettlement of families to a new location – families who had never owned a house or a plot of land prior to the earthquake.

Land ownership is an important question in post-disaster settings (Brown and Crawford 2006; Barenstein and Leeman 2012). No one wants to build a house for a poor family on a plot of land that belongs to someone else. It was a cause of concern – not to say a headache – for most organizations involved in housing reconstruction in El Salvador, and part of the problem could be traced back to the civil war. Depending on each NGO's and donor's procurement methodology, some projects required families to hold official property titles as a condition of receiving reconstruction help. But poor people without property titles were precisely the recipients whom the majority of international NGOs targeted. Most NGOs applied to the Vice-Ministry of Habitat and the Instituto Libertad y Progreso to research and formalize the status of a person as a legal landowner. Projects thus lagged behind schedule while official property titles were obtained and authorities checked whether a plot of land was available to build on. To these delays were added the Kafkaesque bureaucratic bottlenecks that paralyzed progress for months on end, greatly displeasing donors, who were keen to respect deadlines.

Reconstruction in Lamaria meant different things to different people. After the second earthquake, the mayor's office set up a Reconstruction Committee (distinct from the Municipal Emergency Committee), which was comprised of two city councillors, an administrative assistant, and two delegates of *cantones* and *colonias*. Drawing from the lists used for food distribution, which detailed the extent of damage in the housing sector, they established criteria for permanent housing needs. Four categories were identified: renters without land, *colonos de fincas* (labourers living on the land of an agricultural estate), families living in zones at risk, and families sheltered in the temporary encampments. These groups of people were labelled vulnerable populations and were the primary targets of the organizations involved in reconstruction. Many families moved to Los Almendros, namely all of those in the fourth group.

Middle-class homeowners received very little help from the municipality. If they needed to repair or rebuild, they had to do it on their own. For instance, Don Augusto and Doña Leonora, with whom I lived, saw the wall between their kitchen and the interior patio fall down. They decided not to rebuild it (which gave a rather nice perspective to the house, reminding me at first of a Roman atrium!) because they preferred to repair another more seriously damaged and smaller house that they rented out. To do so, they saved over a few months and were able to get back on their feet financially by the end of the year. All shop owners in the *barrio* also managed by themselves. Individuals who owned property, received a pension, or still earned a living were generally not eligible for official aid due to their socio-economic status. In the moral economy of Lamaria's humanitarian venture, they did not constitute a vulnerable group.

Among the other homeowners were much poorer people who for the most part did not live in the urban *colonias* but in the rural *cantones*. Many earned the minimum wage and lived in small dwellings often made of adobe that collapsed during the earthquake. The reason for an NGO to target such individuals was to avoid all uncertainty regarding property titles. The houses rebuilt in the San Antonio area by the Costa Ricans fall into this category. The most significant project of this type was conducted by the Italian chapter of the NGO Terre des Hommes and was aimed at helping eighty-six entitled homeowners in the Los Mangos *cantón*.

The renters who had made it onto the list of the Reconstruction Committee were not only from the urban centre of Lamaria but also from the rural areas, where rents were cheaper than in town. If the owner of a demolished *mesón* (rental unit) decided not to rebuild, the families had to find a new home. More than a third of the La Hermandad families had been renters of *mesones* in the centre of town. Rosa's family spent around two months under a plastic tarp on the very site where their *mesón* had collapsed. "Fue duro, Alicia" (It was hard, Alicia), she told me. Rosa explained that the owner of the *mesón* would look at her old renters squatting on her land with an "evil eye." Initially, Rosa did not want to join the other families in the encampments built by MSF, thinking these would become permanent housing settlements.

Some disaster-stricken families who had not been officially categorized as "vulnerable" nevertheless received help from small-scale religious initiatives. Indeed, reconstruction was not the domain just of NGOs and the government. In general, faith-based reconstruction initiatives were addressed to people whose property title could be easily checked. Certain evangelical churches, such as the Mormons and the Jehova's Witnesses, received funds from their headquarters to help disaster-stricken families by financing a large part of their reconstruction costs. A lady I knew, the ex-mother-in-law of Dr Díaz, received this kind of help from the Mormons. As an ambulant candy vendor, her salary never allowed her to save enough to purchase land or a house. At a cut rate, Dr Díaz sold her a small plot of land, on which she made plans to build a modest house. This woman did not fit the pre-established criteria used to select beneficiaries for the projects in Los Almendros. But as a Mormon, she could benefit from the Mormons' swifter and more generous offer.

Such individualized religious initiatives adopted a framework that was different from those of larger reconstruction projects financed by international and national donor agencies. The activities led by evangelical churches targeted their own members. In this sense, arrangements for gifting could not avoid agreements between preacher and follower; in a single breath, recipients invoked Christ and a house, even if they had to pay their dues. Cynics could say that for a bit of mortar and a few bricks, faith was rekindled. The situation was reversed in the case of small rural churches, which asked their followers for financial contributions. Over months, members amassed the required money to rebuild, bit by bit, their parish. It is a kind of giving and counter-giving that is closer to the Maussian model between exchanging parties who entertain personal relations structured around religious affiliation and belonging. People knew each other and had probably helped each other out before; the parish was a place of ritual but also of support. In a society often marked by mistrust, it provided a space for people to weave relationships of trust. But these small congregations did not receive as much money as the Mormons and the Jehovah's Witnesses. In the general context of post-disaster reconstruction, these micro-scale initiatives operated on the sidelines. Moreover, they were not subject to the same regulations as NGOs, governments, and international donors. They functioned within their own private parameters and reflected the fervour of their members.

This overview of the reconstruction initiatives in Lamaria allows us to flesh out a number of points. First, there was a wide variety of reconstruction activities. In Lamaria, like in other Salvadoran municipalities, the organizations involved in reconstruction established distinct selection criteria to identify beneficiaries, each proposing a particular design for the house – in brick or cement, more or less spacious, modular or not, and so on. The category of "vulnerable population" was subdivided according to the objectives of an organization: the majority of international NGOs targeted poor rural families with or without property titles; NGOs specializing in women's issues sought to involve single mothers; evangelical organizations catered to their members; and others, wishing to avoid administrative deadlocks, preferred to work with entitled homeowners. Donors were the ones who decided. People's only choice was whether to accept an NGO's offer or not.

In June 2002 – more than sixteen months after the earthquakes – only 30 per cent of demolished houses had been repaired or rebuilt,

3.1 Model *techo y piso*, 2001. A cement base, aluminum roofing, and steel bars on which walls can be raised constitute the "roof and floor" design for this type of permanent housing. Some NGOs' reconstruction initiatives opted for this design.

and many of these houses still needed work. Sometimes the new structure consisted only of a concrete floor and an aluminum-sheeting roof, a model called *techo y piso*, which allowed the recipients to raise the walls as they pleased. The rationale for this approach privileged quantity over quality, since a *techo y piso* model cost less per unit than a fully built house.

The role of the mayor's office in housing reconstruction was limited. In 2001 Salvadoran municipalities did not collect their own taxes. The central government allocated 6 per cent of its budget to municipalities, regardless of political representation. Lamaria's City Hall did not draw from these funds to finance any housing reconstruction project at the time of my stay, although it collaborated with NGOs. According to a city councillor on the Reconstruction Committee, no more than 10 per cent of the financial aid received by the municipality came from the central government; the rest came from foreign donors through NGOs.

The mayor's office used the "opportunity" of post-disaster reconstruction to advance a planning project it had been preparing before the earthquakes. Indeed, councillors wanted to provide better access to electricity and drinkable water in the *cantones*, to construct new urban projects – among which Los Almendros – and to identify zones at risk of flooding and landslides. Never before had such an extensive exercise of territorial planning been conducted by the municipality. It took the two 2001 earthquakes for Lamaria to draw its first municipal and cantonal maps.

Compared to more isolated and remote small towns in the region, Lamaria did not have to actively seek the help of NGOs. Questions of access and population composition made a difference; Lamaria is easy to get to from the highway and is not deeply nestled between the hills and valleys of the Cordillera de Balsamo, unlike smaller hamlets. Also, an important percentage of the population has long been composed of professionals (e.g., dentists, doctors, lawyers, computer programmers, engineers, and accountants), but without a proper census, I cannot ascertain their number. Many did not exercise their trade in town but in larger agglomerations like San Salvador, Santa Tecla, or Santa Ana. It was suggested to me that due to their professional relations, they might have influenced the provision of humanitarian and reconstruction aid. According to Mauricio, a social worker who had recently been hired by the mayor's office to facilitate the coordination between the *cantones' directivas* and the NGOs, Lamaria held a definite advantage over neighbouring municipalities because it was a very commercial town. But he also had a more political explanation: he argued that NGOs – especially national ones – tended to be more supportive of municipalities that elected a left-wing mayor than they were of the ones aligned with the Alianza Republicana Nacionalista (ARENA). That Lamaria had recently put a left-wing coalition in power explained why various NGOs were already there when the earthquakes struck. According to Mauricio, this was also true of international NGOs, which had intervened for a long time in El Salvador, assisting the demobilized troops of the Frente Farabundo Martí para la Liberación Nacional (FMLN) after the signing of the peace accord in 1992.

The municipal government used its funds to repair public infrastructure, including the central park. The park was a component of the territorial planning project and held a symbolic value, for it was considered a local heritage site.[1] At the inauguration ceremony for the new park in June 2002, Shafik Handal, an ex-FMLN combatant and the leader of the FMLN in 2002, whom some considered a "communist dinosaur," gave a speech. To his eyes, it was thanks to the FMLN that Lamaria had received enough humanitarian assistance for reconstruction. The political recuperation was flagrant.

Meanwhile, many families had not received any housing reconstruction assistance and hoped that other NGOs would propose alternatives. These proposals came only in mid-April 2002. A commitment to build six hundred houses for the remainder of the disaster victims who held a property title was made by the United States Agency for International Development (USAID) and the Cooperative for Assistance and Relief Everywhere (CARE) through their respective Salvadoran partners, namely the government agency Organismo Promotor de Exportaciones e Inversiones de El Salvador (PROESA)[2] and the non-profit organization Fundación Salvadorena de Apoyo Integral (FUSAI).[3] Another Salvadoran organization, the think-tank Fundación Dr Guillermo Manuel Ungo (FUNDAUNGO),[4] was considering constructing three hundred houses for low-income families without property titles. While the La Hermandad project was drawing to a close in June 2002, over a thousand families were still waiting for some kind of reconstruction offer to come their way.

RECONSTRUCTION AND COMMUNITY PARTICIPATION

So far, I have focused on gifting as a core element of humanitarian configurations. But the gift is not the only value that frames aid initiatives: reconstruction is also suffused with people's desire to do things better, and one of its longstanding features is the involvement of affected communities. In the moral economy of humanitarian endeavours in Lamaria, the participation of the affected communities was a very significant element.

Reconstruction has a particular temporal status in a humanitarian endeavour, as it comes after the emergency period (for which humanitarian action is best known), but it is not quite about development either. It has a narrower focus than development and does not engage with its long-term horizon. The purpose of reconstruction is to rebuild what has been damaged, which usually concerns physical infrastructure. However, most organizations involved in reconstruction – including the state, multilateral and bilateral agencies, and of course, international and national NGOs – would refuse to define it as a mere bricks and mortar enterprise. Other "softer" or "social" dimensions are usually embedded in reconstruction projects that target livelihoods and economic recovery for disaster-affected communities. They can also focus on governance, peacekeeping, and security in areas where conflict compounds the effects of a natural disaster. Reconstruction, in its widest sense, is a concept replete with potentialities: to build better, safer homes; to create stronger, more prosperous and "resilient" communities; and to foster more equitable and just institutions and practices of governance. In the specialized literature on post-disaster recovery, the social counterpart to reconstruction is called rehabilitation, and it refers to people more specifically. Reconstruction and rehabilitation are integral to the overall recovery process (Aldrich 2012). However, these terms are not consistently applied in real-life contexts; they certainly describe the way donors, policymakers, and NGO workers engage in expert knowledge about post-disaster recovery, but the vernacular categories that disaster-affected populations use may not reproduce them. In Lamaria people talked about reconstruction because it was visible, tangible; they also discussed the idea of recovery more generally, using terms such as *superar* (to overcome) and *aguantar* (to endure).

The timeline of the progression from emergency to recovery and development via reconstruction is often difficult to plan precisely since it is common – unfortunately – for reconstruction to last longer than intended. In Haiti reconstruction efforts were ongoing seven years after the earthquake of 2010.[5] And in various parts of South East Asia devastated by the 2004 Indian Ocean tsunami, it took ten years for reconstruction to be completed (Gamburd 2014). In New Orleans people were still living in trailers provided by the Federal Emergency Management Agency (FEMA) seven years after Hurricane Katrina struck in 2005 (Adams 2013). Of course, this enumeration hides the fact that reconstruction efforts depend on the various political and economic forces that shape them. Moreover, these are examples of mega-disasters that require mega-resources. The reconstruction initiatives in El Salvador that followed the 2001 earthquakes were of a lesser scale. What I wish to discuss here is how the notion of participation – particularly community participation – was central to the moral economy of humanitarian reconstruction in Lamaria.

Just like the idea of the gift in contemporary humanitarian action, community participation is a concept that inhabits moral landscapes of "doing good," which gives rise to productive tensions. "Community" and "participation" are ambiguous terms that have received numerous definitions from a variety of perspectives. At its most straightforward level, participation means that people take part in the decision-making processes that concern them. It is difficult to talk about "participation" without mentioning the topic of "community" – a notion that refers both to geographically bounded groups and to looser associations of people who share a common interest. As Heather Fraser (2005) reminds us, the concept of community can refer to many kinds of groupings: virtual communities found online (e.g., a community of cat lovers), geographical communities (i.e., based on territorial belonging), or communities of interest (e.g., a political lobby or the LGBT community). The anthropological literature has shown that we must cast aside visions of communities as unchanging entities that reside in geographically bounded spaces and experience a shared fate. Rather, communities are constantly in processes "of emergence and transformation" (Barrios 2014, 331) tied to wider socio-economic orders of commodity production and circulation and to colonial and post-colonial political orders (Fabian 1983; Gupta and Ferguson 1992).

Who constitutes the community and what activities are performed under the labels of "community participation," "community building," or "community empowerment" are not stable constructs. Not everyone agrees on the identity, scope, purpose, and relevance of community participation, which adds another layer of ambiguity to this notion (Cornwall 2008).

The politics of inclusion and exclusion, as well as the types of activities that are identified as participatory, reveal competing agendas between social actors. So although both conservatives and activists may praise community participation, the knowledge and objectives they respectively mobilize illustrate different political and moral takes on the matter. The same can be said about the dynamics between large donor agencies and small grassroots organizations: the way donor agencies envision the participation of beneficiaries may neither correspond to the latter's expectations nor take into account challenges on the ground.

Community participation has been included in development initiatives for the past eighty years (Hickey and Mohan 2004). It has lately gained renewed impetus, particularly in light of events such as the Arab Spring of 2010 and the Occupy movement of 2011 that followed from previous milestones like Puerto Alegre's model of participatory democracy (since 1990) or Bolivia's Law of Popular Participation (passed in 1994). In their different ways, these examples illustrate how people getting together can effect social change, increase awareness about social inequality, and encourage effective citizenship. In these arenas, participation is about modifying the structures of governance to decentralize power.[6]

A recent World Bank (2013) report qualifies the forms of participation initiated by civil society and social movements as "decentralization initiatives," in that they push for a more equitable sharing of power and decision-making process. The report contrasts them with "community participation," which underpins international development policies and projects such as the ones described here.[7] What we call "participatory development" is now a well-accepted dimension of development policy, but that was not always so.

Although post-disaster reconstruction is not development, its practitioners do harness the ideals of community participation in their endeavours. For some time now, the International Red Cross's *Code of Conduct* for disaster relief has underscored that the organization "strive[s] to achieve full community participation" in its "relief and rehabilitation programmes" (IFRC 1994, 4). In other words, questions pertaining to fostering social capital,[8] enhancing the livelihoods of poor (disaster-stricken) families, and strengthening their capacity to advocate for themselves inform reconstruction agendas (Barrios 2014; Kyamusugulwa 2013). These ideas were not foreign to the La Hermandad project either, even though the central activity remained the building of houses. This situation was not uncommon, considering that the many foreign NGOs building houses in El Salvador were also development NGOs. CARE, Oxfam, Save the Children, World Vision, and Catholic Relief Services, to name a few, were all conducting reconstruction projects in El Salvador. The knowledge base about community participation that shaped their development policies also influenced the programmatic orientation of their reconstruction initiatives.

There is a long history of community participation that anchors its moral legitimacy in the eyes of development and humanitarian experts. For example, the teachings of Franz Fanon (1961)[9] and Paolo Freire (1968)[10] are still considered to be cornerstones for development studies and humanitarianism writ large.

In the 1960s and 1970s, international development did not promote community-driven initiatives. Official development aid intervened to improve the gross domestic product of what were then called "underdeveloped" or "Third World" countries through large-scale industrialization projects. During those decades, top-down development was the norm, governments were in charge of programs funded using official development aid, and their effects were supposed to "trickle down" to the people. In the 1980s things began to change. Evidence was accumulating that development was not performing well: poverty was still rampant, nations failed to "take off" as promised, and after countries like Colombia and Mexico defaulted on their debt payments in the early 1980s, many other countries followed suit. This marked the beginning of the "lost decade of development," as the 1980s have been called. Also, reviews by social scientists and development practitioners critiquing the lack of involvement of local communities in development programs began to make headway in development agencies (Cernea 1985; Hirshman 1984). The work of Robert Chambers (1983) was influential in the integration of participatory development into official policy.[11] A new participatory development movement was gaining momentum.

The recognition of participation in development was probably best exemplified when the World Bank and the International Monetary Fund created the Poverty Reduction Strategy Papers in 1999, which have now been adopted by many countries. The United Nations Development Program also included participatory methodologies when it shifted from the "basic needs" approach, which is narrowly focused on material well-being and definitions of "absolute poverty," to the "capabilities" approach developed by Amartya Sen and Martha Nussbaum (1993), which foregrounds what people can *do* and *be* as a measure of their well-being.

Along with the mainstreaming of participation in official development policy emerged a lively critique addressing its shortcomings. For if participation meant people's empowerment and increased capacity to transform power relationships, the bottom line was that community participation in development projects had often failed to achieve these outcomes. Participation was not delivering the promised goods and required thorough inspection (Cleaver 2001). It is telling that the authors of the World Bank (2013) report on participation arrived at a similar conclusion a decade later.

The critical literature on participatory development grew in part out of the post-colonial and post-structuralist analyses of development by, among others, Arturo Escobar (1995), James Ferguson (1994), and Wolfgang Sachs (1992). Their post-development critique showed that top-down development processes co-opted local knowledge and engendered othering discourses, replete with a biopolitical mechanism of population control, and that unchecked power relations led to pervasive forms of neoliberal governmentality.

By the turn of the millennium, a series of publications addressed specifically the problems associated with participatory development. They exposed the gender bias of participatory initiatives, the reification of the concept of community, and the transformation of political objectives – such as the empowerment of communities – into Eurocentric frameworks (Cooke and Kothari 2001;[12] Gujit and Shah 1998). These critiques wondered whether participatory development had morphed into a techno-scientific practice driven by Western expert knowledge, while contending that community participation stemmed out of a romantic ideal that permeated Western thought (Amit and Rapport 2002).[13]

Nevertheless, many studies conducted during and after the completion of post-disaster reconstruction projects have found that involving communities is preferable to leaving them on the sidelines (Barakat 2003; Barenstein 2005, 2008; Barenstein and Leeman 2012; Fallahi 2007).[14] The finding that participatory methodologies yield better outcomes in reconstruction than donor-driven ones is useful for humanitarian builders, but along with other works on this issue (Davidson et al. 2007; Lizarralde and Massyn 2008), the present ethnography argues for prudence. The reconstruction endeavours in Lamaria certainly point to cautionary findings on the matter. One example is the project in the Los Mangos *cantón.*

PARTICIPATION AND POLITICS OF MISTRUST IN LOS MANGOS

When undertaking a housing reconstruction project, an organization must choose an execution methodology. In many cases, donors encourage the active participation of beneficiaries in building activities for the duration of the project. Participants receive a house, but they have to work for it, and sometimes, as in the case of La Hermandad, they have to abandon outside remunerated work. Of course, during this time they must feed themselves, and the NGO is in charge of providing food on a regular basis, generally through the World Food Programme (WFP). In many humanitarian contexts, the WFP manages the overall provision of food aid. These types of initiatives are called food-for-work projects.[15]

In El Salvador the WFP rented three large warehouses near the capital where food was stockpiled. The WFP worked in ten departments through four umbrella NGOs, which, in turn, partnered with national and foreign NGOs. This is a customary division of labour in the humanitarian aid process. In Lamaria the umbrella NGO was called Action by Churches Together (ACT), which is a branch of the Lutheran Federation, and its local counterparts were the two Salvadoran NGOs Fundación Salvadorena de Apoyo Integral (FUSAI) and Casa de Apoio Paz (CAPAZ). Any reconstruction initiative using a food-for-work system required this organizational arrangement. A similar methodology is called *ayuda mutua* (mutual help). It was also very popular at the time temporary shelters were built. In this case, groups of four or five individuals work together building a house in order to help those who have more difficulty, such as the elderly. In La Hermandad these two methodologies were combined.

WFP representatives in the capital told me they were satisfied with their contribution to the humanitarian emergency and reconstruction effort in El Salvador. However, the beneficiaries' experience of food-for-work projects nuances the WFP officials' positive assessment, as in the case of the Los Mangos *cantón* in Lamaria. In Los Mangos it was the NGO Terre des Hommes that was in charge of reconstruction. It communicated with ACT regarding the distribution of food rations. When the project was presented, families were skeptical. The generalized mistrust of authorities influenced their appraisal, making them doubt that they would really receive a house, for free, at the end of the endeavour. Also, the execution methodology of mutual help seemed somewhat unappealing. People had to work in a participatory manner on everyone's house without the option of occupying theirs before all were finished. The fact that one would not earn a full income at the time rendered the project unattractive. When the families learned that they should present evidence of ownership to the people responsible for registering property titles, suspicion and distrust prevailed. All this was nothing but a "communist plot!" Someone would expropriate the houses, which would not be theirs. It was only after lengthy talks with NGO representatives that the project went ahead.

This example illustrates how the overall climate in one of Lamaria's rural areas was not easily open to the reception of a "gift" fixed by a hierarchical entity – in this case, an NGO. Humanitarian gestures have to be compatible with the cultural values and political culture of a given post-disaster context. In the case of Los Mangos, beneficiaries were private owners ready to defend what they had. Imposing a rule such as forbidding the occupation of one's house once it was restored until all the houses were ready was infringing on individual owners' rights. This was a paradoxical situation: individuals enjoying their private property had to conform to a rule that imposed a suspension of their right of occupation in order to respect a communitarian ideal promoted by donors. As "beneficiaries," all had to work collectively, and no one could occupy a new house until all the houses were finished. The code of conduct corresponding to the ideals of community participation – ideals upheld by NGOs in the aid business – was imposed on the community and clashed with local values. The pooling of resources, namely human labour, was perceived as a scheme, for it suggested a breach of individual property rights. Ultimately, the project was successful, but this example highlights the ways in which NGOs might attempt to legitimate practices that do not correspond, or correspond very little, to local expectations and values at a time of crisis.

What becomes clear is that an execution methodology speaks volumes about an organization's vision and ideals, whether in development or humanitarian work. NGOs often set up participatory projects, and the dominant ideology that sustains them promotes the active collaboration of beneficiaries, who may be involved in building, education, micro-enterprises, and so on. Participation is a credo not only in the world of development but also in the world of humanitarian builders. However, between NGOs and their beneficiaries, as well as within a given group of beneficiaries, it is not easy to create a climate in which the participation of all is equal and fair. Even between NGOs themselves, the working ethos is not best characterized by participation; at the national level, their coordination is rather difficult. Their ways of operating rest not so much on participation and collaboration as on competition – a characteristic that has only intensified in the humanitarian NGO world (Hilhorst and Jansen 2010; Hopgood and Vinjamuri 2012; Stirrat 2006) – even if public discourses say otherwise. Indeed, the glossy annual reports of various NGOs undertaking housing reconstruction projects in El Salvador would unmistakably laud the benefits of participatory methodologies as a means to enhance the well-being of disaster-stricken communities. After almost a year of fieldwork in Lamaria, this rhetoric felt like nothing more than a commercial refrain.

Which brings me to a second point: NGOs often postulate that a communitarian feeling exists or that it should be fostered and that mutual help between people will happen simply because they live in the same neighbourhood or experience a similar trauma. My interest during my fieldwork was precisely to assess the extent to which gaps unfolded between the discourses of humanitarian NGOs and their translation into practice. An NGO that proposes a reconstruction project to a group of people residing in a *cantón* will not necessarily find a collective in which solidarity reigns. In the case of Los Mangos, this disjunction became manifest. Indeed, the many internal migration processes that had occurred due to the civil war and the political polarization that lingered influenced people's behaviours and interpersonal relations. These were often characterized by *envidia* (envy) and *desconfianza* (mistrust) – such as envy because this family received monthly remittances or mistrust because this person was in the army or that one was in the FMLN. Although I do not want to depict a Hobbesian world of animosity, we must cast aside any romantic vision of a community à la Tönnies (1887), at least in this specific Salvadoran setting (Joseph 2002).

The longstanding prevalence of community participation within the work of NGOs reflects a conceptual conundrum. As organizations responsible for development or humanitarian endeavours, NGOs postulate the existence of a social entity that corresponds to their mission, but this expectation does not always agree with reality. The terms "community" and "participation" are commonplace in development and reconstruction parlance and often encompass essentialist presuppositions. The WFP's understanding of community did not correspond, or at best corresponded very little, to what I experienced in La Hermandad. In fact, some NGO representatives I met, but not all, admitted that participatory work was difficult, that people bickered and squabbled, and that they would have to occasionally resort to threats. This was certainly not the kind of information one read in annual reports and funding appeals. Yet it certainly reflected the richness and messiness of social life.

A problem confronting NGOs is their tendency to reify "community" and "participation," despite all the critical work on this question. It is a persistent problem, and there is no blanket solution for it. In Lamaria's *cantones*, where people had experienced a similar tragedy, it did not simply follow that they would act in solidarity toward a common goal. Although there were indeed gestures of solidarity in the aftermath of the earthquake, once the official humanitarian structure was in place, divisions and tensions within groups appeared. This is what happens when some people are designated as receivers of aid whereas their neighbours are not. Those not selected were excluded from the extraordinary activities brought forth by reconstruction and had good reason to feel envious. In addition to pre-existing distinctions, the "community" became divided between the haves and the have-nots of reconstruction aid – even if the "lucky" chosen ones had to work to receive the "gift" of a house.

One must not underestimate the reasons for envy. For many *campesino* (peasant) workers, it was not foreseeable to buy land and materials to build a house of their own. It would require an exceptional circumstance for this to happen, a twist of fate. Those whose house resisted the telluric waves may have received some form of emergency aid, but they were excluded from the initial reconstruction lists – a situation that was not always easy to accept when one's immediate (homeless) neighbour had made it onto that list. This is what happens when the communitarian ideal of an NGO confronts a reality that is partly of its own making: the list marginalized some individuals while electing others as beneficiaries. A new process of inclusion and exclusion was introduced. In Foucauldian language, we could say that the list was an instrument of power/knowledge that delimited a space of representation about deserving disaster victims; it acted as a disciplinary tool that classified populations and was thus a technology of governmentality that engendered new normative orders (Werbin 2017).[16]

Close to a hundred NGOs were managing housing reconstruction projects in different localities across the country. They had to contend with pre-existing social arrangements and with the tensions that their sheer presence engendered. Although tangible elements delineate a community in a geographical and administrative sense (a *cantón* is a territorial entity after all), many disparities can differentiate its population in economic, political, or religious terms. When a humanitarian structure creates new markers and techniques of differentiation (e.g., beneficiaries and non-beneficiaries), tensions can arise that further challenge the NGO's work. Even within a group of selected receivers, where people share a common status as beneficiaries, the situation can be problematic, as the events in La Hermandad showed.

Before turning to a discussion of the La Hermandad project, there is a third point I would like to examine. The "social" component in reconstruction projects was a recurring concern in 2001, especially regarding execution methodologies. The choice of participatory methodologies customarily responded to NGOs' social concerns. They presumed that participatory work would act as a catalyst to reinforce community ties, resilience and social capital, and future collaboration. I would not venture as far as to say that these objectives are chimerical, and indeed almost all humanitarian and/or development organizations entertain a moral horizon that prefigures a better and fairer world. The representatives of NGOs involved in reconstruction told me that they sought to foster collaboration within the groups with which they worked. However, anthropologists working on disaster reconstruction have shown that these concepts cannot go unchecked (Barrios 2014; Cupples 2007; Gamburd 2014).

Yet options other than community participation also exist. An NGO could hire a private contractor to build the houses, which would take much less time. Or it could hire local masons to build the houses, which would also result in a speedier process. But not having the owners of a house physically participate in its making did not correspond to the social objectives many NGOs had set themselves at the time. Including beneficiaries at all levels of post-disaster reconstruction projects was a more logical option for the NGOs – which, moreover, preferred not to disburse their funds to the private building sector.

The communitarian ideal of humanitarian builders is often precisely that: an ideal. A problem arises when they want to produce community, and post-disaster contexts are especially fertile grounds for these kinds of (well-meant) undertakings. "Participation" and "community building" were two intertwined notions deeply ingrained in the discourses of the NGOs I consulted. They are hardy institutional semantics (Abélès 1995)[17] that function as a policy. In their classic work *The Anthropology of Policy*, Chris Shore and Susan Wright (1997) explain that a policy is never neutral but is a core instrument of governance that incorporates values and symbols. A policy can be analyzed under different angles: as a cultural text, as a classificatory mechanism, as a discourse used to legitimize or condemn a certain line of action, or even as a rhetorical measure that empowers or silences the people to whom it is addressed. NGOs' credo of community participation is a form of policy since the concept seeks to orient people's behaviours in a given space-time. The classification of individuals as "beneficiaries" therefore carries a political dimension, which establishes lines of actions and parameters regarding "how things should be done." Although a policy elevates certain notions as symbolic values, it remains a rational device based in techno-scientific knowledge and geared toward action. We then speak of instrumental efficiency. But that is not all. As the authors rightly note, a policy can also have a more diffuse effect when it impacts the ways that people construct their identities and social relationships. Referring to Mauss (1954), Shore and Wright (1997) state that a policy is akin to a "total social fact" since it contains important cultural, legal, and moral elements. We could also say that these are biopolitical effects of a modernist and liberal rationality.

Although participation and community are dominant values in post-disaster reconstruction moral economies, and have biopolitical consequences, it remains that reconstruction has a very specific objective: to rebuild infrastructure and, in Lamaria's case, houses. Hence participation and community building must guide activities that have an explicit aim. To achieve this outcome, NGOs establish an organizational structure and a work regime. But they often also seek to add something more, which the Red Cross officials in Lamaria called the "social component." In La Hermandad this fuzzy category became increasingly contrasted with the "physical" side of the project. Moreover, these considerations were intertwined with narratives about the benefits of participatory work and about the "gift" of a house from distant strangers, creating a moral arrangement of values, objects, and activities aimed at orienting and inspiring people's engagement.

THE LA HERMANDAD PROJECT: RULES AND REGULATIONS

Antecedents

When the German Red Cross arrived in the country shortly after the January earthquake, it was first assigned not to the department of Sonsonate, where Lamaria is located, but to La Libertad. In a humanitarian crisis, the various chapters of the Red Cross divide a country or region into intervention zones to avoid duplicating their efforts, so the German Red Cross does not work where the Spanish or the American Red Cross does and so on. In reality, during the entire emergency period, the German Red Cross was hardly present in Lamaria. The main emergency NGO present was MSF. The German Red Cross got actively involved in the municipality in April, when discussions regarding reconstruction began.

This occurred by happenstance: the German Red Cross was working in nearby smaller municipalities, although these had suffered fewer losses than Lamaria, especially in terms of infrastructure. After talks with MSF representatives, whose mandate did not cover reconstruction, the German Red Cross – which had secured a substantial budget through its national funding campaign – decided to get involved in Lamaria.[18] It took over the management of the three temporary encampments that had been established by MSF. MSF had acquired a very good standing in Lamaria, especially in the eyes of the families who had initially received its help and would end up being housed at La Hermandad. Indeed, they considered MSF a "very generous" donor, one that required nothing in return.

The purpose now was to build permanent earthquake-resistant houses. Temporary shelters, which consisted of basic aluminum sheeting or heavy plastic that could be easily disassembled, had nothing in common with the idea of the *casa digna* (decent house) at the core of reconstruction programs. These *cubículos* (cubicles) were nicknamed *microondas* (microwaves) due to the unbearable heat inside.[19]

Following talks with MSF and the mayor's office, the German Red Cross decided to embark on a housing reconstruction project for one hundred families. The sites chosen for the La Hermandad and La Fraternidad housing settlements were originally privately owned sugarcane fields in the Los Almendros *cantón*. The first families arrived in La Hermandad in May 2001, and the final contract between all parties was signed in July 2001. Unlike many international NGOs stationed in El Salvador at the time, the German Red Cross purchased land using its own funds. According to Gustavo, the Central American representative of the organization, other chapters of the Red Cross were surprised, for this was not common practice. The German Red Cross reached an agreement with the landowner regarding a field of two *manzanas* (roughly one hectare). Legally speaking, a foreign organization could not purchase land, so the German Red Cross partnered with its Salvadoran equivalent to facilitate the transaction. In the case of La Fraternidad, located half a kilometre away, the funds came from the Salvadoran government through the Vice Ministry for Housing, and the deal was sealed after talks between the three organizations that would be working there.

According to Gustavo, the Los Almendros location corresponded to a vision for sustainable development. First, the project's technical team sought a site that was earthquake resistant. Second, local authorities had established their municipal development plan, and Los Almendros occupied a strategic position in it. The *cantón* is on the road that leads to Lourdes and San Andrés, two municipalities that were booming in the early 2000s due to foreign investment in *maquiladoras* (foreign-owned factories). In the mid-1980s Lourdes was just a small hamlet along the highway. In 2001 traffic was steady, many shops had opened, including a mall, and on the road between Los Almendros and Lourdes, various *maquiladoras* hired local workers. San Andrés, further to the northeast, was more industrial than Lourdes. For the municipal authorities in Lamaria, who were tackling a 60 per cent unemployment rate in rural zones, economic development depended on the Lourdes–San Andrés axis. Officials in charge of the reconstruction initiatives in Los Almendros had these considerations in mind when selecting that location.

Project Rules and Selection of Participants

The selection of individuals as official participants followed the criteria laid down by the municipal Reconstruction Committee: chosen individuals had to be disaster victims who did not own a house or a plot of land and had to belong to a nuclear family group earning the minimum wage or less. In 2001 the minimum wage was US$144 per month for the industrial sector, and US$97 per month for the rural sector (UNDP 2014, 126). Most of the people who had been living in the temporary shelters run by MSF fit these criteria. When given the opportunity, eighty-three families from different *cantones* and *barrios* in the municipality agreed to participate in the project. A significant number of individuals came from the "railway tracks." These were families who had fled the eastern zone of the country during the war – which had sustained heavy combat – and who now occupied public lands along the train tracks, living in makeshift shacks called *casas chachas* (slum houses). All these families were selected for the La Fraternidad reconstruction site.

The project was presented in May 2001 as an *ayuda mutua* (mutual help) initiative. If the families wanted to participate, they had to sign an agreement that they would respect a series of guidelines, the most important of which addressed working hours and full participation in "extracurricular" activities. Depending on gender and marital status, working requirements varied: the minimum work requirements were 150 hours per month for adult men, 64 hours for married women (or women living with a common-law partner), and 120 hours for single mothers. And for all women, a (preferably male) kin member aged seventeen or older could do the work instead of them. The wording of these guidelines reflects conservative, heteronormative worldviews.

The German and Salvadoran Red Crosses purchased all the construction materials and hired a technical crew consisting of an engineer from Nicaragua, two foremen from Lamaria (Don Salvador assigned to La Fraternidad and Don Cesar to La Hermandad), and local masons, including seventeen for La Hermandad alone, who would train beneficiaries in the art of bricklaying. Another important figure was Amanda, a social worker from San Salvador hired to develop the "social" aspects of the project. These social dimensions consisted of establishing committees to oversee activities such as food distribution, clean-up operations, risk analysis, health, and hygiene. Amanda, Don Cesar, and the engineer were the main figures of authority present on a daily basis. They did not sleep in La Hermandad but were there every day, except on weekends. Gustavo did not visit often. As for the German officials, we saw them only twice: once at mid-project and then for the inauguration of the new settlement in June 2002.

The families were thus the only ones living day in and day out on the construction site. In May 2001 they disassembled their cubicles, leaving the temporary encampments, and remounted them in designated areas on the cleared sugarcane field. An important clause in the agreement stipulated that no other outside kin member was allowed to live with project beneficiaries since the World Food Programme would distribute food only to official participants. Project leaders refused to allow any additional family members to partake in the arrangement.

A singular clause – singular in the eyes of many men I got to know over months of fieldwork – concerned property titles. The NGO encouraged women to be the titleholder of the new house, something not customary in "this *machista* (macho) society," as Amanda said. This was not a rule but a preference. Nobody was strong-armed, but this social worker's discourse on the matter was clear: she had spoken to all the women at the beginning of the project (between July and September 2001), explaining the advantages of being the primary titleholder. The most important of these was ensuring that in case of separation or divorce, since children tend to stay with their mothers rather than their fathers, the women could retain some claim to the house. Despite this reasoning, the only women who became primary titleholders were the single mothers; all the others declined.

Another proviso stipulated that the new owners would not be allowed to sell or rent out the house for a period of fifteen years. This clause was not unique to the La Hermandad project; many NGOs operated this way. The rationale was that the house should be a family patrimony and that since the families no longer needed to pay rent, their socio-economic situation would improve. Ten years later, the majority of the original families still occupied their houses, but some had left, selling their house or renting it out.

Other clauses covered sanctions that included expulsion in case of theft or loss of building materials, unjustified absences, drug or firearm traffic and possession, and other illegal activities.

The agreement defined formal regulations that families had to follow. It illustrates how a "humanitarian regime" deploys itself in a given context. For many individuals I met in La Hermandad, the rules seemed strict and intimidating at first. But the promise of owning a house outweighed these negative considerations. Some families showed strategic ingenuity in order to fit the project's selection criteria. Couples decided that one would maintain his or her job while the other participated in the construction. Generally, the man would keep his salary, and his female partner would work on the site. Such was the case of a gardener, a shoemaker, a photographer, a surveyor, and a chauffeur. When they did not have any work in town, they would replace their partner on the construction site. But not all men wanted their female partner to lay bricks and mortar. Building is a typically male occupation in El Salvador (as it is in Canada), so they preferred an elder son to do the work, if at all possible. This strategy was adopted by some families to cope with the lack of income. Other beneficiaries had presented themselves as single mothers. The project leaders recognized the particular predicament of single mothers who had to work while raising their children alone, without the support of outside kin members. That is why they stipulated a reduced number of working hours in their case.

The selection of beneficiaries was made between April and May 2001. Gustavo, the engineer, Amanda, William (a doctor affiliated with Lamaria's Red Cross office), Magdalena (a member of the municipal Reconstruction Committee), and an MSF representative interviewed the disaster-stricken families who were living in the encampments. Committee members explained that a reconstruction project of *casas dignas* would soon be underway in Los Almendros, and the contribution of families was laid out: they had to work on the construction site, according to the stipulated hours, until all construction activities were completed. Initially, the project was scheduled to end in February 2002, but it ended only in June 2002. Many beneficiaries thought that MSF would be in charge and were somewhat confused when they learned that the German Red Cross was now taking over. Indeed, MSF had been "good and generous" to them; it had been present in their direst hours and had given them shelter and security for weeks without asking anything in return. The NGO had acquired a strong credibility in the eyes of the families. Rosa was sure that MSF was going to build the houses, that the *casa digna* would be a "real gift," without any counterpart expected from the people, "because the people had nothing to give!" Although the project logic disappointed her, she nevertheless decided to go to La Hermandad with her husband, Maxwell. There was a period of adaptation for the families and the new NGO in charge. In such situations, people become accustomed to the support of a given organization, to its operating style, and to the individuals who represent it. When another NGO takes over, relationships between "beneficiaries" and NGO personnel have to be started from scratch.

The reconstruction program had established that all the selected families from the urban zone of Lamaria, mostly renters from the *mesones*, would relocate to La Hermandad. Others, such as the families from the *casas chachas* and from more remote rural areas, would go to La Fraternidad. Over time, different atmospheres developed on the two sites. Not everything could be foreseen at the beginning of the project, but one thing became apparent quickly: for the "urbanites," the move to Los Almendros seemed like an exile. Lamaria may have been a small town, but it was much more alive and attractive than La Hermandad, which at that point had no electricity or sanitary structures, no water or sewerage system, no regular public transport to town, no *molino de mixtamal* – a public mill to ground corn flour that women use to make tortillas.

The majority of the families moved between May and July while the *cubículos* were progressively being taken down and reassembled. The first to arrive had the thankless job of clearing the sugarcane fields. Sugarcane has deep and strong roots that are difficult to weed out. The people from the *casas chachas* performed this task on both sites, without any particular compensation, as though their being accustomed to farm work designated them for the job. The families from the *mesones* arrived in La Hermandad once the clearing was over. The life experiences of individuals in these two groups had been distinct. Amanda and the engineer explained that the people from the *casas chachas* were used to hard labour, as they toiled daily under a scorching sun, unlike people like Rosa who had spent all their lives in the city. It did not take long for project leaders to establish an opposition between rural and city folk, in which the former were valued positively and the latter were believed to be lazier and whiny, a distinction that reflected the stereotypical beliefs that the project leaders already held about social slotting rather than the actual performance of the individuals in these two groups.

Eighty-three families were selected at the outset, and the remaining seventeen spots were filled over time. The German Red Cross had asked Lamaria's local Red Cross representatives to identify potential participants, who were later called "beneficiaros de la Cruz Roja" (Red Cross beneficiaries). Dozens of people presented themselves to the mayor's office to put their names down. In fact, the selection process did not require a lot of administrative work. If someone met the criteria, they had a good chance of being accepted. Nevertheless, in a few cases, the candidate's socio-economic status differed substantially from the criteria. For instance, the last person to join the La Hermandad group in February 2002 was a single mother who received not only monthly remittances from the United States but also support from her ex-husband, who worked in the capital. Few families received regular remittances, and various women told me they thought this lady was not as much "in need" as they were. Another Red Cross beneficiary (a single father this time) had been trained as a first responder during the civil war; he was also a photographer and was knowledgeable in masonry work. During the months of construction, he rarely stayed in La Hermandad overnight because his designated lot was used as a storehouse, and he often left the construction site to earn money in town. As the months went by, people thought he was receiving preferential treatment.

People's perception of newcomers depended on the way that the latter adapted to and integrated themselves into the work: would they endure the intense labour, the heat, and the dust, which filled every nook and recess when the wind blew? This assessment was made particularly of women who joined construction activities. When they showed that they were as able as their male colleagues to bear these demanding, albeit temporary, living conditions, and that they really *needed* a house as much as the next person, they passed the peer-appraisal hurdle.

Hence, from the get-go, distinctions between families were established according to whether they lived in La Fraternidad or La Hermandad, the way they were selected, whether they came from rural or urban zones, and their socio-economic status. The latter factor may surprise the reader since these families were all poor, owned neither shelter nor land, and had minimum income at their disposal. Although these characteristics applied to the majority – except for the two cases previously mentioned – even within that group, some families were poorer than others. This was not necessarily perceptible at first glance, but over the time I spent in La Hermandad, it became apparent that the greater poverty of some was another marker of social differentiation within the group, which was more diverse than one would expect.

THE PROJECT LOGIC

By the notion of project logic, I refer to Marc Abélès's (1995, 73) view of "institutional logics." Considering that an institution is a set of "public rules of thought and action," the expression encompasses, "on the one hand, a process that leads to the production of rules; and on the other hand, the organization that stems from this process and that integrates its members in a system of constraints" (ibid., my translation). To analyze an institutional logic is to look at a process that puts into action three types of relationships: a relation to time, a relation to space, and a relation to power.

In terms of the relationship to time, there were important distinctions between humanitarian NGOs. MSF acted only during the emergency, although it remained present elsewhere in the country. It arrived three days after the earthquake, undertook epidemiological controls, and erected temporary shelters in designated encampments. From the receivers' point of view, this NGO gave in a generous manner, freely, in a time of desperate need. Under these circumstances, "beneficiaries" did not reduce MSF's gifting gestures to a well-rehearsed humanitarian script expressing the reproduction of technical knowhow.

With the arrival of the Red Cross reconstruction project, the relationship to time changed, as the emergency period gave way to reconstruction, thus marking a new temporality, a new chapter in the unfolding of humanitarian procedures. Defined as a transitory stage between emergency and "development," reconstruction was estimated by many experts with whom I conversed not to last more than two years. When the topic of reconstruction was raised, the German Red Cross presented a participatory housing project. For the families involved, the temporal marker of reconstruction conveyed the promise of not only a return to "normalcy" but also an improvement on their previous "normality." Indeed, the Red Cross would *give* a house, and people would *receive* a property title. The future was laden with possibilities. But at the same time, a counterpart was asked in exchange: their labour. With MSF, nothing like that was expected from disaster victims. The time of reconstruction introduced a new moral economy of gifting, a new humanitarian configuration.

Regarding the relationship to space, both NGOs created distinctive humanitarian spaces in which they intervened. MSF created living areas – the encampments – but they were temporary, at least by definition. Ultimately, most disaster victims living in the camps were rehoused in one of the three reconstruction projects in Los Almendros. The language used to describe the initiatives was also revealing. At the beginning, they were described as *asentamientos* (settlements), whereas in June 2002 people referred to Los Almendros as a *nueva urbanización* (new urbanization).

How the question of power transpired in reconstruction is at the heart of the remainder of this book. But one thing needs to be made clear: from the very beginning, the framework of the project harnessed the language of gifting when project officials conversed with the selected families.

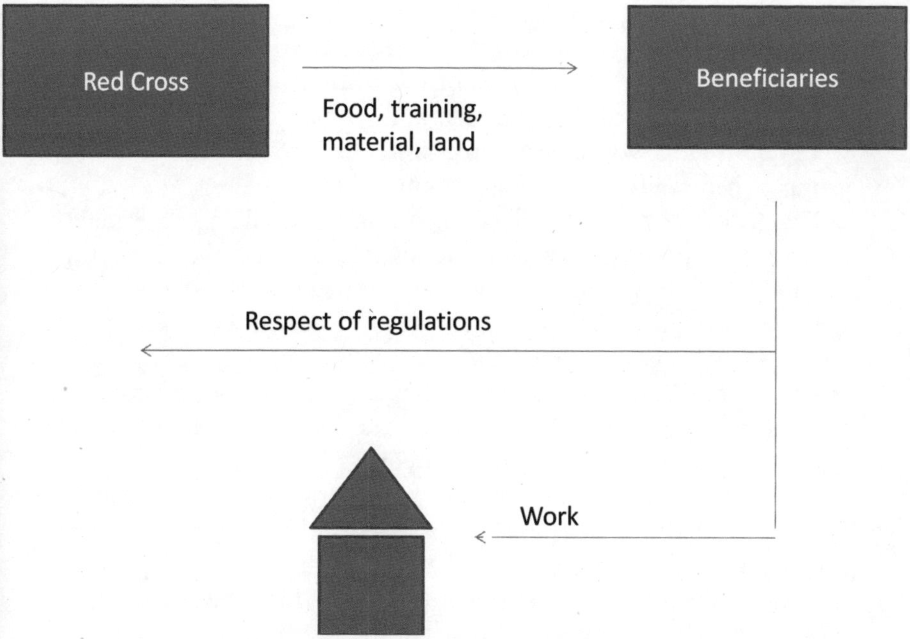

3.2 Project logic. The project's parameters rested on a non-monetary framework where the Red Cross provided materials, food, training, and land. In return, beneficiaries were expected to help build the houses and to respect rules and regulations.

As shown in figure 3.2, the Red Cross provided the land, materials, technical training, and monthly food rations, and at the end of the project, the families would become titleholders of a new house valued at US$4,500 (such was the estimated market value of a finished house in La Hermandad). In exchange, they had to live permanently on the construction site, respect the various rules and regulations, and of course, work. At the outset, there was an ambiguity: was this relationship really about gifting, or was it not more akin to that of a non-monetary exchange? In fact, both coexisted. The language of gifting persisted throughout the project because the object at the centre of the "transaction" was of considerable value. Let me reiterate that owning a house (moreover debt-free) was an improbable venture, financially speaking, for all the families involved. In ordinary circumstances, for the same amount of labour over a similar period of time, none of these people would have been able to amass the economic and material means to begin such an endeavour. Consequently, the object at the centre of the relation between givers and receivers acquired an extraordinary dimension. However, it must also be stressed that the men and women of La Hermandad were not used to working "for free" and "for everyone" – the entire group of beneficiaries – without remuneration.

The project also integrated a communitarian ideal and the valued outcomes of participatory work, as underscored by the execution methodology. Regarding this communitarian ideal, the objective of the "consortium" of institutions involved in Los Almendros was to lay the material basis for creating a new community – hence the construction of two hundred houses, the building of a communal space in La Fraternidad, and the installation of a proper electric and sewage system via national institutions. Moreover, the German Red Cross provided funds to recondition the small primary school located between the two construction sites, as well as for the nuns' hospice project, which was adjacent to the La Hermandad site. The organization also helped to refurbish the offices of the local Red Cross and Health Unit. To capture the project logic, we have to examine it alongside wider initiatives taking place in the municipality.

The communitarian ideal of the German Red Cross reached beyond the sole context of La Hermandad. Although I focus on this site, it was but one aspect of a larger envisioning. In La Hermandad the goal was to create a new community, and even though project leaders did not say they were doing development work, they believed they were laying the material basis of a future community so that others could take over. "We do not do development," explained Gustavo, "but we have a developmental perspective." The Red Cross officials were not naive; they knew quite well that the heterogeneous group of fifty families in La Hermandad and one hundred and fifty families in La Fraternidad did not form a community from the get-go. But I do not hesitate to write that it was in fact their wish to establish a new model community through what would be a post-disaster reconstruction success story down the road. They endeavoured to create this community by actively involving people in the building process in order to encourage a sense of belonging in and ownership of the project. Participatory work was deemed the quintessential means through which to foster a "feeling of community solidarity," explained Gustavo. He hoped that by engaging the families in the very production of houses, the value of the houses would exceed their sole exchange value.

The NGO decided to hire a social worker, whose main purpose was precisely to nurture the communitarian fibre. Amanda was in charge of what were loosely called the "social" components of the project, which, in effect, covered everything and anything unrelated to brickwork. Although the term was perhaps bandied about too loosely, there was nonetheless a clear discursive distinction between the physical and social dimensions of the reconstruction. The social aspect was an important part of the project framework that legitimized the hiring of a social worker, who was given a status equal to that of the engineer, and it conferred to the Red Cross a progressive veneer vis-à-vis its more conservative counterparts working in the country. Indeed, during my various interviews with representatives of other NGOs in El Salvador, especially foreign ones undertaking reconstruction, they were always pleasantly surprised to learn that the German Red Cross had hired a social worker. In a way, it put the NGO at the vanguard of best practices.

Amanda was in her mid-forties; she was dynamic, very politically engaged, and a leftist feminist who was not shy about expressing her beliefs. She had previously worked with women's groups on the assembly lines of *maquiladoras* and with ex-combatants. At La Hermandad she was put in charge of creating social committees that would strengthen the "communitarian feeling." She was responsible for the registration of property titles, and she was also the go-to person when a worker wanted to leave the site during working hours, which occurred with greater frequency as the months went by, especially for health reasons. The Red Cross had an understanding with the Health Unit, which charged beneficiaries a reduced fee for medical consultations.

Amanda wished to infuse a humane dimension into an essentially monotonous and tiresome building process. However, there was no clearly defined way to proceed. She tried to make space and time for outside activities, but she had a very limited budget. Despite all the goodwill and enthusiasm exhibited in the early months, the amount allocated to the social components of the project was less than 2 per cent of the total budget. I do not have the exact figure, for the project leaders did not wish to discuss financial matters with me, believing I would share the information with the families.

Whereas Amanda represented the "social" side of the project, the engineer and the technical crew represented the "physical" one. The engineer had previously worked with the same Red Cross unit in Nicaragua, his native land, in the aftermath of Hurricane Mitch, which had struck in 1998. He was not a humanitarian expert but a civil engineer. The same was true of the La Hermandad foreman, Don Cesar, who was a well-known mason from Lamaria. Everything that pertained to construction fell under their control: the purchase of materials, the organization of working groups, the hiring of masons, and so on. A third person was hired as a supervisor, Luis, a man with a bulky physique who had been a supervisor in a *maquiladora*, a posting that filled him with pride.

The conceptual architecture of the project operated on different levels, not only those of gifting, participatory work, and communitarian ideals but also those of productivity, controls, and outputs – tightly interconnected priorities and concerns that did not coexist harmoniously. It reproduced a dominant model anchored in the techno-scientific knowledge of humanitarian builders that increasingly clashed with the social worker's mandate. The richness of ethnographic fieldwork is precisely that it reveals the paradoxes that emerge between expert discourses and what unfolds in day-to-day practice. "Participation," "community," "gift of a house," such were the keywords that initially structured the relationship between the project leaders and the disaster-stricken families chosen to live in La Hermandad. It was through this rhetorical and moral lens that the rapport between donors and receivers was initially defined. But increasingly, it faded as it clashed with the concerns of the engineer.

To conclude this chapter, let me stress that the project's two rationales – one anchored in humanitarian values and gifting gestures and one focused on the instrumental efficiency typical of labour contexts – were not contradictory at the outset. Only when people began to feel resentful about working "for free" did the two aspects of the reconstruction start to be referred to as the social one and the physical one, and only then did tensions arise between them. The coexistence of the two rationales can be depicted as follows:

Gifting logic/ humanitarian values	↔	Instrumental logic/ productivity and outputs
"Social" dimensions	↔	"Physical" dimensions

In the following chapters, I turn exclusively to the La Hermandad site. That is where I would go every morning, hopping on a truck near the central park that picked up the masons who lived in town. Ten minutes later, we would reach our destination. I would say hello to whoever was up and then generally go to Rosa and Maxwell's house for a cup of instant coffee or see Amanda if she had arrived. During the entire time of my fieldwork, there were few other reconstruction projects taking place in Lamaria aside from the Los Almendros initiative. In this sense, the two hundred families formed a select group. The wider Lamaria population, however, was not particularly concerned with the reconstruction project. When I returned to town at the end of the day, I often visited the family of the doctor with whom I had stayed in February, who enjoyed teasing me, saying that he really did not understand what I could possibly find so interesting in La Hermandad that made me go there all the time! "Why are you hanging around with these poor and lazy buggers?" was a recurrent question. His family said that "those folk" did not even appreciate what the German Red Cross was doing for them. These statements aptly illustrate the divide between social classes in a rural town. By December 2001 the "logic of compassion" that better-off people had demonstrated toward disaster victims had run its course. It was back to business as usual. Conversely, at the enclosed site of La Hermandad, the rhetoric of gifting persisted.

4

Daily Life on a Post-Disaster Reconstruction Site

When I was deciding where to conduct my fieldwork, I felt that if I wanted to get to know people and be accepted by the various parties, I should adopt a traditional anthropological approach: that of an extended stay in one locale to learn as much as possible. In La Hermandad, I sought to create ties with the families. I also wanted to make sure that people distinguished me from the project figureheads, namely the engineer from Nicaragua, his technical crew, and Amanda, the social worker. When I first arrived, many individuals thought I represented a Canadian NGO or a potential source of funding. After a few weeks, once it became clear that I did not have a chequebook or contacts with donor agencies, people accepted that I was undertaking a "social study" about their post-disaster experience. I would spend the days on the site talking to different individuals while going from one working group to another, sometimes helping out with the task at hand. They called me the *gringita* (little gringa). I selected La Hermandad over La Fraternidad because it was a smaller site and housed the "headquarters" of the Red Cross representatives, who converted the first finished home into an office.

This chapter presents an overview of daily life in La Hermandad. The first section describes the physical environment, the composition of family groups, and the spatial organization of living quarters. The second details the building process, as masonry work was the main activity that organized social relationships. The third section discusses the ways in which social relationships coalesced in this rather enclosed space, with particular attention to gender relations and relations between beneficiaries and salaried personnel.

A PLACE CALLED LA HERMANDAD

Three kilometres east of Lamaria, a dirt road branches north from the highway. It marks the entrance into the Los Almendros *cantón*. Buses going to San Salvador or to Sonsonate stop there, just before the billboards that in 2001 displayed the names of the development organizations working in the region. From there, the road dips and crosses a small lush valley. Some modest houses are visible, whereas thick vegetation hides others. This is the centre of Los Almendros – if one can speak of a centre in this rural area – and it is there that inhabitants can shop at one of the two *tiendas* (corner stores) that sell food, beer, and household items. The road then climbs a wooded hillock from which one can see the smoke of a nearby artisanal brickyard. The view is quite nice, pastoral, but this part of the road is treacherous, especially during the rainy season, when rainfalls carve deep ruts. At the top of the hill, the road cuts through two stone walls, a zone declared "at risk" due to frequent rockslides. It then passes an outlet of the Administración Nacional de Acueductos y Alcantarillados (ANDA), the national water distribution agency. The small outpost pumps the groundwater into tank trucks that deliver it to nearby communities. Sugarcane and corn are cultivated in the surrounding countryside. The land is fertile here. Continuing north, the sinuous road crosses a small river, and there on the right is where you would have found the entrance to the La Hermandad reconstruction site. On the left is a huge kapok tree (*Ceiba pentrandra*). And less than a hundred metres away, the nuns were engaged in the construction of the nursing home. At the beginning of my stay, the living quarters were almost finished, and seven seniors were already living there. The construction of the cafeteria and the kitchen was underway, thanks to funds provided by the German Red Cross.

A little farther away is the small Santa Teresa School. It suffered damage in the earthquake, but the Red Cross helped by buying construction material and furniture, as well as dozens of white and blue uniforms for the students. Less than a kilometre away, an armed watchman guarded a large poultry farm against trespassers. And about four hundred metres farther on was the La Fraternidad site. The land on which La Fraternidad is built is at a higher elevation and provides a good view of the Izalco and Santa Ana volcanoes to the east. The road does not end there but continues inland to the heart of the Zapotitán Valley. The valley, which is known for its produce, is divided into different-sized parcels whose landowners hire seasonal or dayworkers. Eggplant, peppers, tomatoes, carrots, cucumbers, beans, corn, papaya, and sugarcane grow year-round. Small waterways crisscross the valley, irrigating the plantations where many *campesinos* (peasants) from Lamaria and bordering villages work. The water table reaches two metres below the surface level. The black volcanic soil on the riverbanks is used for construction. In the very centre of the valley, President Francisco Flores Pérez had bought a cattle farm. During the nineteenth-century border conflicts between El Salvador and Guatemala, the valley belonged to a Spaniard named Emeterio Ruano, who had received it from Salvadoran authorities as a reward for his years of combat and had established there, neighbouring the city of Lourdes, a *hacienda* (estate) twenty kilometres long. It was believed the valley contained gold. Legend has it that Ruano had made a pact with the Devil, who had promised him land and riches; this was proof that Ruano was a strong man, for "one has to be resistant to be able to talk with the Devil himself." This anecdote is well known by local residents, who enjoy telling it. During the 1960s and 1970s, the government purchased the estate and divided it into lots. The Zapotitán Valley was inundated during Hurricane Fifi in 1974 and Hurricane Mitch in 1998.

Composition of Family Groups

The families who moved to La Hermandad did not know each other. They did not all come from the same *barrio*, but some faces were more familiar than others, especially among the thirty-five families who came from the town centre and among those who had been living in the temporary shelters. Although a form of conviviality had developed, it is not because these people had lived a few months together in the encampments that we can speak of a community.

There were hardly any extended families in La Hermandad. One exception was Maxwell and Rosa's family. Maxwell's twin brother, his wife, their baby, and his wife's two daughters from a previous partner were located at La Hermandad. Rosa's father, one of the three seniors selected for the project, was entitled to his own house, as was her sister Martha, who had a four-year-old daughter. Both

Martha and Rosa became pregnant during my stay. Also living there was one of their cousins by marriage, Miguel. When Rosa and Martha were children, their parents had taken five-year-old Miguel into their home. Miguel now had two young boys with a woman named Carla, who had a ten-year-old girl from a previous partner. Miguel suffered from a severe case of hepatitis that gave him a yellowish complexion. Some of the La Hermandad dwellers mocked him, suspecting he had AIDS. This affected Miguel very much. From time to time, he left the site to deliver water in town in order to earn a few dollars, and Carla would replace him on the construction site. Amanda and the engineer saw her as *problemática* (a problem person) because she did not respect working hours and did not perform well at work, something for which Don Cesar, the foreman, regularly scolded her. Amanda explained that Carla's family was among the seven who were "the most vulnerable of all" in La Hermandad.

Kin members did not necessarily live side by side, as cubicles had been randomly assigned depending on people's date of arrival. All the families had children, as illustrated in table 4.1.

The adult population comprised eighty-two individuals, sixty-three of whom were between the ages of twenty and thirty-nine, as shown in table 4.2. The adult population of La Hermandad was thus rather young. However, in El Salvador being thirty does not have the same significance as in North America, especially for women. If women do not have children by the age of thirty, they are considered to have failed as women, and this is truer for rural women. They are seen as lacking something because motherhood strongly defines womanhood. The women with five or six children in La Hermandad had had them with at least two different partners. Abortion was and remains illegal in El Salvador, and family planning was not a common practice, at least not for the women I met in La Hermandad – although the Health Unit did offer workshops on the matter. Many women who had two or three children told me that they wanted to stop but that open talk about these matters with their partners was not always easy.

Of the six individuals sixty and older, three worked full time at construction during the project: Rosa's father, Don Valentin, and his brother Don Lucio. The latter two were registered for one house. In general, their demeanour was circumspect and discreet, and they did not interact very much with the rest of the inhabitants.

Table 4.1 Children under the age of eighteen per family in La Hermandad, 2001

Families	*Children per family*
1	7
3	6
5	5
5	4
10	3
18	2
7	1
Total: 49	Total: 143

Table 4.2 Age range of adults in La Hermandad, 2001

Decade	*20–29*	*30–39*	*40–49*	*50–59*	*60–69*	*70–79*	*80+*
Adults	33	30	11	2	5	–	1
Percentage	40.2	36	13.4	2.4	6	–	1.2

Life Relocalized

When I first arrived in October 2001, I met William, the representative of Lamaria's Red Cross, who introduced me to Amanda and to the engineer in the bare rooms of the locale. The next day, after lunch in a popular diner, the engineer drove me to La Hermandad in his pickup truck, which had the German Red Cross insignia. He was skeptical about my research: why on earth would I want to spend weeks, if not months, in this "desolate" place? He understood that I wanted to undertake a social analysis on post-disaster reconstruction, but the length of my stay baffled him. He thought I was a rich *gringa* with time to kill. There is truth to his statement: I had a doctoral scholarship and generous travel funds to conduct fieldwork. From the perspective of a hard-working Nicaraguan engineer, a weary and homesick father of three, my situation looked unusual and privileged. At the same time, I was never able to shake off the peculiar sensation that he thought something was wrong with me. I was already in my thirties, unmarried, and childless, and I was going to spend time with "these poor families" instead of working at a real job or starting my own family. Something was not right!

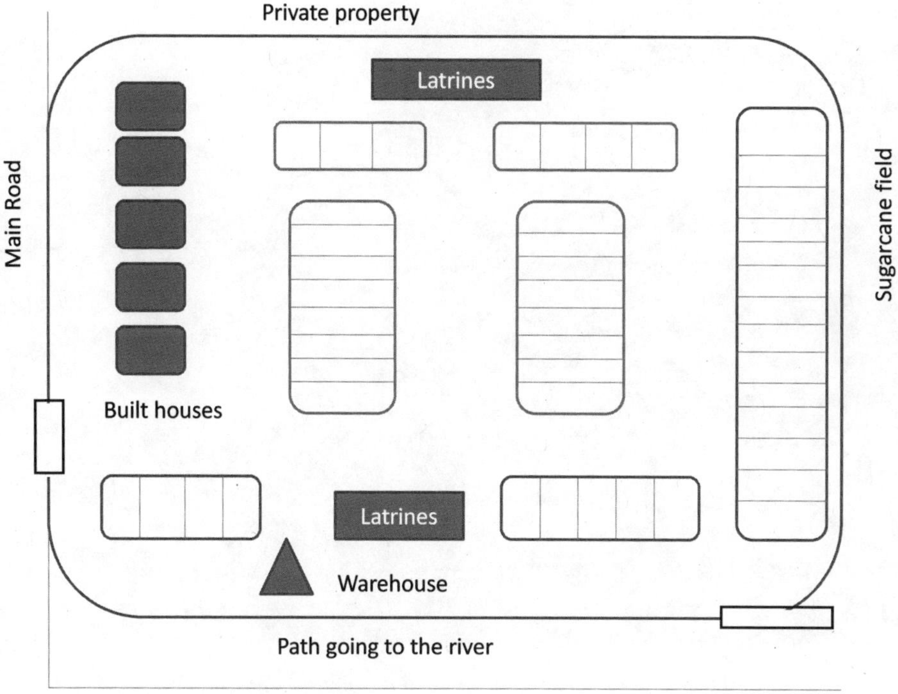

4.1 Ground plan of temporary shelters *(not to scale)*. The aluminum cubicles were mainly found in the two central rows, whereas the shelters of the easternmost row used plastic sheeting.

In any case, he dropped me off at the entrance of the La Hermandad site. The air was hot, and dust stuck to my skin, but the site was lively. Children were running around. Women and men, their faces tanned by the sun, were working in groups on various tasks that I would quickly learn to identify. Amanda approached me and introduced me to Maxwell, who had been elected as the beneficiaries' coordinator. This status was not remunerated, nor did it give him any power over his peers, but Maxwell carried out various tasks that exempted him from construction work. In anthropological parlance, Rosa and Maxwell became "key informants," but in truth, they were much more than that to me.

The first thing I noticed when I arrived in La Hermandad was how barren it looked. Everything had been razed to the ground, leaving a vast sandy field where fifty aluminum cubicles were assembled in rows along the perimeter of the site, except for the westernmost row,

4.2 Row of temporary shelters, 2001. A child is tending to the garden in front of his cubicle in La Hermandad. Families made do with available materials to perform domestic chores, such as drying laundry.

which was made up of heavy plastic sheeting. Behind it was a large sugarcane field. Between the two rows bordering the east-west axis of the compound were the latrines, four pits dug in the ground. Some days, the stench was nauseating. A committee was responsible for cleaning and disinfecting them (with lime), but after Amanda's departure in December 2001, this ceased to be done regularly. Beyond the northernmost limit was a waste ground, and just a little farther away was the nuns' quarters and retirement home project. On the opposite side, past the southern edge of the site, ran a stream where women washed clothing and children bathed.

The engineer had installed a small pump to draw water for building purposes. After months of wear and tear, the hose developed fine cracks, and water sprung out in fountain-like jets – much to the joy of the children. It was a temporary pleasure, for the engineer would diligently seal the holes. The stream was a place of respite for people who sat in the shade of the trees during the hot summer hours. The river was a precious asset for the La Hermandad families, and they were not the only ones to appreciate this spot, as nearby residents also came to it. There was nothing of the sort in La Fraternidad, where families were completely dependent on water deliveries from the ANDA tank truck. There, the technical crew had dug a fair-sized open-air pit to collect water, much like a pool, but it served mainly construction purposes, and anyhow, it was full of parasites. On both sites, empty jerry cans were used to store water for personal use, but it was not drinkable. Rosa, like so many others, used water to dampen the sandy earth at the entrance of her cubicle. During the dry season, dust penetrated the dwellings' every nook and cranny; one could clean the furniture, and half an hour later fine dirt covered it all again. The wind blew particles off the mounds of black earth and white clay used for construction, irritating the eyes of sweaty workers. The tank truck drove back and forth between both sites many times a day, a task Maxwell enjoyed doing until the engineer discovered that his driver's licence was out of date. When the truck honked its arrival, women gathered to fill their jugs.

Two communal kitchens stood on elevated bases adjacent to the southern and northern rows of cubicles. These wooden "ovens" were originally built by Doctors Without Borders/Médecins Sans Frontières (MSF) for the temporary encampments. People fetched wood in the nearby forest, machete in hand, following the trail where it bordered the stream or crossed the main road to fork into other paths. Two ovens were hardly sufficient for the needs of the entire group, especially since those living next to the ovens tended to monopolize them! Many families used a grill on which they placed a *comal* (hotplate) to cook tortillas and beans. A few had a portable stove and used it inside their cubicle. In January 2002 the community kitchens were disassembled to enable the construction of more houses.

There was no corner store in La Hermandad. However, two entrepreneurial women opened small stalls in front of their cubicles. It was rumoured that the first, Ramona – a corpulent single mother whose eighteen-year-old son worked with the masons – had been able to start up her business because she had personal savings, which should have rendered her ineligible for the project. She started small, but her business grew steadily over the months. She sold instant coffee, matches, chicken broth cubes, pastries, candy, and cans of soda

4.3 Communal kitchen, 2002. This communal kitchen was in use until families were allowed to take possession of their homes. To the left, we can see the initial dugout for a permanent house. To the right, temporary shelters are still standing.

pop (an item much in demand), which were kept cold in a large bucket of ice. She also sold eggs, some fresh produce such as tomatoes and carrots when available, instant noodles, soap, and other household goods. But she did not sell alcohol since it was forbidden on the site. Ramona did not get her supplies in Los Almendros but sent her daughter into town every day to buy them. And she had another idea: since she lived in front of one of the kitchens, she decided to prepare hot meals for lunch, for which the technical crew gladly paid, whereas few families could afford such an expense. The second woman to open a stall, whose husband worked on the site, was Laeticia. She had a smaller stall, stocked fewer provisions, and did not cook as much. Nevertheless, five masons became regulars at her place. She also became the main vendor of ready-made tortillas in La Hermandad.

Ramona and Laeticia managed to keep their small businesses going for the entire duration of the project. They became important figures in La Hermandad, and their status was envied by others. Some women treated Ramona with scorn: they did not appreciate her critical tone toward Amanda and the engineer during the monthly gatherings where all would meet. Compared to the majority of women, who remained quiet in front of authority figures, Ramona definitely stood out, not hesitating to openly critique others.

As for Laeticia, she held a grudge against Amanda. After the earthquake, Laeticia had been elected delegate for the *directiva* of the San Damian *colonia*. As a community leader, she had had the opportunity to discuss humanitarian matters with visiting NGO representatives. Once in La Hermandad, she had coveted Maxwell's position as coordinator, but she told me that Amanda had not wanted her to get the position. Laeticia had contacts with a women's NGO in Santa Ana; she understood the language of humanitarian experts and knew how to assert her rights. From the beginning of my stay, when most women were telling me that the project was good and that everyone got along well, Laeticia was already expressing criticisms. By the time I had completed two or three months of fieldwork, others had grown accustomed to my daily presence and confided in me more.

There was no public transport between Lamaria and Los Almendros, but a few pickup truck owners charged a small fee for a ride into town. These were old vehicles passing at irregular hours. The arrival of two hundred families in the *cantón* represented a huge increase in clientele – a window of opportunity – and after a few months, transport was more frequent. The issue of transportation was a big concern, especially for women who needed to go into town to grind the corn kernels received in the World Food Programme's monthly rations – yellow corn, for which they did not much care, preferring the white variety. There was a mill at the entrance of Los Almendros, but women preferred the town market for a change of scenery. In May 2002 the municipality purchased a minibus to travel the route between La Fraternidad and Lamaria. It had red velvet seats, and people found it chic.

When I arrived, five brick houses, facing the main road, were finished. The first one served as an office space for the engineer and sometimes as a warehouse to stockpile the food from the World Food Programme. It was the only house that had electricity – for administrative purposes. The families were not entitled to have electricity just yet, for that would have meant opening an account, and the Red Cross had no budget for the expense. However, a couple of crafty individuals would tamper with the lines once the technical crew had left the grounds in the evenings, one for his radio and the other for an old television. These pleasures lasted until the engineer discovered the stratagem and threatened that wrongdoers would be disciplined.

Without electricity, the compound quickly plunged into darkness at sunset, and night watches would begin. It was a project regulation that men – never women – should make night rounds with torchlight and machete. Maxwell managed the schedule for the two-hour rotations of *vigilantes* (watchmen) that lasted until five o'clock in the morning. Security issues worried many residents: thieves had come one night in November, gunshots were heard, and many people told me they did not feel safe in La Hermandad. After some equipment was stolen, Maxwell called a general assembly, and complaints were heard: *vigilantes* did not patrol the entire site but only their little area, they made too much noise, they did not respect their schedule, and so on. This incident confirmed the need to build a wall around the entire site, but it was not completed until April 2002.

I never spent the night in La Hermandad. Amanda and the engineer believed I would be a perfect target for would-be robbers – or worse – and there was no cubicle available for me anyhow. It was also out of the question to stay in one of the new houses. I never regretted staying in town, for it gave me a different perspective on the project and allowed me to forge relationships with other disaster-stricken families who were never included in the reconstruction projects.

Brief Notes on Cultural Views

Aside from security threats, strange phenomena of a very different nature also occurred, which affected individuals who were more receptive to them. One day, while I was sitting on a bench during lunch break eating tortillas with a group of women and a few masons, a lady told me how she had become extremely frightened one night. Returning from the river, she had seen something like a *chumpe*, an animal with the body of a turkey and a human face that emitted bizarre guttural sounds, as if short of breath.[1] Another lady told me she had come across a blue-eyed dog, the *cadejo*; when his fur was black, it was a bad omen, but when it was white, he was harmless. Many people believed in the presence of evil spirits. The most popular of these forces was the evil eye. After a woman gave birth, an *ojo de venado*, a red yarn bracelet set with a key or a large bean, was attached around the wrist of the newborn to fend off the evil eye. Some people also attached them around the necks of puppies.

Believing in supernatural creatures and their malevolent powers was not seen as going against Christian faith. Around a third of the families were evangelical and the others Catholic, with a few agnostic exceptions; to my knowledge, very few attended church regularly. One man, Don Cruz, planted a large wooden cross in front of his cubicle (he was Catholic), but he was the only person to ever display his faith so publicly. Religion was not an everyday topic of conversation, yet I did have some lively exchanges with Laeticia's husband on our respective worldviews after his day at work. Laeticia would listen to us, a smile on her face. She would not interject much, but I knew she did not miss a word of what we said.

Religious affiliation was not a big factor of social differentiation between residents. Belonging to the same faith could facilitate trust and mutual assistance, but this did not come across as a strong feature during my stay. The prevailing religious presence in La Hermandad was by far the nuns of the Missionary Sisters of Saint Peter Claver, who lived just a few hundred metres away. Sisters Luz Miriam and Elena visited the site on a fortnightly basis and monitored food distribution. Shortly before Christmas, they organized a traditional Christian procession, in which they involved children in a re-enactment of Mary and Joseph searching for a place to spend the night in Bethlehem. A girl and a boy dressed as Mary and Joseph would come out of a house and walk toward another house, followed by the nuns, the parents of the girl and boy, and other adults and children. Hoping to gain entry, the pair would knock on the door of that house, where a nun would say a short prayer, but they would not be admitted. Then another pair of dressed-up children would step out of the group and take the place of the first pair, and the search for lodgings would continue. The scene was repeated a dozen times until the entire site had been covered. It was one of the few festive moments in La Hermandad.

Although religion was a private matter, belief in God came up in my discussions, especially when people talked about the earthquake and its aftermath. I had candid talks with women about their experiences, and many told me they believed the earthquake was a message from God. Although the meaning of this message varied with each person – from divine benediction to punishment – all explained the dramatic events as an act of God, not as a purely geophysical happening. "En primer lugar es Diós" (In the first instance, there is God), said Mercedes, who was evangelical and a member of the Order of Elin; for her, the earthquake was an act of divine intervention that recalled the Apocalypse and the principle of pain that she found in the Holy Scriptures. "Son siempre cosas de Diós" (These are always divine occurrences), said Ana, who saw in the earthquake a call to repent. And Martha explained that God does not provoke these events to punish His children but to remind them of His presence.

One could perhaps agree with the NGO fieldworker who told me that these women were "poor, uneducated, and blinded by their faith," but I heard similar comments from professional individuals working in Lamaria. Although the media had detailed the scientific explanation behind the earthquakes, for many the ultimate cause was divine designs. This view could be seen, for instance, with a group of women who had been invited to participate for free in a training workshop organized by OIKOS (linked to the World Lutheran Federation) and the Unidad Ecológica Salvadoreña on risk analysis and the social dimensions of disasters. The purpose of the training was to show that local catastrophes are partly caused by human intervention in the environment, that disasters are not just natural but also social. When the participants gathered in a diner in town to receive their diplomas, the ones to whom I spoke continued to invoke the hand of God in order to make sense of the disaster. Divine intervention explained not only why the earth shook but also why they were chosen as beneficiaries to receive a new house; and in this light, for some, the house also became a gift from God.

This way of interpreting an unfolding series of events, from the earthquake to the promise of owning a house, rested on widely shared belief systems. As soon as people raised existential questions, as soon as they sought to give meaning to the events shaping their lives, they called upon religion. Regarding disasters, their explanatory narrative wove science with faith and did not feel in the least contradictory.

La Hermandad residents, like many other Salvadorans, were jaded by politics and rarely talked about national political matters. Most of them were in their twenties and thirties, and few had fought during the civil war, although all had been affected by it. There were few sympathizers of the left-wing Frente Farabundo Martí para la Liberación Nacional (FMLN) in La Hermandad, and the party had lost much of its lustre and credibility in the eyes of this population. Although it had been a feat to elect a left-wing coalition to municipal office in 2001, the earthquakes galvanized a national political debate about the political gains and losses following the disaster and its ensuing humanitarian emergency. Institutions providing aid were viewed positively by some beneficiaries and severely criticized by others, and some institutions, such as the army, saw their reputations improve.

The residents sometimes discussed matters related to recent local politics. Their appreciation of municipal authorities depended on whether these bodies had been of assistance to them during the emergency: if the residents had received something, the administration was *buena* (good); if not, they scorned it. One city councillor described the administration's provision of assistance as a pragmatic way of dealing with things. The varied appreciation among residents also reflected customary clientelist ways of relating to municipal authorities.

When I state that people rarely got into political and ideological questions, I mean that such matters did not enter the public space. After a day's work, people wanted to play soccer or just unwind and relax. It does not mean that, in private, individuals did not concern themselves with politics. The politics *within* the reconstruction project are another question altogether. The way power relations structured themselves in La Hermandad is vital to understanding why the project's ideals fell short, and they will be analyzed in the following chapters.

And What about Leisure Time?

On a dusty, dry, and barren site that plunged into darkness at six in the evening, far from town and from local soccer and basketball fields, with no bars nearby and no means to easily visit a kin's house or to just sit in a park and watch people, there were few possibilities to distract oneself in La Hermandad. With the added fact that families had very little extra money to spend on recreational activities, options were limited. Nevertheless, once a week men played soccer on the nearby school field. The Red Cross bought two new balls, which they kept under lock and key with the building equipment. The games were pleasant moments for the group. The project leaders and masons were never present. Sometimes women would join, or they would sit and watch the game in small groups, encouraging their team. On a few occasions, La Hermandad played against La Fraternidad, but aside from these soccer games, the beneficiaries of the two sites did not meet much. Each group worked separately under a different foreman and with different masons. Only the engineer, Amanda, and the truck drivers circulated between the two compounds on a daily basis.

Women did not play sports. For those involved in construction, the end of the workday meant the beginning of household chores: tending to the children, preparing dinner, washing clothes by the river, and cleaning the cubicle. Sometimes, to go to the market or just to get away, they hitched a ride in the large truck that brought the masons back to town. Single mothers were much busier than their married counterparts. Women who did not participate in building activities had more time on their hands, so they would often watch over the children of working women. On occasion, they helped by mixing mortar or by compacting cement. A few acquaintanceships developed between beneficiaries, but friendship was not a dominant characteristic of the social relations in La Hermandad. The amount of gossip and belittling that circulated explains why people did not trust each other much. Women enjoyed gardening in the minuscule plots at the front of their cubicles; they exchanged seeds and cuttings, and improved the sandy compound by adding some greenery, but this had to be cut down when it was time to erect a new house on that lot.

When everyone had taken possession of a house, women quickly started gardening again, in their backyards this time, a space they made their own, enacting what Michel de Certeau (1984) has called the "practice of everyday life." But overall, there was very little distraction during the fourteen months of construction. Weekends were slow and dull – "No hay nada que hacer los fines de semana, que aburrido" (There is nothing to do over the weekend, how boring) – until the engineer made people work on Saturdays.

CHILDREN, EDUCATION, AND HEALTH

Children formed an important group in La Hermandad; there were ninety-eight children under the age of ten and thirty-five between the ages of ten and sixteen. During my stay, three women gave birth. None of them asked a fellow beneficiary to become her *comadre*

4.4 Child in front of temporary shelter, 2001. Shown by the height of the slope of dirt on the right is the elevation required for laying the foundation of a permanent house. The temporary shelter in the background was dismantled a week later. Children adapted to their surroundings, finding relief from the heat as they could.

(godmother of her newborn); trust, which is the basis of the *compadrazgo* (godparent) relationship, had not sufficiently developed between residents. Since *compadrazgo* implies reciprocity between people, it is important to underscore its absence in La Hermandad.

There was no daycare in either La Hermandad or La Fraternidad – an issue that Sister Elena raised at the end of the project. She suggested that the Red Cross build a daycare centre in her hospice where a few project beneficiaries could be employed, allowing women to return to work. Daycare centres were not common in Lamaria, and not surprisingly, mothers were not enthused by the idea; how could they leave their precious ones with total strangers? No one in La Hermandad had ever paid for daycare, as kin members were the preferred babysitters, or perhaps a neighbour. Although many women looked forward to finding work at the end of the project, many were not convinced by Sister Elena's proposal. So for the duration of the project, children stayed in La Hermandad.

Amanda encouraged parents to send their children to the Santa Teresa public school, which accepted children from the age of four. Although in 2001–02 the overall degree of schooling was 89 per cent for primary school (UNICEF 2005, 106), Amanda told me that the parents' inclination to register their children depended on their own degree of schooling and on the gender of their children. In poorer areas of Central America (and elsewhere), parents tend to send their sons, rather than their daughters, to school because boys are expected to become family providers. The accepted future for girls is foremost to become mothers, and "they do not require a diploma for that." Some children stayed with their mothers during the day, and although the engineer and Amanda insisted that children not interfere with building activities, small accidents did occur.

During the initial months of my stay, I would accompany Amanda on her rounds, during which she visited each household. She knew where she would find toddlers running naked covered in mud. She reprimanded their mothers and warned them of the danger of exposing their children to so many microbes. She was right: many children suffered from skin infections and gastrointestinal parasites. I recall the case of a nine-year-old girl, Maria, who had a severe fever. Her mother, who was single, worked, and Maria's three younger siblings either went to school or were left in her care. But Maria began to feel ill and would lie on a plastic bag in the shade of a tree by the river. Her condition kept worsening, and after three days, she was hospitalized for renal deficiency. Adults were also subject to health problems. Considering the less than optimal sanitary conditions of the compound, the intensity of the work, and the absence of a balanced diet due to an excess of carbohydrates and a lack of proteins and vitamins, it is no wonder many people developed semi-chronic health problems. The residents would frequently ask Amanda, the engineer, or even me for a few dollars to go to the Health Clinic. To my mind, there is no doubt that the accumulated fatigue, weariness, and nutritional deficiency contributed to the growing expression of discontent in La Hermandad.

ETHNOGRAPHY OF HANDMADE HOMES

At 6:45 every morning I would hop into the back of the large Red Cross truck that brought Don Cesar (the foreman), Luis (the supervisor), and most of the masons to La Hermandad. In less than fifteen minutes, we were at the building site. The air was crisp at this time of day, and the earth was still humid with dew. A few minutes after our arrival, a whistle call announced the start of the workday. Maxwell would consult Don Cesar to see who would be assigned to which workstation. In theory, at least one adult per family – fifty individuals – had to be present in the morning. Yet on some days, fewer than thirty would be there, and this "lack of commitment" put the technical crew in a bad mood. Maxwell took attendance, and a young administrative assistant typed into a computer the names of those who were there. This allowed the engineer to assess who was a "good worker" and who was not. Indeed, diligence at work became a marker of appreciation – or dissatisfaction – not only between the technical crew and the workers but also between beneficiaries themselves. Industrious workers did not receive bonuses, but when they asked for a leave permit, they were more likely to get one. When a person was not meeting the number of required working hours per month, they received a reprimand, but no one was expelled from the project on these grounds, although the threat lingered.

Masons trained the workers, various groups were established, and some tasks were assigned specifically to women. Around ten of them learned *armaduría*, the assembly of steel reinforcing rods, or rebar, used for the mainframe of the house. Another group of women, the *compactadoras*, mixed and compacted cement and concrete for the foundation of the houses. The men performed heavier tasks: they dug foundations, poured concrete, went to the quarries with pick-axes and shovels, filled trucks with the white clay or black volcanic soil found in the banks of nearby streams, disassembled cubicles to put them back up somewhere else, and built the brick walls under the supervision of experienced masons. Many men had previously done some masonry work.

From beginning to end, the houses were built entirely by hand. There was no heavy machinery in La Hermandad. The drawing for the new urbanization depicted four blocks of houses around a roundabout, with a line of thirteen units along the eastern limit of the site, each separated by dirt lanes. The central path went from the main road to the last row, adjacent to the sugarcane field.

Each family received a lot of 200 square metres. The house occupied 40 per cent of that space, for a total surface area of 80 square metres. In the yard, called the *solar*, families could grow a vegetable garden. The houses were identical and followed a model approved

4.5 First row of houses with adjacent cubicles, 2001. Permanent houses were not occupied until all were built. The small green patch of vegetation in the foreground was a "garden" in front of someone's cubicle, now dismantled to leave space for the construction of permanent houses.

by the families in May 2001 when it was first presented to them. A house had three rooms, two small ones of 20 square metres each and a living room of 40 square metres that led to the *solar*. Each room had windows. On the landing, a prefabricated cement sink stood on a piece of concrete flooring. Toilets, which were outside and consisted of a raised dry-latrine system, were rectangular structures 2 metres high, covered with a corrugated aluminum sheet, and fixed to a cement base 60 centimetres high, smack in the middle of the backyard, and people hated them. A neighbour could see when you were in there! (Thankfully, now that the vegetation has grown, there is more privacy.) A small brick wall enclosed each lot. Roofs were made with slanted aluminum sheeting of better quality than that used for the cubicles since it was supposed to deflect heat. The bricks for the houses were handmade at Lamaria's traditional brickyards. The Red Cross bought tools and materials from local hardware

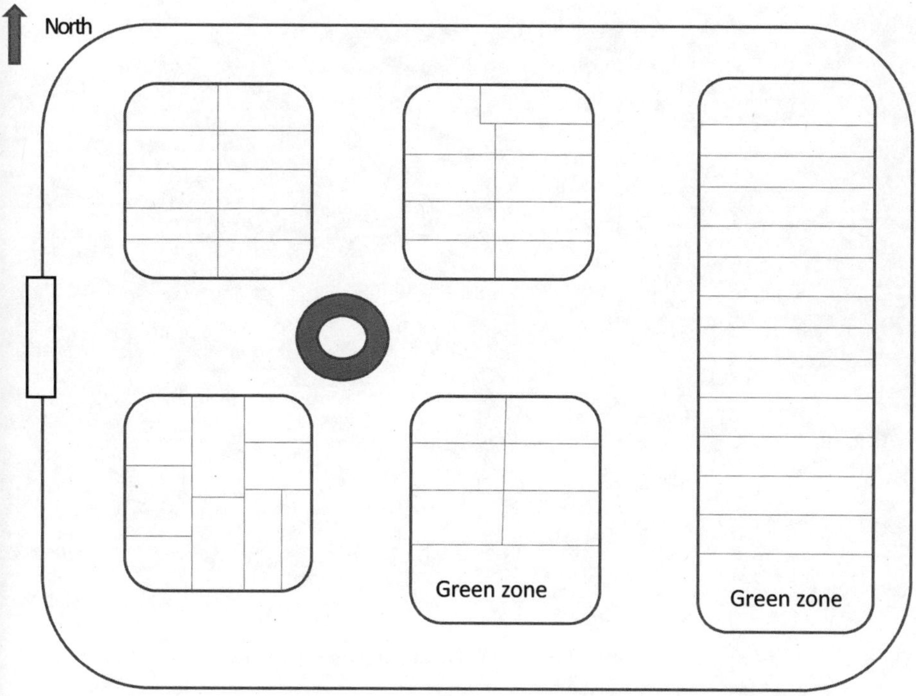

4.6 Ground plan of permanent houses *(not to scale)*. Each lot consisted of 200 square metres.

stores, and the municipality granted free access to the nearby clay quarries. Clay or white earth was used for levelling and landscaping, whereas black earth was used for mixing mortar.

The masons agreed that the houses were structurally sound because the frame was made with a lot of steel. Steel crossbeams strengthened the interior walls, and concrete lintels secured the load-bearing walls. The steel frame, entirely assembled by women, had seven foundation beams in the ground and fourteen load-bearing posts. These houses were designed with anti-seismic structural properties.

The initial step before beginning to erect a building was to measure soil elevation. The entire site was levelled at the start, but the ground was somewhat at an incline and further levelling work had to follow. It was not possible to do it all at once because the families lived on the site. Houses were built by *bloques* (blocks), and when work on a new section began, families had to move. The liberated

4.7 A poor person's adobe house, 2001. This house was on the rural outskirts of Lamaria. The families selected for the La Fraternidad reconstruction site, who had lived along the railway line before the earthquake, occupied similar dwellings. Before the earthquake, there was a national deficit of 400,000 houses.

space was levelled and covered with white earth, which explains why there was constant dust in the air. The foreman used a line level to measure the slope and to mark the contour of the house with twine and four poles. The height of the string indicated the required thickness for the foundations. This operation was done by the *compactadoras*, who compressed large quantities of a mixture of cement, white earth, and gravel using a *bailarina*, a rudimentary sledgehammer made out of a wooden pole with one end cemented into an empty one-gallon paint can. It was a heavy tool, and the task was repetitive and unrewarding. Women used the bottom of the cement-filled can to pound the ground for hours on end, sometimes under a torrid sun, masking their faces with a piece of cloth or an old T-shirt. After trying this out a few times, I can confirm that this monotonous job required strength and perseverance. The foundations had to reach a height of 40 centimetres, sometimes 60 centimetres, which could take more than a week depending on the number of *compactadoras*.

4.8 New anti-seismic house, 2001. According to the masons who worked in La Hermandad, the new houses were well designed using local materials.

Once this step was finished, the proper building began. From the foundation, men dug out holes and trenches in which the masons fixed the rigid structure of supporting steel rods and columns, and then they poured concrete over it. The *armadoras* were responsible for assembling all the columns used in construction. These followed a single model: to make columns of different widths, four steel rods were attached using thinner rods that measured 30 to 50 centimetres long. These thinner rods were placed on a wooden support between affixed nails, and with pliers, the *armadoras* shaped them into a square. The shaped rods were slid onto the four long steel rods to form a hollow rectangle and a very solid column. The *armadoras*, mainly single mothers, repeated this task each day and became a tight-knit group.

Once the iron frame was assembled, the next stage was bricklaying. Experienced masons raised the walls with the help of a few people who mixed mortar on the ground. Watching this pleased everyone. There was no real competition between the masons, but

4.9 *Armadoras* at work, 2001. A group of *armadoras* assembles steel rods under the shade of trees while their children wait in the background.

some beneficiaries enjoyed commenting on who was the fastest or the most skilled, and people laughed. When fourteen rows of bricks were laid, concrete was poured on them. Once dry, another fourteen rows were laid, followed by another layer of concrete. A final ten rows of bricks were then placed, and the top layer had a bevelled edge to give the aluminum roof its incline. When the structure was finished, concrete was poured into wooden forms nailed to the walls to make the doorposts, as well as the non-supporting columns. Once dried, the interior and exterior walls were sanded down. Afterwards, masons poured concrete to level the floor and finally fixed the roof. It took three weeks to build a house. Lastly came the building of property walls and the outer wall surrounding the compound. The latter was harder than expected because trees behind the last row of houses near the sugarcane field had to be uprooted.

4.10 New house and temporary shelter, 2002. La Hermandad was very dusty, and over time, people grew tired of living and working on a reconstruction site.

The majority of people worked on the site, but at regular intervals the engineer designated a few men to take trucks to go dig up clay or black sand. Getting clay was a short and uneventful ride, whereas getting black sand in the Zapotitán Valley could be very pleasant, especially because one could stop and buy freshly picked vegetables. These outings were a nice change from the monotony of work. If I was able to accompany the men, it was only because I was not expected to do labour on the site. Whether or not I was there did not affect the progress of activities, unlike the presence of workers, who could not come and go as they pleased. Construction activities held top priority – above everything else. We must not underestimate the demanding physical effort that was required of people who worked in often gruelling conditions – either scorched by the sun or drenched by the heavy rains that transformed the compound into a pool of mud. Of course, masons earned a salary, but everyone worked hard. When construction ceased and the masons left, their departure created a feeling of emptiness in La Hermandad.

SOCIAL RELATIONSHIPS ON A POST-DISASTER BUILDING SITE

Life in an enclosed space that was dedicated to masonry and home to people with limited means to do much else undoubtedly influenced the way social relations unfolded in La Hermandad. What follows is an outline of the three most significant modalities of group relations that I observed during my fieldwork: gender relations, neighbourly relations, and relations between beneficiaries and salaried personnel. Because one of the main objectives of the project was to foster community belonging, it is important to look at the way social relationships unfolded. These remarks offer a contextual overview useful for better understanding why, over time, interpersonal relationships deteriorated. Social relations between men and women, between neighbours, and with salaried masons are significant to the moral economy of the last humanitarian gifting configuration examined in this book. To recall, the framework of moral economies used here examines the production and circulation of values and affects as they are tied to the acquisition of a substantial resource (a house) in the social space of post-disaster reconstruction. When the humanitarian regime introduces access to new resources, defines new identities based on forms of inclusion and exclusion, and imposes specific codes of conduct on participants, it also engenders values and affects, but these are not divorced from pre-existing cultural views and manners of relating to one another across gender lines or from other interpersonal and hierarchical relationships. In what follows, I discuss in plain language the salient features of different interpersonal relationships in La Hermandad.

Gender Relations

Interactions between men and women in the compound reproduced the traditional gender roles and models found in Salvadoran society. Machismo was certainly very present, and sexism toward women was not uncommon. Amanda shared with me her understanding of gender relations in her country, and although I would not go as far as to say that everyone in La Hermandad fell neatly into her categories, I summarize her points below.

In the poorer segments of the Salvadoran population, such as in La Hermandad, women remain subservient to men. Men are expected to be the providers and women to tend the household and raise the children. Women remain economically dependent on their male partners; they are not expected to own property, access credit, or participate in political decision making. In general, men do not like women to take birth control, and some women told me how intransigent their husbands were in this regard. Intrafamily violence is widespread. In the case of poorer households, many children are born "outside of the bonds of matrimony"; indeed, unions are often made and unmade out of wedlock, and men have a tendency to leave. This puts women in a vulnerable position, and they seek stability by finding another partner. It is a strategy of survival, said Amanda. Although in 2001 United Nations indicators suggested that the condition of women was improving, as a growing number of them participated in the workforce, the situation of poor rural women still corresponded to Amanda's description (PNUD 2001, 39–43).

Take the case of Magda, who told me that none of her dreams had come true: "Here in El Salvador, one can work all their life, we never earn enough, and we stay poor. My husband and my son don't lift a finger; I always have to wait on them." At the age of forty, she said, she wanted to be like me, without children, living in America, having another life. I heard the same type of commentary about me from a single mother: "Que chulo como ella, sin niños" (How cool to be like her, without kids).

Amanda was very loquacious on the subject. According to her, Salvadoran culture depreciated women so insidiously that they had internalized a victim discourse. She believed that women lacked self-esteem and ambition, which explained why they opted to send boys to school instead of girls, projecting their lack of self-esteem onto their daughters and hoping that their sons would take care of them when they got old. Amanda said, "En esa cultura machista, la mujer no tiene mucha oportunidad de desarrollarse, de aprender cosas nuevas, además la mujer pobre como aquí" (In this macho culture, women do not have many opportunities to develop themselves, to learn new skills, and this is all the more true for poor women such as the ones here). Indeed, she insisted that the situation of Salvadoran women was deplorable. That was, in sum, Amanda's sociological analysis of gender relations.

Others, like Sister Elena and the NGO spokespersons I met, shared her point of view. But we need to nuance this appraisal: although project beneficiaries were representative of the bulk of poor Salvadoran families, not all of them corresponded to Amanda's description. The notion of self-esteem is particularly tricky. Most women in La Hermandad recognized they were suffering from endemic poverty and injustice, and they willingly shared with me the stories of their arduous life trajectories. They also critiqued male behaviour, sometimes in that particular joking fashion that can help to foster bonds between women from diverse backgrounds. But I did not conclude from these exchanges that they all lacked self-esteem. Despite the many hardships they had faced, the dominant narrative – or at least what I can extrapolate at a general level – attests rather to their perseverance, endurance, and determination to "deal with things." "Aguantamos" (We endure it), they say. After eight months of fieldwork, I felt I had gained a great lesson in humility from these women's stories. The discourse on self-esteem that had been put forth by Amanda also came up during my interviews with Salvadoran NGO representatives in the capital, especially with professional women. The words "auto-estima de la mujer" (women's self-esteem) appeared to be another policy catchphrase that did not satisfactorily reflect La Hermandad women's narratives about themselves. To postulate that poverty and illiteracy are synonymous with no self-esteem is to cut corners, and for my part at least, I cannot conclude that all La Hermandad women lacked self-esteem. They suffered from a patriarchal system, no doubt about it; however, Amanda's diagnostic of her peers perhaps lacked nuance.

Recall that Amanda was hired to cover the "social" dimensions of the project, a decision attesting to the project designers' consideration for gender matters in post-disaster practices. At the time, increased attention was being paid to the integration of a gender analysis into reconstruction projects. Studies have established that disasters reveal conditions of vulnerability structured along gendered lines (Blaikie et al. 1994; Enarson 1998; Enarson and Morrow 1998), and they have underscored that reconstruction practices can either replicate or redress pre-existing gender inequalities.[2] The negative consequences of ill-conceived disaster management practices that ignore gender, including reconstruction endeavours that focus too narrowly on material relief assistance, are referred to by Maureen Fordham (2000) as "disastrogenesis." Hiring a social worker for La Hermandad was a measure intended to address pre-existing gender inequalities. Through the creation of various committees and consciousness-raising activities, Amanda hoped to organize, if not "emancipate," the female population of the site. However, there is a difference between "practical gender needs" and "strategic gender needs": practical considerations "derive from women's ascribed responsibilities for households and child-rearing chores" (Ensor 2009, 140), so they do not challenge the customary division of labour in a society that maintains women in a subordinate position, whereas strategic considerations seek precisely to modify deeply entrenched structural power imbalances. In the post-disaster context, this means that a project should pay attention to women's legal rights, equal wages, protection from domestic violence, and role as primary caregivers. Marisa Ensor's (ibid.) study of reconstruction in Honduras after Hurricane Mitch reveals that, overall, strategic needs were ignored and that reconstruction efforts tended to reproduce traditional gender inequalities. And although many projects trumpeted a gender perspective, their design and implementation tended to slot women into stereotypical roles, falling short of the intended transformational goals. Sarah Bradshaw (2002), who conducted a large-scale study of women's roles and responsibilities in post-Mitch reconstruction activities in Nicaragua, found that the hurricane's impacts reinforced traditional women's roles rather than transforming and diversifying them. Her analysis of women's participation, including that of women-headed households, in various housing reconstruction projects determined that these did not positively address women's strategic needs. Instead, Bradshaw observed a decrease in women's income-generating activities and in the recognition of their own contributions to both the household and reconstruction activities.

Amanda was aware that the project could easily reproduce traditional gender roles and turn a blind eye to gender violence if she were not present. Her public harangues about machismo and the status of poor women in El Salvador were purposefully provoking; she wanted to "shake things up" a little. Encouraging women to become primary owners of their future house was one attempt to change gender inequalities. Another was to actively involve them in the building workforce; selecting a dozen women-headed households was seen as a progressive measure countering their subordinate role in Salvadoran society. Amanda's comments about La Hermandad women's self-esteem reproduced stereotypical ideas about poor and vulnerable women dependent on men, but she did not fully ignore the subtle ways that identities in post-disaster contexts can change. Indeed, disasters are intense moments when people's identities can become "fragmented or fractured, or they can shift in a more positive manner," as Julie Cupples (2007, 167) shows in her work on women's subjectivities in post-Mitch Nicaragua. The suddenness of becoming homeless, of losing one's sense of place, can profoundly impact people's perception of self. Just as traditional ideas about women's suffering and victimhood can be incorporated into narratives about gender identity, heteronormative ideas about gender roles can be strategically manipulated and performed differently in reconstruction practices. Many women in Hermandad did integrate a discourse about suffering, not only with respect to the earthquake's impact on their livelihoods but also when reflecting on their personal lives. But this does not mean that they had low self-esteem or preclude their pride, their strength, or their aspirations for a better future.

Amanda's overt feminist discourse annoyed most men. But they could not say or do much about it since she was their superior on the site. Also, many men were unsettled by the fact that women were working at traditionally male jobs. Women learning masonry, mixing cement, compacting earth, or assembling steel rods did not tally with the stereotyped roles and status that the men associated with women and that the women had also internalized from a young age. Some men, such as Rosa's husband, Maxwell, refused to let her work at construction. He, and he alone, would fulfil the regulation regarding working hours for his household. Her case was not unique, as there were fifteen women at least who never engaged in physical labour. But others did so all the time, particularly the single mothers and the female partners of men who decided to keep their regular jobs.

Single mothers were assigned to two specific groups: the *armadoras*, who assembled the steel frames of the houses, and the *compactadoras*, who compacted the earth for the foundations. Some women joined in when their male partners were not available, an occurrence that became more frequent in February 2002 when men began to miss work: a few became sick – with other beneficiaries saying behind their backs that they were lazy – and others grew tired of working for no pay and decided to find a paying job elsewhere. This did not please the engineer, but as long as working hours were met, he would not mete out any sanctions.

Working women were spending a lot of time with the masons and with other women's male partners. This became a tremendous source of gossip, even badmouthing. Some women saw single mothers as threats and potential rivals who could seduce "their man." In fact, three single mothers had flings with masons (if the masons were married, their wives lived in Lamaria, so it felt safer). The *desconfianza* (mistrust) that is typical of relationships between strangers took a particular turn and became centred on the way (some) women interacted with (some) men, such as how José had made Irena laugh and how, after work, they were seen leaving the compound together, or how Raimunda was trying to seduce Gustava's husband. "Ah! What a nasty person!" These types of remarks were made daily. Men gossiped less, but at times small talk would take on such proportions that they took part in it as well.

Gossip functions as a form of social control. It reproduces the cultural models and markers that categorize people and their behaviours (Kapferer 1990, 1992; Stewart and Strathern 2004). In La Hermandad differentiation was quickly established between single working mothers, seen as free, and married women. It was most apparent in the case of five single mothers who sometimes went on outings with the supervisor, two truck drivers, and the engineer. That they had more freedom (relatively speaking) and could go "picnicking at the beach" with project officials irked others. Rosa was vehement on the subject; she was happy to criticize their bad morals to whoever would listen! What began as a subtle process of differentiation between single mothers and married women evolved into a real separation between the two groups. Because gossip could be so damaging, people employed all kinds of strategies to avoid being the object of gossip: they would try not to make eye contact with members of the opposite sex and would refrain from talking or showing too much interest in other people's stories. More than modest reserve, this behaviour was a strategy of self-protection not unique to the La Hermandad residents.

In Neighbours We Trust (for a While)

Relations between neighbours acquired a gendered dimension in La Hermandad. Cubicles had been assigned to people regardless of family ties. The compound was not very big, so one could walk around it in fifteen minutes, making it easy to pay a visit to a resident. Nevertheless, feelings of proximity and distance developed depending on location, especially between families living near the road and those occupying the last row of temporary shelters. People defined the near and the far within the site's limits, thereby marking their own sense of personal space. Rosa found it *lejos* (distant) to visit her sister living in the last row; those near the river believed they were luckier than others. Recalling the seminal work of Henri Lefebvre (1992) on the production of space, these comments illustrate that even in a liminal space such as a post-disaster reconstruction site, people produce place: they create categories of closeness and distance, and their immediate surroundings are invested with their creative labour, be it tending a small garden, organizing cooking quarters, or simply adopting a particular shaded spot to sit as one's own.

This kind of appropriative place-making process is precisely what is at stake when humanitarian or development projects seek to foster a sense of belonging in displaced communities. I have so far refused to use the notion of displacement in this book, for there is a distinction to be made between forced large-scale movements of populations due to conflict, famine, or mega-endeavours – such as the construction of hydroelectric dams – and the type of relocation process that occurred in Lamaria, even though it was after a disaster. The move of two hundred families to the Los Almendros *cantón*, although not undemanding and trouble-free, was significantly less challenging than many cases of contemporary forced displacement, not least because after a year's time people's socio-economic status had objectively improved: they were now property owners of new anti-seismic houses. Nevertheless, as modest as this relocation process may seem, the individuals involved had to adapt to a new environment and to new faces. They had to learn to make this place their own. This is what project leaders counted on: that the chosen families would slowly exhibit the signs of community building.

Relations between neighbours were visible mostly between women, in part because women had more time to engage in neighbourly relations than did the working men, whose socialization took another form. Women lived mostly outside since, under the Salvadoran sun, the aluminum cubicles would heat up too much to stay indoors. They shucked corn, cooked beans, laid out clothes to dry, and chit-chatted while keeping an eye on the children. Neighbours exchanged cuttings of small bush or flower plants. Exchanges of small services between neighbours stood in for well-established mutual aid networks. But this was not true for all the families, and it depended on trust. Many single mothers lamented the absence of a kin member to help them with the children while they worked, but such arrangements were forbidden as long as the project was ongoing. When neighbourly relations were positive, they were valued greatly.

But these living configurations frequently changed, as the site was in constant movement. People had to disassemble and move their cubicles at some point to make way for the construction of houses. Rosa's family relocated three times, and all the families from the last row moved at once. The shuffling of households meant that one would lose a neighbour. People could not say anything about this situation, as the technical crew made the decisions according to the needs of the *obra física* (structural work), and this arrangement sometimes caused disappointment.

In April 2002 families learned which house would be theirs, following a draw that had happened in January. They were not invited to the draw, except Maxwell, since he was their representative. Assigning houses in this manner avoided potential accusations of favouritism. The draw had taken place in January because the Vice-Ministry of Housing had needed the names of the families for the registration of property titles. Bureaucratic paperwork takes time. But in April, when the families learned where they would live, the houses were not ready. Roofs, windows, outdoor latrines, and the low brick walls enclosing each property still had to be done. But at long last, families knew who would live where and beside whom. They still had to wait before taking possession of their new home, but knowing the identity of their future neighbours influenced people's conduct.

Of course, knowing about permanent living arrangements did not necessarily produce helpful relations between future neighbours. Many times, I had heard Rosa and Marielos comment on families next to whom they would not like to live. Marielos said, "No me gustaría vivir cerca de la gorda que no cuida la casa y no cuida a los niños, tampoco de la Reina. Aí, que chucos" (I would not like to live next to the fat lady who does not tend to her house and does not watch over her kids, or next to Reina. They're so dirty). So when Marielos learned that she was going to be living next to the *gorda*, she was quite disappointed.

Marielos's observation introduces another way people created distinction: through the category of cleanliness. This was not the sole affair of women; project leaders would also comment on the matter. On paper, all beneficiaries were the same. They were all poor and vulnerable families. But in reality, not all had the same level of education or the same access to financial resources and support networks. Amanda said that the "poorest were the dirtiest" and that the point was not to blame them but to educate them, thus giving them the "capacities" to improve their living conditions as well as "their way of life." Amanda targeted the "most vulnerable" women from La Hermandad and La Fraternidad, trying to recruit them for the different social committees she headed. She said, "Hay que capacitarlas involucrándoles en los comités" (You have to train them and involve them in the committees). She explained that in La Hermandad there were seven extreme cases, and among them were the families of the *gorda*, Reina, and Carla. Even though these families were *problemáticas*, disregarding many project regulations, it was out of the question to kick them out because "it is after all for such families that humanitarian projects exist." When I questioned the engineer about them, he grumbled a few words, shrugged his shoulders, and headed off. My queries irritated him.

During the inauguration of the site in June 2002, the engineer had to pick a house for the German Red Cross officials to visit. He decided on Marielos's house because it was "well kept." She also had some furniture, contrary to many other residents: a quaint dining set, two armchairs, and an old refrigerator that did not work.

Not all officials had the same views on the matter. Gustavo, the German Red Cross representative for Central America, thought that project officials should not expect people to maintain a house like they would themselves. The subtext hinted at notions of cleanliness. Families received a *casa digna* (decent house), but project leaders doubted whether they would live with dignity in them, if by dignity one meant living dirt-free. Statements such as these rendered the officials' patronizing – almost contemptuous – sentiments palpable.

Relations between Beneficiaries and Salaried Personnel

Seventeen masons, the foreman, the supervisor, the engineer, three truck drivers, and Amanda: that makes twenty-four salaried individuals for fifty families in La Hermandad who did not earn a dollar from the project since they were "benefiting" from it. La Hermandad was a humanitarian initiative, at the outcome of which families would receive a new house as the fruit of their labour.

The relationships between working beneficiaries and masons were usually cordial. Unlike the engineer, Amanda, and the foreman, the masons were not authority figures. Some masons – such as the more jovial ones and the ones with better professional skills – were liked more than others. The mason who trained the single mothers in the art of *armaduría* (assembling rebar) was very much appreciated by his "students." He showed them how to assemble steel rods into columns, which was an important part of the process. Masons earned close to US$300 per month, a salary three times above the minimum wage. During the last three months, a small number of women had developed intimate relationships with masons. One whose partner had been kicked out of the project in December for incest later had a liaison with a mason. Once she took possession of the house, he moved in with her. Another single mother had "befriended" Luis, the (married) supervisor, and although she tried to hide the affair, everyone knew about it.

The good-natured relations that the beneficiaries enjoyed with the masons contrasted with the more tense ones they had with the supervisor and foreman. Amanda, however, was not slotted into the same category as the technical crew. She was in charge of the "social aspects" of the project: she formed the committees, encouraged illiterate adults to attend free reading classes in the evening, managed the paperwork with the Housing Ministry, organized activities for the children, such as a Christmas party with piñatas, and was the one who signed the authorizations to leave the compound during working hours. Many women called her *niña* Amanda, not the more formal *doña* or *señora*. But no one called the engineer by his real name and always referred to him through his profession. Amanda forged friendly relationships with Rosa, Maxwell, and Miguel, as well as with many single mothers, a situation she herself knew all too well. Although she remained an authority figure, she was much more approachable than the engineer. But I was surprised to learn that five months into the project, she had never once lifted a tool. When she picked up a *bailarina* to compact soil, a tool that a few women used quite often, she mumbled, "This is much heavier than I imagined!" In my field notes, I wrote that for someone who prided herself on being close to the people, she seemed indifferent to the nature of their labour. In retrospect, I realize that I projected a personal judgment that was overly harsh, but I record it here to underscore how, in contrast to Amanda, I desired to get to know and be accepted by people. It also illustrates how, in the moral economy of post-disaster aid, the novice anthropologist did not escape making valuations of her own. I understand now that Amanda cared, even if she did not toil like the others.

The distance provided by time and memory calls for a reflexive pause. The data that anthropologists record in situ are the raw material from which we draw. I have now been living with this experience for over a decade, and during this "gestation period" a process of sedimentation has occurred. My fieldwork has acquired a narrative rhythm that differs from what I perceived in the moment of initial recording. Hence today, I question my earlier interpretations. I ask, for example, whether Amanda was really uninterested in the work of the people? For I also remember an afternoon in La Fraternidad when she told me how hard the *compactadoras* toiled. The interpretations I made then seem less secure now. Perhaps Amanda had neglected to pick up a tool not out of indifference but because it did not cross her mind until the moment I was with her; or maybe it related to her status as one of the project leaders. I can second-guess myself only so far. Since I did not ask Amanda why she had not tried to compact soil before, I am left with speculation. And I clumsily console myself with the fact that there can rarely, if ever, be a completely fail-safe ethnography.

In October, Amanda asked for a paid holiday and flew to Cuba with a delegation from the mayor's office. This episode was the end of her. I learned afterward that the engineer thought her completely irresponsible for leaving before the official Christmas break. The antagonism between this "macho man" and the "feminist social worker" had been strong. Amanda was dismissed from the project in December – to the great surprise of the rest of us.

The relations between the engineer and the beneficiaries were characteristic of power relations. He was usually distant and in a hurry. He did not have time for small talk or to deal with people's personal problems. He focused on the demands of the construction. Once Amanda was gone, people had no choice but to see him in order to get a leave permit. Not wanting to be bothered, the engineer asked Maxwell to hand them out, which put Maxwell in a delicate position more than once. Indeed, if Maxwell declined a request, the concerned individual would contest his authority: "He is just a beneficiary like the rest of us after all! Who does he think he is to deny us the right to come and go from the site?" This was the kind of recrimination Maxwell wanted to avoid.

As months passed, the project fell behind schedule. The engineer became taciturn, stressed, and displeased with the beneficiaries' *falta de compromiso* (lack of commitment). From February until June, he could be found having lunch with the foreman at the house of a single mother with whom he went to picnic. This was seen as favouritism, and many were envious. But no one dared challenge the engineer, except Laeticia's husband, who boldly and publicly accused him of abusing people's human rights. The motive of his anger always concerned working conditions.

Ultimately, the confined nature of the compound amplified small differences between families. Distinctions between people's socioeconomic status, the ties some created with the salaried personnel, and the manifestation of mistrust and envy, combined with the circulation of gossip, all generated tensions and divisions within the group: single mothers versus women with partners, workers versus non-workers, and beneficiaries versus project officials. Friction also appeared between Amanda and the engineer, between the families and Maxwell, and between Maxwell and the engineer. In other words, the politics of the project, which sought to place everybody on an equal footing in order to create community, created schism instead. The participatory nature of the work, which was supposed to foster a feeling of common belonging, reflected the ideals of the project designers. But this arrangement clashed with people's lived conditions, and mistrust between individuals lingered, holding back the efforts of project leaders to cultivate a communitarian feeling through participatory labour.

Thus a significant feature characterizing interpersonal relationships in La Hermandad was that of mistrust. It also occupied an important role in the moral economy of this humanitarian endeavour. Families left homeless by the earthquake relocated to a barren site without history on the promise of gaining a new house from a humanitarian organization they hardly knew. Amanda was not from Lamaria, nor was the engineer, and the Red Cross was a newcomer in the municipality's humanitarian response. A first vector of mistrust can be associated with people's uncertainty about the project's outcome and the manner in which project leaders would treat them. This form of mistrust reflected people's lack of knowledge about, and familiarity with, the hierarchical authorities with whom they now had to interact on a daily basis. Yet they were also regularly reminded of their status as beneficiaries – an identity category that required trust in benefactors and that families and project leaders alike could strategically manipulate. However, people expressed the most mistrust between each other. As becomes clear in the following chapters, the regulatory nature of the project, with its sustained work regimen – combined with people's relative isolation from kith and kin, their lack of privacy, and the absence of prior community ties – set in motion different processes of differentiation that intensified to become overt expressions of mistrust between micro-groups.

Mistrust is neither the mere opposite nor the negation of trust, and it should be understood on its own terms, not as the lack or absence of a positively valued trust that has to be restored. Such binary thinking is sterile and fails to explain the affective, strategic, and phenomenological value of mistrust in given ethnographic contexts. Whereas many studies on trust have been published over the years (Gambetta 1988; Hardin 2006; Luhmann 1979; Putnam 2000; Simmel 1950), as a general rule, mistrust has received less attention and has too often been conceived as something destructive to be remedied or avoided. Recent anthropological works on mistrust, however, take a different approach, underscoring its generative qualities: mistrust can be good for social life in that it can protect from dangers, contribute to people's knowhow in different fields of practice, and function as a political and civic virtue that keeps power in check (Allard, Carey, and Renault 2016, 7). Mistrust can take on strategic qualities when people find themselves in unforeseen circumstances where there is an element of uncertainty or doubt – a situation that well characterized the new residents of La Hermandad. Initially, they did not know what to expect from each other or from the project leaders beyond the promise that they would receive a house – and believing in a promise from strangers also rests on a delicate balancing act between trusting and doubting (Giraud 2007). In his ethnography *Mistrust*, about the Berbers of the Moroccan High Atlas, Matthew Carey (2017, 16) considers mistrust to be a disposition that is not necessarily corrosive or alienating for social relationships and that can be, on the contrary, quite useful as a way to "manage the freedom of others." This perspective fits my purposes because it does not postulate two incompatible antithetical worlds. Mistrust in La Hermandad stemmed not only from people's lack of familiarity with hierarchical authorities, coworkers, and neighbours but also from a lack of control over their environment – that is, the project itself with its various regulations and parameters – and ultimately over their own labour. When mistrust is understood as a disposition, it is easier to appreciate its affective and strategic expressions, especially when people are called to recreate social relationships in foreign settings. In La Hermandad it meant protecting oneself not only from the unfamiliar but also from possible disappointment. I return to the topic of mistrust in the book's concluding comments.

CONCLUSION

My intention in this chapter has been to paint a picture of the general atmosphere in La Hermandad. Unsurprisingly, work influenced the way social relationships evolved. It was defined as a participatory activity, in which all built houses without knowing which one would become theirs – at least not before April 2002.

Although the project was founded on a communitarian ideal, the space was subjected to a series of specialized calculations: it was surveyed, mapped, and divided into geographical, architectural, and economic units that defined the nature of the site. And from this matrix, from this space without history and memory, a communitarian feeling was supposed to emerge. But in a context that was overdetermined by construction considerations, spontaneous and personal appropriations of space were limited. They were constrained by a series of regulations and codes of conduct that aimed to maintain a formal equality between individuals and to define what was allowed and what was forbidden. People were not in a position to "invent their everyday life," especially in this highly regimented environment. The invention of daily life rests on the weaving of social and intersubjective relations, and it is deployed through anodyne gestures that mark one's "home" in an otherwise rather impersonal space.

I have said that many things were defined top-down: working hours, night watches, people's movements, food distribution, and so on. It is no wonder that the quasi-omnipresence of a hierarchical authority influenced the unfolding of social relationships. Moreover, project leaders had expectations of beneficiaries in terms of their behaviour, their diligence at work, the emergence of a form of social cohesion, and their gratefulness for being chosen for a humanitarian endeavour. Indeed, all these elements made up aspects of a "counter-gift" that project leaders anticipated. And they constituted central dimensions of the moral economy of post-disaster reconstruction in La Hermandad. But unlike the mechanics of house building, which the project leaders had the power to coordinate, the genesis of a communitarian feeling or expressions of gratefulness could not be commanded. A gifting logic partly framed the official discourses that defined the project, but as the next chapters show, it dissolved itself in the exercise of authority and in the sweat of daily labour.

5

Engagement and Estrangement in La Hermandad

La Hermandad was the last and lengthiest humanitarian configuration that the displaced families experienced. The Red Cross had developed an operational logic that rested on participatory work and communitarian ideals that it believed would facilitate the entire endeavour and render it meaningful for participants. The initiative was presented as a non-monetary exchange, but another discursive layer was superimposed on this ideal, one that harnessed the notions of gifting to which project leaders referred, especially when the situation became challenging. This chapter takes an in-depth look at different dimensions that illustrate what participatory work truly looked like in La Hermandad. Living for months in an enclosed space where the priority was building houses was not only monotonous but also generated tensions between micro-groups that appeared over time.

A key feature was the integration of women into building activities, and in this respect, the German Red Cross incorporated lessons it had learned on the importance of involving women in reconstruction projects. As I mentioned in the previous chapter, an important critique addressed to post-disaster reconstruction initiatives seeking to foster community participation has been the lack of attention paid to gender as a crosscutting dimension – a problem of which the German Red Cross was aware. The organization had targeted single mothers in its selection process, trained women in masonry work, and hired Amanda to encourage women to participate in various committees. Project officials also hoped women would put their names forward as property titleholders. There was deliberate attention to gender matters in what was essentially a civil engineering project. But gender relations on the site revealed the extent to which programmatic frameworks and good intentions encountered setbacks. Relationships between working women and men became an unforeseen source of tension. When we analyze what people's participation entailed in La Hermandad, various dimensions have to be taken into account, among which is the gendered dimension of participatory work. I therefore pursue the earlier discussion on gender in post-disaster reconstruction at the beginning of this chapter.

Mainstreaming gender in reconstruction can be challenging; there are frequently divides between the way it is envisioned and how it is realized in concrete settings. In this regard, the Red Cross's operational framework reproduced a dualistic understanding of two spheres of activity, namely the physical and the social aspects of reconstruction, which the engineer and the social worker respectively incarnated. This opposition meant reconstruction work was considered a "non-social" occupation. Undoubtedly, this work was the most significant activity at the site; it gave beneficiaries their raison d'être and represented their main contribution toward receiving a house. However, this is also where contradictions appeared and intensified over time. At the conceptual level, work was defined as a contribution, but in practice other questions prevailed regarding the speed of completion of the project, security on the site, and overall "personnel management." Because work was not considered part of the "social" dimensions of the project, Amanda was not entitled to say anything about it. Work was a unique micro-environment where a few women and many men interacted on a daily basis, and it was the most visible way for residents to show that they participated. Work is the second dimension of participation in La Hermandad that I unpack in this chapter.

I also address a specific issue concerning food distribution that further strained the relationships among people. Under the project's framework, food was understood as a return for people's labour. When food rations failed to arrive, it exacerbated economic divides. It made visible to all who got by and who did not. Finally, I relate a telling example that speaks to the power of relationships and their effect on what was the first and only expression of a collective proposal for community building. All in all, these different frames of analysis illustrate processes of differentiation within the small collective that tested the communitarian ideal entertained by project designers.

LABOURING ACROSS GENDERED RELATIONS

As I mentioned, gender is important in the field of disaster and reconstruction; it is also a key dimension of community participation. It is now well established that dismissing the gendered dimensions of disasters, at all cycles of a disaster, causes unnecessary harm and violence. Gender relations had a tremendous impact in La Hermandad, much larger than what I had anticipated.

Research has proven extensively that disasters affect women disproportionately and in a more pernicious way because in many societies women are less mobile than men and have less access to capital and other resources after a disaster. They are also much more at risk of being subjected to gender-based violence when their customary help networks are jeopardized or have collapsed (Enarson and Morrow 1998; Felten-Biermann 2006; Jenkins and Phillips 2008). Patriarchal structures and stereotypes limit women's opportunities, and international aid, in the heat of the action, has tended to distribute aid to men because they are usually identified as the "heads of families," although this is now changing.

Local culture, the sexual division of labour, as well as political, socio-economic, and ecological conditions, all have an impact on women's capacity to overcome the effects of a disaster and reduce their vulnerability. In other words, disasters have a differential impact depending on gender. In light of this situation, international organizations have begun to mainstream gender in their policies.[1]

The political, economic, and social subordination of women (but also of other marginalized groups such as the elderly, homeless, undocumented, LGBT, and ethnic and religious minorities) diminishes their access to the resources that come with reconstruction initiatives. Inequality produces a downward spiral wherein the chances of overcoming a dire situation are impacted negatively. These findings hold especially true for women in developing countries, which has been underscored many times since Elaine Enarson (2000), a leading figure in the field of gender and disasters, reported it to the International Labour Organization at the turn of the century.

Nonetheless, after decades of research and policy work on women's experiences in disaster, "gender blinders" persist (Enarson 2012, 2). We might have expected gender equality to be better integrated into post-disaster reconstruction, not as a normative and rigid framework disconnected from local realities but as a priority without which the success of reconstruction initiatives remains partial. Indeed, all gender-mainstreaming frameworks reiterate that the participation of women, in a way that takes their needs into account and recognizes their rights, is essential to reducing discrimination and gender-based violence. Alas, this objective is far from accomplished. On the contrary, gender inequality is still pervasive, as the most recent human development report explains (UNDP 2014).

Although the reasons for the persistence of gender disparity are complex, two factors can help us to appreciate how the situation has evolved with regard to post-disaster reconstruction. The first is the reification of the concept of gender in policies, and the second pertains to the heavyweight influences of what Naomi Klein (2007) has called "disaster capitalism."

Feminists from the Global South have voiced an important critique about the manner in which gender has been adopted in policy frameworks. They point to the fact that power does not express itself along single axes but at the intersection of issues of class, gender, race, and caste (Mohanty 2003). If the goal is to empower women in development and reconstruction projects, gender alone is an insufficient category of analysis. It needs to be considered alongside other crosscutting dimensions that contribute to the reproduction of gender inequality.

There has been much research on these matters since the turn of the millennium. It has scrutinized the normalizing effect of policymaking and explained that ideas that were meant to empower women lost their mobilizing force once they became integrated into official frameworks (Moser and Moser 2005; Mosse 2003). For many feminists working in development and in disaster-related domains, the dulling of gender's emancipatory potential – due, in part, to a naive belief in an imagined women's solidarity (Cornwall 2007, 2008) – is a setback. Even more pernicious factors explain this failing. Notably, patriarchal systems have displayed a great adaptive capacity to generate new forms of institutional discrimination (Luft 2010). Furthermore, with the rise of neoconservative forces in recent decades (Sen 2005), large agencies integrated gender mainstreaming in ways that were subject to neoliberal macro-economic prescriptions that promoted Western ideological paradigms and canons (Syed 2010).

In a similar vein, post-disaster reconstruction projects have tended to isolate gender as a unit of intervention without comprehensively linking it to questions of class, race, localization, ethnicity, or religion, which can be just as significant (Hyndman 2008). When the men-women binary opposition reproduces heteronormative standards, gender mainstreaming becomes a normalizing procedure that obscures the other expressions of identity and forms of violence that stem from political and economic processes (Jauhola 2010). It then falls short of recognizing the differential impacts of disasters on gender; it leaves us wanting in our understanding of how power relations and related processes of dispossession and impoverishment are reproduced. A narrow perspective on post-disaster reconstruction risks taking gender as the sole, rather than a single category, of analysis – as though it were divorced from questions of political economy, social justice, access to resources, and so on. To better appreciate the plural construction of identities and forms of exclusion during disaster cycles, gender must be linked to other correlative factors.

Another way that reconstruction can marginalize groups at risk (including women) is through the investment and funding opportunities that are offered to governments and businesses wishing to build large infrastructure, which then allow them to extend their ambit over affected populations. When the logic of the market supplants the humanitarian rationale (which itself is not problem-free), pre-existing inequalities are often exacerbated (Gunewardena 2008a, 2008b). Critiques of humanitarianism have shown that reconstruction – as an institutionalized transnational practice – remains enmeshed in logics of empire (Donini 2012; Rufin 1986) and global governance (Kennedy 2004). Thus works that examine the influence of neoliberal doctrines on development are pertinent for reconstruction precisely because reconstruction is supposed to lead to development (Appelbaum and Robinson 2005; Duffield 2007; McMichael 2008). No doubt, the stakes are high when hundreds of millions of dollars are pledged. Mega-disasters have been instrumental in expediting the introduction of private sector interests, which are seen as *the* motor of development and, by extension, of economic recovery. This was the case for the tourism sector in Honduras after Hurricane Mitch in 1998 and in Sri Lanka after the tsunami in 2004 (Gunewardena 2008b; Stonich 2008). Business models that seriously limited and complicated people's access to financial assistance also defined reconstruction in New Orleans after Hurricane Katrina in 2005 (Adams 2013; Button and Oliver-Smith 2008). When reconstruction adopts technocratic initiatives with little input from affected communities, it tends to reproduce forms of marginalization. At worst, it becomes a vast enterprise of social re-engineering. Again, scale is important: between massive displacement processes and more modest projects like the one discussed in these pages, the impacts of reconstruction will differ. We need to be mindful of the effects, both large and small, of disaster capitalism on social groups, and we should not romanticize community bonds or blindly accept the more simplistic assertions of the gender-mainstreaming agenda.

In La Hermandad the most visible instance of gender mainstreaming was the involvement of women in masonry. Issues around disaster capitalism were not particularly relevant, but the tendency to regard the involvement of women in construction as a way to empower them and improve relations between the sexes was at times a gross miscalculation.

Every morning, close to twenty women were present at the roll call, sometimes more. Aside from the single mothers who had to work regular hours, married and accompanied women sometimes joined the group, depending on circumstances. Project leaders commended single mothers for their "endurance," and it was clear that these women were proud of their contribution. Because single mothers worked alongside the men on a daily basis, a form of camaraderie developed between some of these men and women. But this apparent friendship looked suspicious to other women, who thought their male partners were being too chummy with other (single) women! Friendship between the sexes is not that common in rural Salvadoran society, where stereotypes about men and women hold strong. Among the residents of La Hermandad, some came from the countryside and others from the town. The single mothers who became the object of gossip were from the centre of town: two had worked in a *maquiladora*, one had been a cleaning lady, a fourth was well known because before joining the project she used to deliver freshly baked bread, and a fifth had tended a mill stall in the market where people came to grind corn. Their work experiences distinguished them from those of rural women, who usually laboured on agricultural estates. Women who came from town joked around more easily with men, and the men replied in kind. These exchanges appeared too flirtatious, giving rise to gossip about some single women's "outrageous immoral behaviour," and such accusations only intensified after the departure of the social worker.

5.1 Residents at work, 2001. A *compactadora* brings sand in a wheelbarrow while masons and workers lay the steel foundations of a house.

Gossip, aside from the amusement it may bring, is an important mechanism of social control at the level of groups (Gluckman 1963) and also in terms of psychological control over individuals (Paine 1967).[2] These characteristics were magnified in the enclosed space of the reconstruction site. With little to do in terms of recreational activities, talking about a third party became a way to establish a tie with an interlocutor. Chitchat was very common between women in La Hermandad: they talked about work, the weather, their children. Amanda and I regularly conversed with women; because we were, respectively, a social worker and a foreign researcher, we could easily walk around, visit different households, and sit for a bit of conversation.

But a more pernicious form of chatter developed in La Hermandad: due to the sexual *celos* (jealousy) and the *envidia* (envy) that the "free women" inspired, malicious gossip and accusations spread quickly. For example, one morning we found a note on a latrine door that said La Roja was sleeping with Juana's husband; Rosa was accused by her sister-in-law of fooling around with her husband (who was Maxwell's twin); and then there was Morena, who joined a few young men on a weekend outing, which upset Rosa because she suspected Morena of flirting with her man. Gossip of this nature is of course commonplace, and people develop different coping mechanisms, but in La Hermandad's enclosed living quarters, it had particularly negative consequences. To avoid being the object of spiteful gossip, some individuals developed prevention strategies. For example, Morena became utterly exasperated with being at the centre of the rancour and completely withdrew from others. Rosa and her sister-in-law did not speak to each other after the incident during the entire time of my stay, and the same occurred between Rosa and Juana. The point is not whether rumours were well founded but to recognize the extent to which they affected this small collective. And their reach was significant. Over time, a climate of suspicion weighed heavily. "Todo el mundo es hipócrita" (Everyone is a hypocrite), said Karlita and Rosa. Morena was seen crying one afternoon: "No puedo más suportar toda esa platica de la gente" (I can't stand this talk anymore). A lasting coldness evolved between, on the one hand, a few working women who were perceived as taking excessive liberties with men and, on the other hand, some of the married women who were more prone to jealousy.

The divide in La Hermandad between working and non-working women even morphed into accusations of witchcraft, which happened twice, both times after Amanda's departure. Amanda had managed to calm people down and mediate conflicts, and after she left, the overall atmosphere in La Hermandad definitively deteriorated. This was another way that the constraints tied to the working environment altered the lived experience of the humanitarian framework.

Anthropologists have noticed for a long time that gossip can be a significant mode of informal social control (Herskovits 1937; Kluckhohn 1944). Sally Engle Merry (1984) explains that gossip is more powerful in morally homogeneous and close-knit social groupings, where escape and avoidance are not possible, than in large scale societies, where it is more fluid. Other researchers argue, on the contrary, that gossip is more important in complex, urbanized, and stratified societies because it allows us to better negotiate complex organizational structures, facilitates access to information and resources, and more generally, satisfies people's desire to know their social environment (Demerath and Korotayev 2015). Although the residents of La Hermandad did not compose a close-knit society, the confined setting in which they lived made avoidance extremely difficult. And although Lamaria was not a highly industrialized city, its residents had been navigating for decades complex political and economic institutions and structures (e.g., clientelism and wage labour). Merry distinguishes between two forms of gossip: information-sharing and judgmental. It was this later form – full of criticisms, evaluations, and malicious undertones – that grew in La Hermandad. Habitually, gossip is about reputation, about "fitting morals to ambiguous situations," and it "thrives when the facts are uncertain" (Merry 1984, 51–3). Having single women work so closely with other women's men for weeks on end was perceived as a morally ambiguous situation that became intolerable for some. The result was badmouthing and personal attacks on the reputation of targeted single mothers. But there is another side to this situation: judgmental gossip can also be a signal of trust between the speaker and the recipients of gossip, a form of closeness that rests on the sharing of certain moral views about other people's behaviours. It then operates as a device to manage relationships, establishing boundaries between intimates and outsiders. Gossip in La Hermandad became toxic due to the lack of trusted social outlets through which people could express grievances and stress. Because mistrust was a common strategy of protection through which to test out social relations, judgmental gossip was a singular instantiation of mistrust that established "cognitive maps of social identities and reputation" (ibid., 55). And these expectations extended to domains other than that of objectionable flirtatious behaviour.

THE VALUE OF HUMANITARIAN LABOUR

Praise and Blame at Work

In the project's non-monetary exchange framework, manual labour was the most significant contribution from the families. Without it, nothing would materialize. Receiving the house was entirely dependent on people's manual labour, and consequently work was their greatest preoccupation. Work was upheld as an important social value. The language of gifting framed the overall project in its most general terms – as a gifting gesture from distant Europeans. Gifting was not a daily subject of conversation, but it surfaced regularly during monthly assemblies or when a person became "difficult," a tag that was given to someone when problems impacted construction activities.

Having a decently paid job was highly valued by all. The lack of jobs and their precariousness reinforced the importance that people ascribed to work. Even though there was a lot of work to be done on the site, this was not considered a *chamba* (job). Instead, it was seen as unpaid labour in return for food, shelter, and the promise of becoming a homeowner.

At the beginning of the project, work was welcomed with enthusiasm. Conditions were not optimal – especially for the townspeople, who were less accustomed to toiling under a tropical sun – but people nevertheless got along relatively well during the first few months. There was a feeling of anticipation in the air; the excitement of seeing the first houses completed was palatable. The majority of the families to whom I spoke during this time said they were content to be here, finding daily life on the reconstruction site not that bad. They thought overall that social relations were fine; they would say, "The Red Cross is good for us." Another aspect that they emphasized was their status as "beneficiaries" who had suffered a lot, noting that "they" – the different humanitarian actors – had come to help them. In this regard, women's conversations, more than men's, were punctuated by words of gratitude. "Gracias a Diós, gracias a la Cruz-Roja, gracias a usted" (Thank the Lord, thank the Red Cross, and thank you) – although I had nothing to do with any of the help they received! But not all women spoke this way. Ramona, one of the women who opened a stall in front of her cubicle, said that she was entitled to receive a house because she had been poor all her life and because she was an "official beneficiary." She saw it as only fair.

During my first weeks of fieldwork, when I prompted them, people often expressed words of recognition and appreciation regarding the project, especially toward the Red Cross and the "good people of Germany." Indeed, project leaders had explained to the families that the funds came from ordinary German citizens who, having seen the destruction in El Salvador, gave "from the goodness of their hearts." If families had any misgivings about the project, they would not have expressed them in front of me since they did not know whether I had ties to Germany or whether I occupied some kind of official position.

In November the first signs of fatigue began to appear. Amanda granted more and more leave permits, especially for health reasons. In December two families left the project for economic reasons: not being able to earn money while working full time on the site had become too big a burden. "No les gustan trabajar" (They do not like to work), some people said. Diligence at work evolved as a marker of differentiation between people. It gave project leaders a way to distinguish between "good" and "lazy" workers. Since working hours were counted, the technical crew could easily evaluate how "dedicated" each individual was. The good worker was a person who always showed up on time, who did what he or she was told, who respected project regulations, and who would not shy away from doing extra tasks. When a person was diligent, demonstrated effort, and did not complain but "endured," that person was generally appreciated as a *buen trabajador aguanta* (good worker who endures). Among the most valued workers were the three men over sixty-five years of age, in particular Don Romero, who at eighty years old never missed a day's work performing the single and repetitive task of sifting sand through a sieve. "The young ones today do not really know what work is," he told me. "Me, I am used to hard labour, I've done it my entire life, and even if I am old, my body endures better than theirs!"

New recruits had to show that they could handle the work if they were to be accepted by others. La Roja, who joined the group of *armadoras* in February 2002, felt that her colleagues were judging her on her endurance since she came from the city. Newly arrived beneficiaries had to quickly prove their ability to adapt and keep up with the pace.

Diligence at work was a shared moral value that became a criterion for assessing who was "really in need." To a foreign observer, everyone in La Hermandad seemed to be in need. However, divisions evolved within the site. Those who consistently laboured without fuss demonstrated that they were really in need: "En el trabajo se ve quienes tienen necesidades" (Through the work, one sees who is really in need). It was through labour that people could show they were "in need" and be recognized as such by their peers. Work was the most tangible expression through which people demonstrated that they partook in the gifting logic that framed the project. During the first six months, the majority of the families seemed to accept this rapport; it was only later that things deteriorated.

In this context, individuals who began to miss work – mainly from February onward – and who overtly complained about labour conditions would rarely receive open support from others. On the contrary, too many grievances and recriminations could lead to rejection and isolation. People avoided the person who complained, and in the worst cases, this person would be labelled *problemático* (a problem person). Having lost the respect of their peers and of the technical crew, these (few) individuals moved about silently, wondering whether they would be evicted from the project. These "problem people" tended to be men, and the case of Don Cruz was the most telling. This devout Catholic had been a member of the Alianza Republicana Nacionalista (ARENA) during the civil war but had left it when he became disillusioned with politics. "Religion saved me from politics," he explained. Don Cruz suffered from severe back pain. He took a six-week sick leave and requested that his young wife, who was pregnant with their fifth child, replace him. "I have no other choice if I do not want to be kicked out of the project." After two or three weeks, other residents looked at him with scorn; he had become an example of laziness. Don Cruz had been toiling as hard as the others, but his reputation suffered. The same thing happened to a man we called the photographer: due to his worsening health condition, his wife replaced him for seven weeks, and he was also judged as lazy. Miguel's case is different – and much more dramatic. He suffered from a severe strain of hepatitis, and with his yellowish tone, others mocked him, saying he had AIDS. With his partner, Miguel was part of the "seven most vulnerable" families of La Hermandad. Miguel had to leave the site on a regular basis to undergo medical exams and treatments that sometimes involved short hospital stays. When he left the compound, his partner replaced him, but she was said to be "among the most undisciplined workers," and it was not long until she was labelled *problemática*.

The most *problemático* of them all was Don Julio, Laeticia's husband. With a strong and resilient physique, he was often assigned the heaviest tasks. He liked to joke and enjoyed a good conversation. More than once, I joined him in front of his cubicle after work, sipping instant coffee. He would question me about my life in Canada, making jokes about the Inditos (a pejorative way to refer to Indigenous people), while affirming that he was himself of Pipil descent. Sometimes we talked about religion, and neighbours would listen to us, but no one ever voiced their opinion on this delicate subject. Don Julio had done jail time, five years for involuntary homicide. He had a fiery temperament, slept in too much, and arrived late for work. He was also quite vocal in his criticisms of the conditions at La Hermandad. He contested the supervisor's authority and even that of the engineer. This happened more often in February and March, when the project was supposed to end.

Considering someone *problemático* was not the sole affair of those in charge; residents also applied this label to each other. People who underperformed, complained, or showed weakness at work were contrasted with those who showed diligence, which had become the dominant value in people's everyday moral reasoning about the project. Work was the concrete expression of the value set that framed the humanitarian project and the clearest embodiment of participation. Working "well" proved you cared, were in need, and abided by the project regulations. In other words, work was a significant value in the moral economy of this humanitarian configuration, leading to judgments that would eventually question it.

To minimize "labour issues," Amanda and the engineer organized general assemblies, usually once a month at the end of the afternoon. The engineer always spoke first, saying that he recognized they were all working hard, and were tired, but that this humanitarian project was for them and that they should try to get along better since they would all be residing in La Hermandad for the coming years. He would also invoke the notion of gifting and the idea of community building:

> It is thanks to the gift of the German people, through the Red Cross, that you, the beneficiaries, are receiving these houses. They are giving you the chance to start your lives anew, to improve your living conditions. You are here, together, you've worked hard, and it is a shame that there is so much grumbling and disunity in La Hermandad. When we leave, you will have to form a new community, and you will return to your usual occupations. But in the meantime, there is still work to do before the inauguration.

Such speeches urged people to see in La Hermandad a new beginning and to rise beyond their "petty tensions." Perhaps officials hoped that through repetition, these ideas would end up influencing people's conduct. During general meetings, project leaders repeated that families ought to overcome their grievances and think about the "collective good." The more they focused on work, the faster they would take possession of their new homes. Although well intentioned, these encouragements failed to galvanize enthusiasm for more than a few days. Some problems do not disappear with uplifting words.

"We Are Humanitarians": Between the Physical and the Social

The distinction between the physical and social dimensions of reconstruction was a discursive device that complemented the gifting semantics of the project's framework. To my mind at least, the difference is more heuristic than a proper characterization of reality in the sense that it fixes boundaries between rhetorical spheres of value. It originates in a managerial way of understanding post-disaster reconstruction. But words and concepts do influence the experiential, and insofar as there was regular talk about the "social" and "physical" sides of the project in La Hermandad, this distinction did shape social relationships, spheres of activity, and expectations.

Construction work was the domain of the engineer. He incarnated the "physical," or "material," side of the project. Amanda was hired to foster a communitarian feeling, which various committees were supposed to encourage. Conceptually, the creation of committees demonstrated that the project designers cared about the "social" well-being of the families. Involving small groups of people in various activities was believed to stimulate group belonging, but aside from the food distribution committee, these groups hardly functioned at all. There are different explanations for why.

First, Amanda had mostly recruited women, and most of them felt uncomfortable with this situation in relation to their male partners. Amanda was a feminist and liked to say out loud that Salvadoran society was *machista* (chauvinist), that women were subjected to men, and that family violence was rampant, particularly in poorer households such as those found in La Hermandad. For all these reasons, she deliberately targeted women for the committees, both single mothers and married women, in the belief that it would strengthen their self-esteem. But Amanda's discourse intimidated people. After she left, both men and women confided to me that she scared them a little. From the beginning, some men adamantly forbade their wives from participating in any committee.

Second, the committees did not function properly because they were not led with a clear sense of direction. The committee in charge of food distribution was operational because all wanted their rations once they arrived – and they had to be distributed one way or another – but the committees for the environment, health, and education existed more on paper than in reality. In the words of the engineer, beneficiaries' "lack of initiative" or "indifference" regarding this particular aspect of the project had negative consequences.

Amanda's responsibilities were limited and did not correspond to her ambitions. Only 2 per cent of the overall budget was allocated to the "social" aspects of the project, so Amanda's room to manoeuvre was restricted. She had been active at the beginning of the project, in May and June, during the selection process, and she had established relationships with other NGOs working in Lamaria. In November, however, she mostly managed the files for the registration of property titles and signed requests for leave permits.

Amanda intimidated people not only because of her overt feminism but also because of the power she wielded. In early December a beneficiary was removed from the project and arrested for sexually abusing his stepdaughter. He had threatened that he would kill her mother if the stepdaughter said anything. Amanda was able to gain the trust of the girl, who confided in her. The girl was sent to a specialized shelter while authorities incarcerated the stepfather. After this incident, no one doubted Amanda's authority over the group. Later, Amanda explained to me that people were not accustomed to denouncing others because "civil society was scared." And it is precisely because this problem existed all over the country that she sought to create a security committee: "One must defend the area where one lives."

But on a day-to-day basis, Amanda spent most of her time talking to people who came to see her in the mornings with complaints about a health issue or a personal problem, and she would decide whether to grant a leave permit or not. Sometimes she mediated quarrels and disputes. She encouraged mothers to send their children to school, but not all complied; the main reason, they said, was that they could not pay for the exercise books. Amanda thought that in general "la gente es envidiosa" (people are envious) and that problems would only increase with the Red Cross's departure. Often she stayed with Rosa during the hot afternoon hours, sighing about how *aburrida* (bored) she felt since she was unable to carry out her projects for the residents of the site. Seeing the apparent amount of "free time" Amanda had, the engineer began to wonder about the merits of the project's "social" component.

By November, Amanda was receiving more and more complaints related to work issues, and she was taking them seriously, which irritated the engineer. He was growing displeased with the fact that she was defending the workers in their grievances since it diminished the labour force and weakened his own authority. Moreover, her feminist discourse upset him. In mid-December the tensions between the two were at their height, no doubt worsened by the visit of external evaluators who came to assess the advancement of the project, which was lagging behind schedule, and asked about the social worker's "valor agregado" (added value). She replied that all was "running its course."

Sensing that she would be fired and feeling uncomfortable on the site, she told me what she truly thought of the entire endeavour. The project was overemphasizing the *obra física* (structural work). Sure, the objective was to build houses, but this was not a small business! "Somos humanitarios!" (We are humanitarians!). In her perspective, the technical crew treated the workers like cheap labour and disregarded all the other aspects of the development. She felt that Luis, the supervisor, admonished people from the *campo* (countryside) too often and that the engineer exercised his authority in a way that did not respect the humanitarian ethos, where the contribution of beneficiaries ought to be acknowledged beyond their manual labour. She also believed that the masons did not realize they were working in a humanitarian context and failed to treat people on an equal footing. Amanda did not mince her words.

The masons' situation requires some clarification: they worked daily with the beneficiaries and were under the direct authority of the foreman, Don Cesar, who had hired them. It was "a good opportunity," concurred the masons I interviewed, particularly in a period of job uncertainty. Masons believed the families were lucky to have been selected for this project and to receive a house they themselves would have been incapable of acquiring easily. The mason who had trained the *armadoras* thought it unfair that humanitarian organizations disregarded people like him for reconstruction projects. In many cases, masons had also suffered from the earthquake. But as they owned either a plot of land or the house in which they lived, they were ineligible for the first reconstruction initiatives that arrived in Lamaria. They probably felt some *envidia* toward the beneficiaries, but they did not show it; indeed, they were instructed to avoid conflict with the "non-salaried workers." When the pace of work intensified, however, some tended to scold workers. I recall an incident where a mason harshly reprimanded a man in front of all the families lined up to receive their food rations. The culprit had let the cement dry and the mason had needed to liquefy it again, "and all this for five pounds of corn!" he screamed, red-faced.

According to Amanda, being a humanitarian meant focusing first and foremost on the beneficiaries' well-being. Her comparison of the project with a small business venture illustrates the tension between instrumental reasoning and the logics of compassion. According to her, project leaders had to "be at the service of the people," something at which the technical crew failed. But the extent to which she herself was "at the service of the people" remained vague to me. Without being a professional humanitarian expert, for it was the first time she was hired by an international organization, she endorsed humanitarian values, which she integrated into her personal concerns. She strived to change class and gender relations. She wanted to combat poor people's *asistencialismo* (welfare dependency) – an objective more commonly found in development projects. "No doubt, the Red Cross was not going to tackle these problems. Such 'ambitions' are beyond its program," she told me. She lectured on social change, but in La Hermandad the audience was limited, except for the engineer, who so obviously disliked her feminist bravado.

On 18 December 2001, at a meeting with the evaluators in the offices of the small Red Cross in town (where I was not welcome "because it is private," said the engineer), the decision to terminate Amanda's contract was made final. She admitted that she was relieved and told me that she was applying for a job at another foreign Red Cross (which did not come through). For the next six months, the project continued without a social worker. The engineer became the main authority figure on the site, and his priority was to finalize construction as quickly as possible.

This situation illustrates various points. First, just because one calls a project humanitarian does not mean that the individuals in charge endorse similar humanitarian values. Aside from Gustavo, who was the Central America representative of the German Red Cross, and to a much lesser extent the engineer, who had done post-Mitch reconstruction work in Honduras, no one had any professional humanitarian experience. The technical crew was unfamiliar with the institutional culture of transnational humanitarian NGOs, so they did not seek to incarnate any particular values. They tended to behave according to the parameters of a regular paid job. The middle managers, such as the foreman and the engineer, were under pressure to be as speedy as possible. Although there are often significant differences between the laudatory discourses of humanitarian professionals who pull the strings from their foreign offices and local personnel hired to work in the field – something relevant to this case study – a pragmatic attitude would be to acknowledge that each side had its own worry: the institutional humanitarians sought to finish the project in due time and within budget limits, whereas the priority of local masons was to do a decent job (so as not to be fired), hoping that in the future the foreman would hire them again.

Second, the tensions between the visions of the engineer and the social worker recalled the national considerations regarding the effects of reconstruction on society. In post-disaster El Salvador, civil society was in the midst of debates regarding the impact and nature of reconstruction. It is worth recalling that the notion of reconstruction itself was replete with meaning. After the signing of the peace accord in 1992, the nation had embarked on a five-year national reconstruction plan, which sought to reactivate economic activity, especially in former conflict zones, and to repair damaged infrastructure. However, the plan's two most significant programs were "the creation of the PNC [local police force], separate and distinct from the armed forces, and the land program for former combatants on both sides and for supporters of the FMLN [Frente Farabundo Martí para la Liberación Nacional] who had occupied land during the war years" (del Castillo 2008, 111). As Castillo explains, underlying the plan was the belief that lasting peace could be secured only through economic stability and growth, and she reminds us that at this time, the International Monetary Fund induced neoliberal macro-economic policies (ibid., 112). These policies regarding land distribution, poverty alleviation, and the reduction of inequality did not properly address the root causes of the war. Instead, they favoured an export-oriented growth strategy. Salvadoran civil society organizations, many of which had been or still were FMLN supporters, had thus been engaged in a long ongoing debate with the government regarding what reconstruction meant for the nation.

After Hurricane Mitch in 1998, the Inter-American Development Bank put forward another reconstruction plan for Central America, which specified that "reconstruction must not be at the expense of transformation" (quoted in Large 2005, 279). Reconstruction is never value-neutral and had not been so ever since the end of the war in El Salvador.

Back in Lamaria, activist NGOs such as OIKOS (linked to the World Lutheran Federation) and the Unidad Ecológica Salvadoreña conceived of reconstruction as a lever to change social structures. In a certain way, Amanda reproduced this mobilizing discourse, and the engineer disregarded it. He avoided politics. To his mind, reconstruction meant the building of houses for disaster-stricken families, no more and no less. Even if Amanda could only voice her desire for social change, it was enough to spark antagonism between the two. And since the project could not do without the engineer, Amanda was let go.

I learned later that at the very beginning of the project, German officials suggested that a micro-credit component be integrated. It would certainly have given more viability to the social dimension. Amanda had been in favour of it, but Gustavo and the engineer had opposed it, arguing that it would have taken too much of people's time away from building activities. Therefore, from the beginning, Amanda had seen her scope of action limited by the priorities of the *obra física*. I realized this when I met her again in April 2002; she was still bitter over the way the project had been handled.

The beneficiaries' perception of this polarization was not homogeneous. Many were wary of Amanda. Her incursion into people's daily lives was not always appreciated. She made overt comments about how filthy one resident's cubicle was, how another mistreated her children, how a third was *problemática*. It is not surprising that people were resentful. She also had some who supported her, such as Rosa and Maxwell, because she had chosen them to occupy certain functions: Maxwell to be coordinator and Rosa to be personal assistant.

I also found that people were quite observant of orders of precedence. Hierarchical statuses impress and inspire deference. In La Hermandad very few individuals dared to publicly confront the two main figures of authority, except Maxwell, who felt he was "one of them." Although people respected Amanda and were grateful to her when she granted them a leave permit, they never interfered in the misunderstandings or quarrels that opposed her to the engineer. Not only was this "not done," but also, no one wished to receive a sanction – or worse! When the balance of power was leaning dangerously against Amanda, families remained quiet. But there is more: Amanda's discourse on social change did not resonate with the families. Rosa told me that she had "learned a lot" from Amanda, but putting into practice her teachings was a step she could not take. More generally, people did not want to jeopardize their ownership of a house, so they avoided disagreement with project officials, except for in a few isolated cases.

I saw Amanda a few times after her departure. She enjoyed meeting at the Unicentro, the new air-conditioned commercial centre in Lourdes. "Mall culture," I remember saying to myself. Malls are appreciated in El Salvador, at least by those who have shoes – I saw a barefoot man being refused entrance by an armed guard. In April 2002 Amanda vented her feelings. She told me that everyone on the project had a *mala fama* (bad reputation) and, specifically, that the engineer and Gustavo were stealing money "on the backs" of the masons. She did not have proof but would not hesitate to testify that they were corrupt, and in the meantime, if she had not left the project earlier, it was because she "cared about the people." (In my field notes, I wrote, "She wants me to think she cares." And in hindsight, it looks like I, too, internalized the ambient suspicion that circulated against her.) She added that William, the young representative of the local Red Cross, had found a cheaper supplier for the bricks but that the engineer and Gustavo had declined to pursue that option. She said that the accounting books ought to be shown to the German Red Cross leaders, for she believed they would reveal many irregularities. Even Sister Elena was in her line of fire: when I asked her whether Sister Elena might help her to find work, she replied that Sister Elena had a *mala fama* for reputedly diverting humanitarian food aid to resell it on the black market! According to Amanda, the entire municipality had a *mala fama*. Lamaria was a place of mistrust and corruption, starting with the mayor, who did not hold any real power. Instead, it was a councillor from the FMLN who pulled the strings.[3] The small Red Cross was not exempt from Amanda's vehement critique: it also had a *mala fama* because of William, "a real homophobe," who supposedly smoked drugs, and Mario, another volunteer, who was apparently involved in a car theft network. It was simple: Amanda believed everyone was corrupt, especially in the development world. "The development sector in El Salvador is a network of corruption ... We should have the project audited because there is a lack of transparency."

Amanda did concede that at the "physical level," the houses were excellent. "There is no better project in the country. These are the best houses, but there is no viability at the social level." Amanda's firing had a very concrete effect on one crucial aspect of La Hermandad's collective life: food distribution.

PROBLEMS WITH FOOD DISTRIBUTION

The German Red Cross was responsible for providing monthly distributions of food rations. According to the project framework, this was a contribution from the institution in exchange for people's manual labour. There was a significant loss of income for families since an adult member had to be dedicated full time to construction, and a family could find itself completely dependent on the Red Cross for its sustenance. The majority of reconstruction projects in El Salvador that were headed by an international NGO and that had adopted a "mutual aid" or "food for work" execution methodology had established links with the World Food Programme (WFP). The German Red Cross had an understanding with the NGO Action by Churches Together (ACT), a branch of the World Lutheran Federation, which served as an intermediary with the WFP. In theory, distributions were to happen on a monthly basis. They comprised the same amount of food as what was given during the emergency period: 22 kilograms of corn, 22 kilograms of rice, 5 kilograms of beans, and 2.5 kilograms of vegetable oil. Amanda was in charge of the logistics, and when the food arrived by truck, the members of the food distribution committee had to divide up the bags into family rations. When everything was ready, Maxwell would ask everyone to stop working and line up to collect a share.

There was another food distribution. It was targeted at children under the age of seven of insufficient weight and height. All children in La Hermandad qualified. It mobilized a different organizational network, through CARITAS (the social mission branch of the Catholic Church) and the Missionary Sisters of Saint Peter Claver, whose role during the emergency had been so prominent. Every six to eight weeks, the nuns received food aid from the Fundación Salvadoreña de la Tercera Edad (FUSATE), which was then transported to the compound. Parents had to pay seven *colones* (75 cents), and they received the same type of food as in their WFP rations but in lesser quantity (1.5 kilograms per bag), as well as powdered milk, flour, *mezcla* (corn flour), and sometimes semolina. Perishable food items were never included. During the first three months of the project, from July to September 2001, families also received food aid from a religious order of nuns based in Santa Ana who had given them soap, plastic plates and bowls (very sought-after items), and various personal hygiene products. The Red Cross also came at the beginning to give out provisions, utensils, and household accessories.

Residents told me that at the beginning of the project, distributions came as planned, every month. But after months of hard labour, with the project lagging behind schedule and Amanda gone, their assessment was quite different. In February 2002 a majority of individuals told me – although they never officially complained about it – that their situation had become almost unbearable in terms of food sufficiency. It was definitely the case for the seven "most vulnerable families," most single mothers and their children, the elderly, large families, and those without any outside income – which represented half the individuals. The lack of money meant that families could not easily purchase supplemental food items, and everyone suffered from vitamin deficiency. This was due to the quality of food rations, which were high in carbohydrates and low in protein and vitamins, but also due to the irregularity in deliveries.

Regarding food for the disaster victims, something always struck me: since La Hermandad is so close to the Zapotitán Valley, why did the organization not consider buying produce from local growers? It would have complemented the food rations and been a definite "value added" to the "social" dimension of the project. I never received a clear answer to this question. Of course, the WFP networks are humanitarian systems, and it would have implied a greater financial investment. In other words, the Red Cross did not have to pay for food since it was undertaking a reconstruction project. As for the irregularity in food deliveries, this mainly became a problem after Amanda was fired. The smooth functioning of deliveries was one of her chief responsibilities; she managed the logistics and coordination between institutions. With her dismissal, the engineer took charge of food deliveries, and the situation deteriorated. Distributions were late in March and May, and although the nuns' food deliveries arrived on time, they were insufficient to feed a family for weeks on end.

No doubt, this state of affairs had consequences. To overcome the lack of food, some families borrowed money from kin members but also from better-off individuals on the site, such as Ramona and Laeticia, and got into debt. The women whose partners were working outside the compound were not in the same situation as the single mothers who had no choice but to work on the site. Not all single mothers went into debt, but some did. These were small sums, and no interest was charged, but at the end of April some women owed over US$100. If this seems a negligible amount, borrowers found it a burden nonetheless. Juana, whose husband had left her after an altercation between him and the guards at City Hall, owed over US$100 to Ramona. This amount corresponded to one month's salary at minimum wage. Juana came from a distant *cantón* and had no choice but to borrow money from Ramona for daily expenses. Shortly before the inauguration of the project, Ramona wanted Juana to start repaying her in instalments, knowing that she would not be able to settle the entire loan in one payment. But even that was difficult for Juana. Josefa, a single mother, had also run up a significant debt with Ramona, but since they were neighbours and had become friends, Ramona did not ask the same of her. These examples illustrate the economic challenges some people faced.

Credit transactions were a private matter. Perhaps Amanda would have been more likely to get involved, but the engineer did not wish to interfere in personal business. It is not that he was an insensitive man; I saw him more than once hand out some bills from his wallet to alleviate someone's hardship. In fact, throughout all these months, it was not uncommon for Amanda, the engineer, and me to act in this way. We regularly gave money to help a person pay for medical fees at the clinic or food at the market. These gestures happened on a spontaneous and one-off basis, but even so, people talk, and there was gossip again and *envidia* about who received money from whom! In the context of a humanitarian project, where all are supposed to be on an equal footing, these modest gestures of financial aid could sour interpersonal relations. Because money given by the engineer was seen as a form of favouritism, it turned the wheel of *envidia*.

Regarding food aid, families were the ultimate receivers in a long chain of institutions involved in humanitarian action. This "food chain" began with donor countries, via the WFP, and then branched out through various NGOs to finally reach families involved in participatory housing reconstruction projects. Food was defined as a return contribution that would be used for the generation of "assets" that would allow "vulnerable populations" to rebuild their communities.[4] The assets were the houses. If at the conceptual level food aid ought to be considered a return contribution in exchange for work provided (the property title being the main and final transaction), the fact that it was insufficient to satisfy the nutritional needs of the families was a problem. It was not just an intellectual matter about the semantics of the project logics: it had significant consequences for people's very bodies and lives. The entire biopower critique is certainly relevant here. What I want to highlight, however, has less to do with the politics of bare life and the technologies of power (Agamben 1998; Foucault 1991) and more to do with the pernicious results such forms of governmentality created in La Hermandad, namely envy toward better-off individuals and general discontent.

One last point relates to the quality of corn. There are different varieties of corn, and the WFP corn was yellow. A few families from Lamaria did not like it, preferring the white variety that came with the children's food distributions. A small group of friends persuaded a merchant in town to buy the yellow "humanitarian" corn at nightfall once the project leaders had left in order to get some cash to buy what they really wanted. The scheme grew to involve a dozen or so families. Selling food was not illegal, but it did contravene project regulations. Something that was defined as a counterpart in a non-monetary exchange was then integrated back into market circulation.

Hence, on the one side were very poor families who barely made it with the food distributions, and on the other were crafty individuals who, disliking the quality of one staple item, cheated the system with a clever stratagem. I never knew whether the engineer discovered the scheme, but in March 2002 the men stopped selling their yellow corn.

In retrospect, it is clear that everyone lacked sufficient food, but this condition was not unique to La Hermandad. Thousands of poor families, in pre- and post-disaster contexts, show signs of malnutrition and vitamin deficiency. Under this particular humanitarian regime, however, food aid and access to extra food became another source of distinction between residents, and comparisons were unavoidable.

COMMUNITY BUILDING NIPPED IN THE BUD

Whereas the previous points explain unfolding processes structured around work, gender relations, and food aid, this last section concerns a telling occurrence that is illustrative of power relations. It concerns the creation of a community association, called an Asociación de Desarrollo Social Comunitario del Cantón (ADESCO). In the *cantones* of the Salvadoran countryside, residents elect local delegates who officially represent the community. An ADESCO is a legal entity that voices the community's needs and claims to official governance bodies. Before the earthquake, not all *cantones* and *caseríos* in Lamaria had an ADESCO. Immediately after the earthquake, in order to count the number of damaged houses and people per household so that emergency aid could be organized, they created *directivas*, some of which became formal ADESCOs. Some ADESCOs are more influential than others. Lamaria's rural areas were not among the most political in the country, contrary to the province of Usulután, for example, where I witnessed how savvy and articulate community leaders were in playing one foreign NGO against another. ADESCOs in Usulután were strong and organized (due to the reinsertion of ex-combatant communities), which was not so much the case in Lamaria, aside from two or three that existed before the earthquake and whose members regularly petitioned the mayor's office.

In La Fraternidad an ADESCO was formed in January 2002 at the construction site with which the German Red Cross was involved. The other two initiatives – one led by the Italians and one by the Marist Brothers – were finished. They had hired a private contractor to do the heavy work, and the houses were built with cement blocks instead of bricks. The building process was much faster, and the demands on beneficiaries' manual labour were fewer. Mauricio, the social worker hired in the New Year by the municipality at La Fraternidad to coordinate future reconstruction and development initiatives in Los Almendros, encouraged the creation of ADESCOs.

One hundred and fifty families resided in La Fraternidad, but there was an obvious difference between the Red Cross project and the other two. The families involved with the Italians and the Marists received a smaller house on a smaller plot (170 square metres instead of 200 square metres), but they had to work much less than their Red Cross neighbours. *Envidia* manifested itself on both sides: on the one hand, because the "gift" of the house seemed less generous; on the other hand, because some were still building after others were done "with this construction business."

According to Mauricio, an ADESCO fosters community cohesion since people have to meet, discuss, elect representatives, and formulate requests to City Hall or to an NGO. Initially, the Red Cross at La Hermandad had no objection, but by December, Gustavo and the engineer were against it and frowned at the mere talk of an ADESCO. Indeed, an ADESCO might have delegitimized their authority. Of course, they did not express themselves in these terms in public, invoking instead the priority of the *obra física*. The engineer had spoken to the most influential residents, such as Maxwell and Ramona, explaining that it was not the right time to form an ADESCO in La Hermandad; there was still much construction work left, and it would be best not to "disperse people's energies in political matters." Gustavo and the engineer also spoke to the mayor about their position. The situation in La Fraternidad was different: there were three NGOs, including the Red Cross, and Red Cross officials could not forbid a representative of the Red Cross beneficiaries to be part of the newly formed ADESCO – it would have been clearly unfair – so a Red Cross representative was elected. Due to La Hermandad's enclosed nature, project leaders had more influence over people. When I questioned them about the thwarted ADESCO initiative in La Hermandad, they said that they wished to keep "everyone on an equal footing." What they did not acknowledge was that they wanted to avoid dealing with a formal entity that could challenge their authority.

I found it quite telling that an international humanitarian organization wishing to foster the communitarian ideal decided to nip in the bud the only true manifestation of grassroots collective expression. Humanitarian builders sought to develop a new community, but its members would not be able to organize as a collective until they were given permission to do so. Plainly stated, authorities on site sought to maintain control. After his confrontation with Amanda, the engineer wanted to avoid potential altercations with an ADESCO. Families hardly protested; Laeticia was among the few who complained, believing it was a good idea to create an ADESCO at mid-project, but Maxwell disagreed. Ramona presumed that she was the object of too much envy and was reluctant to be elected.

When the question was revisited in May 2002, the overall atmosphere was so negative and tense that no one wished to take part in an ADESCO. Ironically, the engineer now tried to influence some individuals he wanted as members of an ADESCO. The truth is that toward the end of the project, people were utterly tired of the interpersonal strife. Maxwell repeated that "la gente está pleitista" (people are quarrelsome), and he was drained. There was no way he would take part in an ADESCO. His role as beneficiaries' coordinator had left him disillusioned: "To constantly be the object of *envidia*, I am fed up!" For months, he had been the target of people's spite because he had a different status and knew about certain decisions before others. He described his experience as being constantly torn between people's demands and the supervisory controls of those in charge. Instead of the burgeoning of a new communitarian ethos, La Hermandad was descending into divisionism, moral fatigue, and physical exhaustion.

Amanda's dismissal was undoubtedly pivotal. It revealed the ways that the project's framework collided with people's expectations and worldviews. Indeed, the project logic, structured around the principles of community participation and reciprocal exchange, was constantly being challenged, and interpersonal relations soured. There were other crises, which I present in the final chapter, that further illustrate the difficulties that awaited the social microcosm of this enclosed post-disaster reconstruction initiative.

6

Weathering the Moral Economy of Aid

With Amanda's departure, the group came under the authority of the engineer, whose topmost priority was to finish the houses as quickly as possible. In January, with the the dry season at its peak, building was advancing slowly and health problems intensified. In February, when the project was supposed to end, only thirty houses had been built, and they still lacked windows, roofs, and doors. The delay exasperated the engineer, who complained about people's *falta de compromiso* (lack of commitment). Amanda was not there to arbitrate quarrels, so they multiplied and gossip swelled. Jealousy, and in particular sexual jealousy, took on large proportions, especially toward a few single mothers. Many deplored the climate of "hypocrisy" that now spread over the site. It was a recurrent theme in my conversations during these winter months. One would accuse another of being a gossip-monger, much like in the story of the biter bitten. In mid-February the engineer decided that people should work on Saturdays to finish the project faster. He announced it during a general assembly, saying that he was requesting a "surplus" from people, whose ultimate objective remained "receiving the gift of the house." From February to May 2002, the overall atmosphere in La Hermandad steadily deteriorated.

In this chapter, I recount particular incidents that further illustrate the erosion of the moral economy of humanitarian reconstruction.

WORK, TAKE 2: DOLDRUMS IN A HUMANITARIAN REGIME

One April afternoon while the engineer was driving along the dirt road leading to the site with La Roja and her son, two men wearing balaclavas and pointing shotguns halted the pickup truck. They ordered the passengers to step out of the vehicle and empty their pockets, and then they left with a little bit of money, two digital cameras, and of course, the Red Cross truck. This type of incident was not uncommon in El Salvador, where members of the Salvatrucha or La 18 gangs regularly stopped motorists, even long-distance trailers.

The incident triggered a lot of chatter across town. The police conducted an investigation, but it did not provide significant results because the thieves had likely taken the truck to the countryside, quickly stripped it down, and sold the parts. Suspicions pointed to a Red Cross volunteer who was associated with a vehicle theft ring, but no charges were laid for lack of evidence.

This incident had an impact not merely on the engineer's mobility but also on his patience. "Estoy canzado de todo, del proyecto, de la gente pleitista, de estar lejos de mi familia, de la falta de compromiso de la gente, de toda la gente aquí" (I am tired of everything, of the project, of the quarrelsome people, of being away from my family, of people's lack of engagement, of everyone here), he said to me a few days later. He saw the holdup as a sign that it was time to leave, but construction was far from over and he could not just pack up and go. However, there was a solution: compel beneficiaries to work faster.

The lateness of the project was due to three factors: an error in judgment in evaluating the necessary time required to complete the houses, the reduction in manpower due to people's withdrawal, and the exhaustion of workers after many months of hard work.

The engineer began to distribute penalties, he sometimes uttered threats, and a few individuals received warning letters for contravening a project regulation. The most significant group sanction was to limit the height of individual property walls. He said to the families, "Since you are lazy and since you do not want to work anymore, then no more than a height of ten bricks for the walls!" Even though building the walls was quite costly, the Red Cross could not depart from the original design that had been approved months earlier and forgo building the walls altogether. The engineer was particularly exasperated with La Hermandad's "city folk," whom he thought complained a lot more than the families in La Fraternidad. The distinction between town and country people was evident in the engineer's comments, and he did not hesitate to criticize the former to their faces: "You are used to the least effort, you have absolutely no gratitude." Maxwell concurred, even though he too was now categorized as one of the "undesirables." By the end of March, all the houses were built but lacked roofs, doors, windows, and latrines. Among the work that still needed to be done was also the levelling of the roads and the installation of pipes and street lamps – all financed by the Salvadoran organization Fondo Nacional de Viviendo Popular (FONAVIPO), which arrived in La Hermandad at the end of March.

Despite the steady activity, the threat of not receiving a house hung in the air. Aware of the engineer's and foreman's growing irritation, families began to wonder whether they were really going to receive a house. "Has this project been a lie? Have we been working for nothing," wondered some people. I would try to reassure them and tell them that they had nothing to worry about, that it was impossible that they would not receive their house, but the risk continued to seem real for some. For his part, Maxwell never doubted the outcome of the project, yet he did wonder whether some individuals would be expelled. The case of Don Julio is informative. This man of tempestuous character did not appreciate the way authority figures treated him. It is true that he was far from being a "model worker": he arrived late in the morning, took long breaks, and chitchatted too much with others. In the eyes of the technical crew, he "took it too easy." One day when Don Cesar, the foreman, was rebuking him for something, Don Julio replied menacingly, machete in hand, "Te voy a matar" (I am going to kill you). It was the second time Don Julio had flared up, and Don Cesar, who knew how impulsive the man was, never spoke to him again. A month later, Don Julio exploded again in front of the engineer. By that time, I had developed an easy talking relationship with him, and he explained why he believed beneficiaries' human rights were being abused. They were not cheap labour, and the technical crew should not expect him or anybody else to behave as a salaried worker. There was no boss in La Hermandad, but the engineer and the foreman tended to forget that. No doubt, Don Julio's resentment reflected a sentiment shared by others, but he was the only one to confront authority figures publicly.

These incidents challenged the project's moral framework. For many workers, the status of beneficiary had become draining, both physically and financially. By openly critiquing the project logic or withdrawing from it altogether, the "labour power" was disavowing the non-monetary exchange rationale meant to orient social relationships and the reified gifting rhetoric used as a motivational discourse. With the heat, lack of money, and talk about not receiving the houses, tensions increased and became palpable.

In the hopes of lifting people's spirits, a general assembly was convened in early April with the mayor and representatives of the Red Cross. Gustavo, the German Red Cross representative for Central America, announced that the families could take possession of their houses as soon as the roofs were secured. This decision was made not only to smooth things over but also to facilitate the movement of two levelling machines from FONAVIPO. Two weeks later, families began to access their new homes. The first to move were Ramona, her sister, and two single mothers, whose new houses where in the row facing the road, a prime location for Ramona's business. Josefa, one of the women who moved in, did not believe that the houses had been assigned by luck of the draw. If the *armadoras* received "the best houses," it was because they had worked hard. By now, the heavy work of the *armadoras* and *compactadoras* was over, and the engineer allowed the single mothers to return to other occupations.

Work dynamics changed once families began to move in. In May more than half the group halted all work activities, believing that now that they had their house, their contribution was over and done with. It was not a planned tactic but a shared refusal to pursue the "game" of donor and receiver any longer. "Ahora que tienen la casa, todo el mundo se vuelve individualista" (Now that they have the house, everybody is becoming individualistic), said Karlita and some others.

From then on, the division of labour changed. When the walls for all the houses were built, all the masons left, which created a feeling of emptiness. It also indicated the end of participatory work, as people had needed to work collectively to build the walls. The engineer hoped that some beneficiaries would still behave as a team, but that did not happen. Don Julio was in fact encouraging his peers to refuse to work "for free," arguing that now that the houses were built, the leaders could not expect any further involvement from them. The logic of participation had run its course. To remedy the situation, the Red Cross decided to pay a few experienced beneficiaries to mount the latrines at a rate of US$29.71 per latrine.

6.1 Moving from the cubicles to the new houses *(last row)*, 2002. Once the residents were allowed to occupy their new homes, they needed to clean up the space left by the temporary shelters. Individual property walls separating each lot are not built yet, but the wall surrounding La Hermandad is visible.

People were unhappy with the dry-latrine system. The latrines were an eyesore. Septic tanks could not be built because of the nearness of the water table (2 to 3 metres deep). None of the families were familiar with the dry-latrine system, and the Red Cross offered training on its proper usage.

FONAVIPO was a second source of potential remuneration. Men had overheard that the organization would recruit people at a rate of 25 to 30 *colones* per day (around US$3). The wage was finally set at 15 *colones* per square metre of moved earth, a pay rate Maxwell found low since it was the same as five years earlier. Various men accepted the contract and began work in mid-May.

During the last six weeks of the project, there was no participatory work. Families lived in their respective houses, retreating to their private sphere. Some decided to lay coloured cement on the floor, a common home-improvement practice. Women began gardening, and

6.2 Building the roundabout, 2002. Toward the end of the project, people were tired of working for no pay and disengaged from participatory work. The NGO paid a few beneficiaries to build the roundabout.

new neighbours exchanged seeds and plant cuttings. The masons' departure had an economic impact on Ramona's and Laeticia's hot meal businesses, and Laeticia closed shop.

The residents of La Hermandad became progressively more disenchanted. As the dialectics of participation disappeared, so did the pretence of a gifting morality. On the side of the receivers, there were complaints and negativity, and on the side of the givers, there were also complaints and negativity, notably regarding people's lack of gratitude. This matter requires some attention.

In analyses of the unilateral and free form of giving (Godbout 1998), gratitude and recognition are often described as a form of return that confirms the social relationship between the individuals participating in the gifting "transaction." Recognition is an intersubjective acknowledgment of value assigned to gestures, objects, or people. Other works examine the question of recognition differently.

Bourdieu (1996), for instance, emphasizes the dissimulated strategies that social actors use to establish and reproduce social ties. For him, gifting is a case of misrecognition that, if plainly exposed, would reveal how similar it is to monetary exchanges because it manipulates different forms of capital.

Questions about recognition and gratitude resurfaced regularly on the site, starting with Maxwell and the engineer. The latter had mentioned to Maxwell, Rosa, and others that he preferred La Fraternidad to La Hermandad because people there were more grateful, which could be seen in their diligence at work. Maxwell held similar opinions, and he also developed a critical view of collective life: "Aquí la gente no agradece, es demasiado pleitista, hipócrita, siempre quieren más" (People here are ungrateful, they fight too much, they are hypocrites, they always want more) – as though dissension meant a lack of gratitude.

Once the families had moved into their houses, I asked them what they thought of the entire endeavour. Women in particular answered that they found it regrettable that the group was so divided and did not show more appreciation toward project leaders. I was actually surprised to hear them echo the engineer's words.

To my mind, the "lack of recognition" reveals the erosion of the moral underpinnings framing the project. Social relationships within a humanitarian reconstruction regime such as this one are organized around the establishment of a hierarchical power structure that project leaders incarnate, and participation is the mode of operation. The exercise of power, which was manifest in expert knowledge, working conditions, regulations, and constraints, curtailed the "gifting spirit" between partners. Donors and receivers did not share the same status: donors were hierarchically superior and defined the rules of the game, whereas receivers had to agree to the rules if they wanted to secure a house.

Receivers accepted these conditions because they felt the "gift" was worth it. But opportunism and individualism were as important (if not more so) than the desire to entertain a social rapport geared toward community building and defined in terms of a gifting relation. If people were blamed for being (supposedly) hypocrites, it was because they refused to uphold the moral grammar of the project and opted instead to withdraw from it – hence the frustration of those who still had to defend it.

An example to illustrate these comments: at the end of the project, the Red Cross wanted to redistribute the aluminum sheeting used for the cubicles – which had initially been given by Doctors Without Borders/Médecins Sans Frontières (MSF) for the temporary shelters – to other people in need. When the families heard that Gustavo had decided that all beneficiaries had to return them, they were vexed: "Es mío, la gente de MSF me la dio, la necesito" (It is mine, the people from MSF gave it to me, and I need it). Gustavo's decision particularly irked the women, who would have liked to use sheeting for a makeshift roof while cooking outdoors under the scorching sun. Regardless, there was no choice, each family had to select someone they knew to whom they would give their leftover aluminum sheeting. The engineer wanted to organize a committee composed of two or three people, including the coordinators of both sites, to oversee the process. However, since both Maxwell and his counterpart in La Fraternindad now inspired mistrust, the engineer asked me to compile a database – which I did. This was the only time I had an official role in the project.

From an institutional point of view, giving away the aluminum sheeting was an altruistic gesture, but it also served an aesthetic purpose: Red Cross officials wanted the site to look nice for the photographers, journalists, and German Red Cross administrators who would come for the inauguration on 6 June 2002. Gustavo did not want the model settlement to display too many signs of poverty and deemed rusted aluminum sheeting unfitting. His second argument called upon the idea of gifting. The organization had "given" each family a house, and a very well-built one at that, so why not extend the gesture to other unfortunate people who could make good use of the aluminum? It was a "surplus" that could "help more people," said Gustavo. But if the main objective of the German Red Cross were truly to assist *as many people as possible*, it could have opted for another execution methodology and house design or used cheaper materials, for instance, in order to build more houses.

During the last months of the project, social relations continued to sour. Resentment was now (also) targeted at men who were paid by the organization to finish up masonry work. The case of Raul, a mason hired to build the roundabout, was a case in point. Raul had arrived recently. He was Ramona's "hidden" husband; she had presented herself as a single mother – a strategy that a few other women had also used – in order to increase her chances of being selected for the project. Raul worked alone on the roundabout and was paid. One morning, his wife found a threatening note saying that Raul would be killed if he did not leave. She told me that to protect herself she had a gun in her house. Toward the end of my fieldwork, as often happens, people shared more personal details with me. And so it was that I learned that at least half the men in La Hermandad owned firearms. If I, a foreign anthropologist, was aware of these things, no doubt rumours about guns and death threats were rampant. Many individuals now had a *mala fama* (bad reputation): the *problemáticos* like Don Luis, the favoured ones like the single mothers, the better-off ones like Ramona and Laeticia, the lazy ones like Rosa, who never once did any physical work, and so on. And of course, the engineer had a *mala fama* too: "This guy is weird and shady," confided disgruntled individuals.

We are far from the romantic communitarian ideal that humanitarian builders hoped to foster. Division characterized relations here, which should not surprise us, considering the circumstances. It is important to remember that the only real tie that linked people together was their status as beneficiaries, which was both recent and temporary. Community ties take longer to materialize. During the last stretch of my fieldwork, two events occurred that speak to the deleterious atmosphere that reigned in La Hermandad.

These two occurrences concern Miguel, who killed himself in April 2002, and Rosa, for whom this tragedy marked her total withdrawal from the group. On a reflexive note, I would like to say that this is the first time I have written about Miguel's suicide since I first recounted the events in my doctoral dissertation. Many years have passed. And I still believe, as I did before, that Miguel's death is indicative of what can go terribly wrong in humanitarian endeavours, even if no one was directly to blame. It is, rather, that this particular reconstruction regime aggravated a person's pre-existing vulnerabilities, and he committed a radical act. My involvement in his burial left a profound impression on me.

Miguel's Story

Miguel was a tall and thin young man who spoke little and smiled little, a solitary and worried fellow who had been diagnosed with a severe case of hepatitis. Amanda always showed him solicitude and reminded him to take his medication, but he often lacked the money to purchase it. He was married to Carla, and they had two young boys together. His mother and Rosa's mother were *comadres* (godmothers to each other's children), and he had been welcomed by Rosa's mother and raised in her household for a few years when he was a boy. Rosa did not like Carla, and the feeling was mutual. Carla thought Rosa was prideful and a gossipmonger, and Rosa thought Carla was dirty and vulgar. In February and March, Miguel returned to his previous employment as a water deliveryman in the city, leaving Carla to replace him at work. Sometimes Miguel stayed in town overnight because he had to get up early to deliver water in the *colonias*. Carla integrated into the group of *compactadoras*, and her peers noticed that she made an effort "to look nice" (e.g., wore lipstick). Carla had the reputation of being a flirt, even at the beginning of the project. When Miguel started working in town, the gossip escalated: Carla was seen with another man in the central park, with one of the masons, and so on. Miguel was a jealous type, very jealous, and the rumours of his wife's infidelity hit him hard.

On Saturday, 13 April, he confronted Carla, who was supposedly drunk, and she denied the rumours. She told him to leave her alone. He refused and threatened to kill himself if she did not put an end to her liaison. She snickered. Miguel was holding a jar of rat poison. He opened it and swallowed the contents. He died a few hours later on his way to the hospital. That night, Betty, who was Rosa's sister and had therefore grown up with Miguel, confronted Carla threateningly. Fearing for her life, Carla called the police, and Betty spent the night in jail. Sunday morning, Rosa knocked on my door – coincidentally, I lived across from Betty's *mesón* (rental unit) – to tell me what had happened. She was in tears, and she was furious. That morning, Miguel's body had been transported to Betty's *mesón* and people had called the engineer at his home.

The wake was to take place on Sunday evening at Betty's *mesón*. When someone dies, it is customary to hold a wake in the house for family and friends to pay their respects. The deceased is surrounded with flowers and with effigies of Christ and the Virgin Mary. At nightfall, women recite the rosary. My friend Yanira's teenage daughter liked to visit wakes, where there are always coffee and biscuits on offer. It is a social gathering.

Doña Leonora, with whom I lived, agreed to lead the prayers, but the body had to be prepared. It was hot and Miguel's family did not have the money to pay for embalming. Rosa asked the engineer whether the Red Cross could help, but there was not much money for "extra expenses." The Red Cross nonetheless did purchase a burial site, a coffin, and the chemical solutions required to prepare Miguel. For this task, the engineer called on Paco, one of the beneficiaries who had worked for the local Red Cross. Paco knew the rudiments of the practice, as did Luis, the supervisor. During the afternoon, while the engineer went looking for Luis, Paco asked me to help him.

Rosa's mother nodded, meaning that she gave her approval. I was stunned but dared not refuse. I entered the room where Miguel was laid out. Paco was filling a syringe with formalin, and he wanted me to hold the bottle of formalin while he injected Miguel. Paco explained that he had to inject liquid into the vital organs and into the abdomen especially. The air was hot and heavy, saturated with the odour of formalin. Luis arrived and took over; I stepped outside to sit on the sidewalk. A while later, Luis and Paco joined me. Luis was satisfied. He told me that it was doctors from the American Red Cross who had shown him how to do this during the civil war.

When I attended the funeral the next day with Amanda (who had been notified), the men from La Hermandad who had been asked to dig the grave reeked of sweat and alcohol and had not finished digging. The grave had to be at least eight feet deep, and the soil – wet, heavy, and compact – resisted the shovels. It was a scorching day. The engineer had given the families the day off so that they could attend the burial, scheduled for two o'clock, but few showed up. Neither Carla nor her children were present. Perhaps this was because Carla knew how angry the whole family was with her. She also wondered whether she would be expelled, so she chose the day of the funeral to get her *cedula* (identification card), eight months after she had joined the project. "She had lost her husband; she did not want to lose the house" – that was the word.

As dictated by Catholicism, the customary funeral mass could not be performed since Miguel had committed suicide. When his coffin was placed in the ground, no words were pronounced. The silence saddened me. Two hours later, everybody returned home. The next day, the engineer acted as though it were business as usual. He did not address the families in a general assembly but remained silent about the tragedy.

The experience seemed surreal to me, starting with my involvement with Paco. I describe these events not only to illustrate the different roles and statuses that anthropologists may encounter in the field but also to mark a turning point in the way social dynamics progressed in La Hermandad.

Miguel's tragedy illustrates how a man's sexual jealousy, fed by the rumour mill, acquired such proportions that he took extreme measures to end the conflict between him and his wife. With Miguel often away from the site, Carla could behave like a "single woman," and gossip about her misbehaviour did the rest.

Spells, Curses, and Rosa's Evil Eye

Rosa was very affected by Miguel's death. The following weeks, she became extremely tense and nervous, criticizing everything and everyone. Rosa held Carla personally responsible for Miguel's death, and she was baffled as to why the engineer did not take action against her. Although she was angry at the engineer, she was in a subordinate position, so she refrained from expressing her irritation. Instead, she began a cold war with Carla and with anyone who stood up for her.

Four weeks after Miguel's death, Rosa became pregnant with her second child. She was twenty-seven years old, and her first daughter was seven. Although Maxwell was overjoyed, she received the news with mixed feelings: how were they going to feed another mouth now that Maxwell had no job? Aside from this pragmatic consideration, as soon as she discovered that she was pregnant, Rosa was worried for her child, fearing that someone would cast the evil eye on it. Rosa did not want anyone to know about her pregnancy, especially the "witches" who lived in La Hermandad. But everybody knew because like any proud father, Maxwell was happy to announce the news.

Rosa knew who the *brujas* (witches) were: her sister-in-law, who had accused Rosa of sleeping with her husband; Ana, the young single mother who got along so well with the engineer; and Ramona, the plump entrepreneurial woman from the "front row." According to Rosa, all three women had a *mala fama*. Rosa explained that now that she was pregnant, she was more vulnerable to the evil eye and to the nasty spells that could be cast on her unborn child. Not surprisingly, what she dreaded occurred: she developed a huge abscess under her left eye.

One might have thought that Maxwell had beaten her, which she vehemently denied. She tried to pierce the absess and rubbed it with garlic, but it only got worse. Wary of doctors, Rosa let the boil fill with pus, and it swelled to the size of an apricot, putting her vision at risk. Convinced that she was the victim of witchcraft, she repeated over and over that "these women" had cast a spell on her. She finally ceded to recommendations that she go to the clinic; the doctor told her to immediately consult an ophthalmologist in San Salvador, which she did four days later. "What a stubborn woman," sighed Maxwell. On her way back from the capital, Rosa stopped in Lourdes to see a *hermana curandera* (sister with healing powers). Between members of a given evangelical church, people call themselves "brother" or "sister." The woman was an evangelical healer whose prayers had curative powers. They prayed together facing an altar festooned with rose petals. The *curandera* took a petal and rubbed it against Rosa's sore eye, assuring her that an *hechisera* (sorceress) had cast a spell on her. Rosa cried and the *curandera* said that the Lord was with her. When Rosa, flushed and feverish, returned home the next day, she told me what the *curandera* had said to her: "You cannot stand where you live anymore; these people are driving you crazy!"

Rosa decided that she would not live in La Hermandad during her pregnancy. She went to stay with her mother in town and did not set foot on the site for as long as I remained there. The boil disappeared.

The intense stress that Rosa experienced may have manifested itself physically. Rosa was envious of various women, and as time passed, her feelings of hostility intensified. Evoking the evil eye and witchcraft was a way to express her hostility toward others. The boil provided her an opportunity to leave the site and live with her mother, avoiding for some time the stress triggers that bothered her. Accusations of witchcraft are inherent to the grammar of *envidia* (envy). Rosa's refusal to live in La Hermandad did not last long. Less than a year after the events, I spoke to her on the phone, and she told me that she was back in La Hermandad. But she did not feel any more friendliness for her fellow beneficiaries: "La gente tiene mala fama. No me gusta vivir allá. Prefiero la ciudad, hay luz y agua y está mejor para la Natalia, el bebé" (The people have a bad reputation. I do not like to live there. I prefer the city, where there is light and water, and it is better for the baby). Conversely, other residents felt that her ability to go live in town with her mother showed that she was "less in need" compared with them.

GIFTING A HOUSE: WHEN MORAL ECONOMIES COLLIDE

Housing is considered a human right, as per article 25 of the Universal Declaration of Human Rights. The notion of "a decent house" emanates from this guiding principle, and most NGOs in El Salvador referred to it when undertaking post-disaster reconstruction. NGOs had different options: some chose a minimalist model, some used traditional materials like adobe, and others preferred non-traditional materials like reinforced steel polystyrene. The model adopted at La Hermandad fell into the more expensive category due to the choice of materials and the construction technique. In this sense, project designers emphasized quality over quantity.

Many reconstruction projects in El Salvador limited the sale of newly gifted houses for a given period; in La Hermandad it was ten years. The recipients were also not allowed to lease or exchange their new houses. The Red Cross offered poor families access to private property but restricted the full enjoyment of this right. In property law, this proviso is called "restraints on alienation." Since the goal was to better ensure sustainable livelihoods, the house was considered an economic asset that would liberate families from rental expenses. Thinking about future generations was certainly on Gustavo's mind when he explained the underlying rationale for the project. The house was a family patrimony that humanitarian experts wanted to make inalienable for a period of time. In other words, they sought to restrict the exchange value of the house in order to enhance its use value.

From the perspective of sustainability, the argument is defencible. But I also found it strange to limit people's rights over their private property, especially after the months-long discourses on "the gift." Project leaders' gifting rhetoric intimated that when the object arrived at maturity, receivers would have full enjoyment of it: "This is your house, it belongs to you now," they said. And families said the same: "Es mi casa ahora, mi propiedad" (It is my house now, my property).

Humanitarian builders sought to lay the material basis for a new community. Limiting beneficiaries' right to sell their houses was meant to further this objective. As I have shown, top-down community building encountered significant challenges in La Hermandad, which is why I refer to it as a humanitarian reconstruction regime.

Gifting practices reveal types of socialization and particular forms of moral economies, and in La Hermandad the utilitarian component was evident. Ultimately, instrumental interests predominated because they leveraged important survival strategies. Owning a house was what drove families' involvement; it was accessing private property that was their motivation, much less the desire to form a community. When leaders harangued people to work harder, while drumming into their heads that this was about humanitarian gifting, contradictions arose.

As Arjun Appadurai (1986) has argued, we face two regimes of value: the first is that of humanitarian donor-builders seeking to limit the house's exchange value, and the second refers to receivers-beneficiaries for whom the monetary value is an important feature. I am not inferring that families denied the patrimonial value of the house, but they would have never put forward the idea of its inalienability. The moral reasoning of humanitarians can be expressed as follows: in the name of communitarian ideals and sustainable livelihoods, the house should not be a commodity, at least not in the immediate future. Perhaps they also wanted to protect families from greedy real estate agents and speculators.

When families took possession of their houses, they appreciated their new status as homeowners, and a general atmosphere of "to each their own" prevailed. Gustavo worried whether they would "take care" of their houses. For him, as well as for others who visited Los Almendros over the year, such as development workers from the Salvadoran Red Cross, the International Federation of Red Cross and Red Crescent Societies, and FONAVIPO, a concern remained: "Since poor families are generally content with any kind of shack (*son tranquilas con una champita*), are they really going to value and maintain a decent house (*casa digna*)?" Gustavo alluded to the "cultural issue" of cleanliness, but in this respect, not all residents acted similarly. He noticed that the more "vulnerable" families left garbage to rot on the floor. He was also worried about people's personal hygiene. No one had cared about such issues besides Amanda. Gustavo explained that the German Red Cross espoused a "vision of social change without doing social change per se." He hoped that development NGOs would take over and offer *capacitación comunitaria* (community training) in order to "teach people how to maintain a house." In my field notes, I wrote that project leaders considered people to be like playdough, seeking to mould them into "proper" owners.

This brings me to another point: the consortium of institutions that undertook the Los Almendros initiative wanted the *cantón* to be hooked up to basic services such as electricity, water, sewage, and so forth. The first step was obviously to build the physical environment. But many people did not have the money to pay for these services. More than a year after my departure, Maxwell told me that there were not many families that were hooked up to the electric grid because of the cost of connection (US$70). And fourteen years later, in 2016, there was still no running water. Humanitarian builders sought to construct a modern settlement, but its residents are not able to enjoy its full benefits, which is why Gustavo had hoped that development NGOs would come to Los Almendros with micro-credit projects. As for the families themselves, they wanted to find a job. Some worried about what was going to happen after the departure of the German Red Cross. And so ended the reconstruction experience for these Salvadoran disaster victims. New houses may be "gifted," but the problem of structural poverty remains.

It is like Gustavo and the director of the World Food Programme said: there are two El Salvadors, the capital and the rest. In 2002 social and economic indicators were improving, but malnutrition, poverty, underemployment, and homelessness were still rampant. These problems existed before the civil war and are ongoing; they are structural issues to be found in many developing countries, and humanitarian builders cannot eradicate them. Poverty is not a humanitarian problem but a political one.

In the enclosed space of this regulated humanitarian endeavour, various social actors confronted the impossibility of maintaining a moral framing based on exchange and gifting. The project's grammar had defined people's manual labour as a return in a non-monetary relationship, but it morphed into its opposite: a quasi form of wage labour, which was not real wage labour, for there was no pay, at least from the workers' perspective. Over time, the celebrated identity of being a "beneficiary" was eroded, and the institutional semantics of the project were challenged, revealing the contradictions inherent to the project's framework. The living conditions in La Hermandad exacerbated *envidia*.

6.3 Digging canals for water pipes, 2002. Water pipes were laid once people lived in their houses.

The fifty families who lived in this microcosm might have been considered relatively homogeneous in terms of socio-economic status and cultural worldview. This study has shown how microprocesses of social differentiation can have harmful effects in overdetermined humanitarian spaces. In La Hermandad they generated tensions, in one case with tragic consequences, and were counterproductive to the emergence of a communitarian feeling among residents. In terms of the gifting rhetoric, what transpired was mainly the obligation to give back, or rather, to give back without balking.

One of the reasons the institutional semantics of the project failed was that the project leaders did not embody the values associated with the organizational culture of humanitarians. After the departure of the only person who tried to uphold them – Amanda, with her stance that "we are humanitarians!" – the remaining individuals, who were construction workers really, did not abide by, or know about, humanitarian codes of conduct. The representations of a communitarian ideal, participation, and gifting relations

6.4 La Hermandad in 2014. Residents have built extensions onto their houses, and a lush vegetation now covers the grounds.

were perhaps just fictions. This judgment might be too severe, since there is a usefulness to fictions that orient and inspire people's actions. This is not to accuse humanitarian action of being laden with sentimentalism (although it certainly exists) but to highlight the reified aspects of the practice. In this regard, my long-term fieldwork documented the impossibility on a daily basis of enacting predetermined moralities.

We could say that there was a friction between moral fields. In line with my framing of humanitarian configurations in terms of moral economies, in which affects and values are assembled and come into conflict, a productive way to address the question is precisely through the topic of moral reasoning.

The onset of humanitarian practices generates new social dynamics and calls on a particular set of moral and ethical encounters. An important value that structures the humanitarian moral complex is that of *giving help* to suffering victims. The gift is one among many underlying values that shape the moralities of humanitarianism; another is the notion of people's rights – to aid, to development, and so on. For months, this moral complex defined the flow of goods and services and shaped the roles and identities of humanitarian providers and receivers, including the nuns, City Hall, families, and various national and international NGOs. With the routinization of aid, what began as a strong institutional moral discourse was distilled into a more embodied way of enacting the "everyday ethics" of humanitarian transactions.

Moreover, once in La Hermandad, people were faced with two interrelated narratives that described their daily lives: one upheld a non-monetary exchange, based on their manual labour in exchange for a house; the other professed the idea of humanitarian gifting as an overarching symbolic and moral frame. The first foregrounded the material object at the centre of the transaction (the house), whereas the second foregrounded service and transnational generosity (i.e., that of the Germans). Both informed the humanitarian moral complex, and they were not mutually exclusive – at least not at the beginning. But they did polarize as the relationship of beneficiaries with the technical crew soured and working conditions became strenuous.

They polarized because reconstruction transformed the previous parameters of gifting relationships. For months in the immediate aftermath of the earthquake, while living in the temporary shelters built by MSF, families had grown accustomed to a particular kind of humanitarian rapport; they had been positioned as receivers of gifting gestures with little expectation of return on their part, certainly not material forms of return. Food, clothing, and shelter were theirs to keep. The first configurations of aid I described manifested a humanitarian morality wherein the gift became a central value in that it legitimized new identities, roles, and relationships between local humanitarian actors and "deserving," "vulnerable" disaster victims. Of course, this humanitarian morality does not preclude other interpretations, such as having the right to aid. How utilitarian and altruistic motives were combined depended on whether the donor was the government (represented by the mayor's office), the nuns, or a foreign humanitarian organization.

Over time, we can say that the families developed a familiarity with, or a certain embodied attunement toward, this situated humanitarian morality. I would not go as far as to say that during the initial months they never questioned things, but when they arrived in La Hermandad, they did not actively question the project's framework. They recognized it as a humanitarian project, as did the Red Cross personnel. Acquiring a house and title in land represented an extraordinary opportunity, another type of humanitarian gift, even if they had to work for it.

Participatory reconstruction projects are often characterized by a non-monetary exchange. La Hermandad was an extreme situation because participation meant full-time dedication to labour with no salary for over a year. During the last months of construction, most residents felt that they were being exploited and that there was nothing humanitarian about the way that they were exhorted to work. This frustration was further exacerbated in February, when two-thirds of the families in the adjoining construction site took possession of their houses. Two of the three projects on that site had ended earlier because the managing NGOs had rented heavy machinery and used prefabricated materials. Hence many of the people in La Fraternidad were able to return to their normal lives earlier, unlike in La Hermandad, where the process seemed interminable.

Comparing their situation to that of their neighbours, and contrasting the Red Cross's and MSF's dynamics of humanitarian gifting, individuals began to question the project, taking a conscious step away from the official discourse and disputing its conceptual underpinnings. This was a form of ethical reasoning, a point at which people made more and more judgments about the project, contesting its moral grounds. The tensions that emerged between various micro-groups led to the revision of the humanitarian moral value complex put forth. All the unrest, strains, and struggles, and most importantly the demands on people's chief counterpart (labour), led to an explicit critique of the project's use of gifting rhetoric and participatory work. This situation differed from the previous moral grammars of aid because with reconstruction the conditions became similar to those of wage labour.

Might the notion of alienation or estrangement better characterize the situation? I use the concept in a general manner, referring to a market sphere of exchange wherein subjects sell their labour and do not control the means of production. In everyday life, this certainly describes the labour conditions of the poorer segments of Salvadoran society, but it rarely describes a humanitarian initiative. However, during the time of reconstruction, people found that working conditions became akin to the forms of labour they experienced elsewhere, leading them to consciously reflect on what was expected of them. That said, wages and commodity production were not the dominant idiom of reconstruction, and workers would end up controlling the product of their labour once property titles were transferred.

The problem lay in the friction between (moral) expectations, as people made judgments based on the conceptual grammars that defined a series of humanitarian configurations. In La Hermandad participatory work and social harmony became values through which donor representatives measured people's gratefulness and fidelity to the humanitarian moral complex. They became tokens of value, as actions came to be understood as sources of value (Graeber 2001). Diligence at work, community spirit, and social harmony were at once ends in themselves and the means whereby people could show they accepted the moral underpinnings of the organization's humanitarian gifting gesture. Since they were performative, they made morality visible, giving meaning to the "spirit of the gift."

Studies on gift giving from Mauss (1925, 1954) onward have underscored that an important function of a gift is to establish expectations between exchange partners and to ensure reciprocity. In other words, one function of the gift is to enable trust. An initial gift is a gesture inviting another into what could become a trusting relationship; it is an anticipatory move intimating a future relationality as yet uncertain and indeterminate. When there is a failure to reciprocate, trust is relinquished and distrust sets in. In the liminal context of La Hermandad, where the exchanging partners knew their connection was temporary, the inaugurating gifting gesture was the promise of a house of one's own. It was a credible promise. Once the houses were done, the NGO would leave.

In the meantime, the NGO had to execute the programmatic objective of fostering a community spirit through participatory technologies. The expression of a community spirit would confirm that recipients valued and internalized the project's unstable moral grammars. However, by way of their labour, they were already acknowledging their indebtedness to foreign givers and to the authority figures' own investment of time and effort. Whether recipients trusted project leaders personally was not so much at issue as the fact that they displayed enough mistrust and *envidia* among themselves to erode the idealized goal of the project. If participation was the technique meant to animate community, it did not live up to its potential.

On the contrary, participation resembled a Foucauldian technology of government, a technology present in many humanitarian spaces and policy discourses. For instance, the committees Amanda was entrusted to facilitate are "an example of what Niklas Rose (1996) calls a 'politics of community,' where populations constructed as problematic and vulnerable or 'at risk' are enjoined to perceive themselves as a community" (Olivius 2013, 48).[1]

In La Hermandad speeches reifying the trope of a "gift from strangers" scolded residents for being unruly and failing to express a collective spirit. Ultimately, working proved insufficient to fulfil their obligation, their short-lived desire to form an ADESCO was overdoing it, and the many squabbles and personal crises were perceived as a lack of gratefulness by those in charge. The return that project leaders awaited and would validate depended on exhibiting prescribed forms of participation and subjectivities, namely as members of an obedient, appreciative, and manageable workforce. Residents knew what a "good" beneficiary ought to be or do – but there were limits to what they considered acceptable and fair.

When desired forms of participation and subjectivities predefined by humanitarian organizations do not materialize, people on the receiving end of the aid chain – whether refugees or post-disaster victims – are deemed recalcitrant or ungovernable. They are blamed for not following sanctioned scripts. Policy efforts that seek to realize the holy trinity of community participation, social capital, and resilience in post-disaster contexts often produce a value complex that magnifies, in situ, refractory forms of socialization among vulnerable populations at risk. At worst, they feed suspicion and distrust in "uncooperative" subjects – a topic on which there is ample literature, particularly in the case of refugees (Daniel and Knudsen 1995; Harrell-Bond 2002; Hynes 2003). More commonly, they reproduce depoliticized building practices ill-equipped to address the traumas, histories of violence, and dispositions of mistrust people may carry. Aseptic humanitarianism is a "cruel optimism" (Berlant 2011).

Yet these frictions (and fictions) do not stop there. In La Hermandad residents played with moral categories, too, as they navigated the project's rhetorical tropes, leaders' expectations, and people's personalities – all the while acclimatizing to their new surroundings and testing the worth of others.

These remarks are not unique to this ethnographic context. But what discussions of humanitarian configurations in post-disaster reconstruction generally discount is the generative role of mistrust. Instead, when addressed, mistrust is seen as a barrier, a hindrance, a group problem, a personality fault, or the like – in short, as an undesirable to be transformed and conquered. Additionally, when the trope of the gift is instrumentalized as a signal for future relational trust, and participation becomes the means through which mistrust ought to morph into its healthy functional opposite, this repeats, to my mind at least, the application of standardized moral frameworks that are believed to "work" and be "good."[2] "Are we not happier and more efficient when we trust one another?" is a trite aphorism of neoliberal governmentality. Here is not the space to delve into these matters. What I do want to dispel, however, is the pervasive idea that mistrust is *necessarily* an adverse relational form.

Writing about refugees, E. Valentine Daniel and John Knudsen (1995, 2) state that there is an important contrast to be recognized between mistrust as a cultural value "available for invocation into conscious ideology or normative recitation" and the heightened magnitude of mistrust into which refugee populations are propelled, an experience that "bars [them] from settling back into a state of comfortable and largely unconscious comportment with the surrounding ... world." La Hermandad residents, of course, were not refugees, but the project's disciplinary moral logics framing their involvement amplified a disposition they already had, albeit in certain individuals more so than in others. Mistrust was strongly expressed along gendered lines but also toward the technical crew when people, tired and irritable, doubted the houses would be theirs. Authors discussing the features of trust in different ethnographic contexts, such as Palestinian refugee camps (Schiocchet 2014), Luo livelihoods in Africa (Shipton 2007), and the use of the gift as an invitation to trust in managerial practices (Mathews 2017; Raffnsøe 2015), underscore that to trust is to risk betrayal and disappointment. Trust is described as always containing "an element of uncertainty, unknowability and indeterminacy" (Miyazaki 2015, 209). But mistrust does not completely protect one from disappointment either. Nor does it mean that a judgment or knowledge about someone's or something's trustworthiness is set once and for all.

In La Hermandad mistrust was not just a coping or survival strategy in a time of crisis but also a disposition of people's being-in-the-world (Carey 2017). Mistrust is intimately tied to people's history and everyday hopes and struggles. The pre-earthquake lives of La Hermandad's residents were not typified by general trust or by sustained community engagement toward a common good. But nor would I say that they lived in a "dog-eat-dog" world. Rather, they were trying to get by, making a living, raising kids, falling in and out of love, and taking care of ailing parents while dealing with limited resources in a political-economic climate in which they had little traction. Indeed, the post-war situation of El Salvador in 2001 remained fraught with structural, symbolic, and everyday violence (Binford 2002; Bourgois 2001). It marked people, and no one in La Hermandad was left unscathed by the armed conflict, the intensifying gang violence, or the incoming challenges of neoliberal poverty (recall that in 2001 the country made the US dollar its official currency). From herein arises the terrain of mistrust as an affective disposition akin to an embodied precautionary principle that does not foreclose new relations but sets its own pace in making, or not making, the other's mistrust understandable.

This situation was not something the moral grammars at play in La Hermandad could avoid. The promise of a house of one's own as the inaugurating gift of a new humanitarian configuration, signalling a commitment to a common future, did not efface the habitual way that people related to strangers, whether to their peers or to those in a position of authority.

Humanitarian configurations like these have limited capacities; any assumption they may have about restoring apparently broken or weak "social bonds" must be treated with circumspection given their failure to counter the wider social systems that reproduce people's vulnerability to disaster. Also, there may be nothing to fix in the first place. Mistrust, instead of signifying avoidance and an obstacle to curtail or overcome, can be a generative force in the tentative exploration of future meaningful social relations.

Moreover, what I venture should be dispelled is an understanding of mistrust as antithetical to the world of the gift. Mistrust is a competency when seen as an affective capacity to make one's life more secure or as a shared disposition that inflects people's relationships to their wider political, economic, and social milieu. It is a way to dwell in the world that does not ipso facto spirit away the recognition of the gift. Borrowing language from Zigon (2014, 17), I maintain that mistrust is a form of attunement to the world, part of people's "fuzzy, fragmentary and oftentimes contradictory" moral assemblages. Certainly, much more about this statement can be debated, but this book is not an essay on the role of mistrust in moral economies of gifting. Nonetheless, in La Hermandad at least, despite all the mistrust, tensions, and processes of differentiation that unfolded, recognition of the gift as a relevant idiom did not just disappear.

A GIFT TO BE THANKFUL FOR

To conclude, I revisit the matter of gratefulness and rituals of "giving thanks" that generally mark the completion of a housing reconstruction project. Not only do these ceremonies signal the end of a humanitarian configuration and of a particular relationship between humanitarian donors and receivers, but they can also be touching moments.

Such was the case on 6 June 2002 when German officials, Salvadoran dignitaries, and the media attended the inauguration of La Hermandad. The site was decorated with garlands and coloured paper, the engineer had placed stickers of the German Red Cross on each house (as the politics of visibility required), and a tent was set up to protect people from the sun. When the visitors arrived, the children – wearing their white and blue school uniforms – clapped their hands and sang songs. The president of the German Red Cross looked delighted. On the podium, he complimented the families, emphasizing their diligence and commitment. He pronounced commending words on community, on the successes of participatory work, on the importance of humanitarianism, and on the future development of La Hermandad. Josefa, one of the *armadoras*, nervously read a short and heartfelt text: "Gracias a Dios, gracias a la Cruz Roja alemana, gracias a usted" (Thank the Lord, thank the German Red Cross, and thank you). Eight individuals were invited to go up on stage to receive papers recognizing them as homeowners – symbolically because the official deeds from the ministry were not ready yet. They shook hands with the delegates and smiled for pictures. After applause and questions from journalists, the two-hour ceremony fizzled out. Some people wanted to organize a party, but that did not happen. The next day, newspapers described the project as a success.

These types of occasions have been described as humiliating for people on the receiving end of the aid chain. For example, Benedikt Korf (2007) has argued that ceremonies of giving thanks in Aceh, Indonesia, after the 2004 tsunami perpetuated donor domination, especially as they were obligatory and scripted performances of gratitude in exchange for commoditized gifts. Along with others (Scheper-Hughes 2000), he suggests that post-disaster aid should be a universal right, and although I completely concur with this critique, I also agree with Annemarie Samuels (2013, 10) that "claiming such a right seems far from possible in actual post-disaster situations. Meanwhile, 'gifts' have the potential to do many things other than humiliate."

In La Hermandad the inauguration was indeed scripted, and it was expected that someone from the "beneficiary population" would say words of gratitude. But in La Hermandad, contrary to what Korf found in Aceh, it was the lack of ritual that felt underwhelming: people wanted to dance, to really mark the moment, and to have some fun, together, but no one had taken the lead to organize a *fiesta* (party).

It is true that during the building process, project leaders complained about the lack of gratitude, something residents themselves would repeat: "La gente no agradece" (People are not grateful). But this did not foreclose future desires to show gratitude. It was one thing to be expected to show reciprocity daily through labour and behaviour and quite another to display thankfulness during a formal event putting you face-to-face with foreign donors.

In this sense, the idea of gifting did not completely lose its relevance. Samuels (2013, 8) explains that for her informants in Aceh, the "gift" of reconstruction from foreign NGOs was perceived more positively than government assistance and that disaster victims' recognition of foreign NGOs was a means through which to frame Aceh as a "place-in-the-world." Even if only imagined to be a gift, reconstruction established a relationship between the Acehnese and the rest of the world.

There are parallels between Samuels's account and what I experienced in La Hermandad. The donations of German citizens, via the German Red Cross, to Lamaria's disaster victims, which culminated in a house, composed an imagined aid chain that fed the gifting narrative, and people accepted that. What they did not accept was being forced to perform gratefulness as "docile bodies."

Different moral economies may very well coexist. The case of La Hermandad illustrates the gaps between project leaders' and people's underlying expectations. Whereas the former tried to uphold customary humanitarian ideals (Amanda more so than the engineer), the latter's foremost desire was to secure a roof over their heads and acquire private property. In this perspective, the discourses evoking the idea of the gift were instrumentalized and incorporated into a penalizing discourse that exposed and blamed people's supposed ingratitude and lack of engagement.

But at another level, the gift stayed resilient: through the opportunities that emerged from a disaster, families received houses. Whether a gift of God or a gift from strangers – individuals invoked both – the significance of the object being offered, even if its form was moulded from their sweat and labour, was not reduced to instrumental and economic valuations alone. Everyone recognized the special nature of their situation.

Between gift and power lies the entire humanitarian endeavour. Humanitarian action, as witnessed in this Salvadoran context from emergency to reconstruction, is neither wholly one nor wholly the other, as people's subjectivity and agency thread through both realms, creating various symbolic orders to frame social action.

I was scheduled to leave shortly after the inauguration. The day before my departure, Karlita invited me to her home for a goodbye lunch. When I arrived, her house was decorated with balloons and garlands – it was a surprise party for me! Maxwell, Morena, La Roja, and their children were there, cheering. They had pooled their money to buy a chicken and some rum. After a delicious meal, we cleared the tables and danced, to the great delight of the children. It was the first time that someone from La Hermandad had invited me for a salsa! After a few rum and cokes, Maxwell lowered the volume and gave a moving speech. I expressed my heartfelt thanks to them. I was sad to leave. At the end of the day, I toured the site one last time to bid families farewell.

This account of the trajectory of fifty disaster-stricken families through the humanitarian aid chain is not exceptional. Similar kinds of situations are revisited each time a calamity affects the livelihoods of populations at risk who are then obliged to relocate to more or less distant locales. As post-disaster scenarios are on the rise, providing humanitarian relief is essential, as are the reconstruction programs that follow. But aid always comes at a cost, not merely a financial one but also in terms of time, labour, and future possibilities. It is my hope that this book has shown that anthropological fieldwork at post-disaster sites can renew our appreciation of the seminal categories, such as that of the gift, that help us to understand the multifaceted dimensions of the costs and hopes of aid.

Notes

INTRODUCTION

1 The names of places and people have been changed to respect privacy and preserve people's confidentiality and anonymity.

2 The FMLN was the main guerrilla organization fighting the government during the twelve years of civil war from 1980 to 1992. It then became an official political party.

3 For example, at the request of some of its units and delegations, the International Committee of the Red Cross has been reflecting on how to mainstream sustainable development into its practices. The committee has published three reports on this matter so far, an indicator of the changing paradigm of humanitarian action (ICRC 2015).

4 Maskrey (1993), a well-known figure in Spanish-language disaster studies, explains that these earlier studies were still marginal compared with the pre-eminence of well-established and better funded science-based analyses of disasters. Latin American researchers suffered from isolation because their works were rarely translated and hence not widely disseminated (relative to research in English). Their access to bibliographic sources was limited, and they lacked adequate institutional structures to pursue their research. These factors explain why there were relatively few specialists in Central America occupying academic or professional positions at the time. To remedy the situation, practitioners and researchers with a common interest in the social analysis of disasters established a multidisciplinary and interinstitutional network in Costa Rica in 1992 called La Red de Estudios Sociales en Prevención de Desastres en America Latina (LA RED). Today, this network is a go-to platform for people working on

disasters in Latin America. It has published many works on the subject, has organized international conferences, and was buoyed by the fact that during the 1990s the headquarters of the International Decade for Natural Disaster Reduction (IDNDR) was located in Costa Rica.

5 Lavell (1999) explains the centrality of the relationship between disasters and development: "The theme has now become an almost obligatory point of reference and reflection when discussing the topic of disasters. This is the product of various circumstances amongst which, particular importance may be attributed to: a) the IDNDR and it's [*sic*] emphasis on risk reduction and mitigation; b) the outstanding economic losses associated with Hurricane Andrew, the Mississippi floods and the Kobe earth-quake during the first half of the decade; c) the generally accepted fact the human and economic impact of disasters is rapidly increasing at a world level, with the developing countries and their poorer populations suffering an undue amount of the burden; d) the idea that such factors as a global climatic change, the introduction of new technologies and increased social vulnerability may provide conditions for more and larger disasters in the future." These comments have not lost any of their relevance since the mid-1990s.

6 As Terry Cannon explains, "much of the conventional work on disasters had been dominated by 'hard science' ... this 'physicalist' approach is also a result of the social construction of disasters as events that demonstrate the human condition as subordinate to nature" (Cannon 2000, 46).

7 The concept of resilience came to the fore in the 2004 issue of *World Disasters Report* (IFRC 2004). It has gained tremendous ground, especially in discussions about climate change adaptability.

8 Blaikie and colleagues (1994, 9) define vulnerability as "the characteristics of a person or group in terms of their capacity to anticipate, cope with, resist, and recover from the impact of a natural hazard. It involves a combination of factors that determine the degree to which someone's life and livelihood is put at risk by a discrete and identifiable event in nature or in society."

9 Gustavo Wilches-Chaux (1993, 22) describes vulnerability as a "total social state" in perpetual fluctuation. He explains that vulnerability covers the political, economic, ideological, social, technical, cultural, and symbolic dimensions of a people's way of life. Similar comprehensive perspectives on vulnerability are now well established (Phillips et al. 2010).

10 These estimates are reproduced by Rodolfo Barón Castro (1942). A more recent estimation by William Fowler (1988) suggests that the precontact population of 1519 was between 700,000 and 800,000 and that it diminished to between 400,000 and 500,000 during Pedro de Alvarado's conquest in 1524.

11 The Spanish Crown represented the supreme authority, but the Catholic Church, notably through the Franciscan and Dominican orders, was the principal instrument of domination over Indigenous people. Steadily, a new social hierarchy consolidated itself with the peninsular Spanish at the top (those born in Spain), followed by the *criollos* (whites born in El Salvador), the Mestizos or Ladinos (at the beginning, only sons of Spanish men and Indigenous women), and finally the "pure" Indigenous person. Barón Castro (1942) notes that single Spanish women were not allowed to travel to what were called "the Indies" without the authorization of King Charles I (ordinance of 23 May 1539) or his successor Philip II (ordinance of 8 February 1575). This effectively contributed to the mixing between Spanish colonists and Indigenous women. The Spanish considered the Mestizo to have many faults (ibid., 150). The process of "ladinization" occurred all over the Central American isthmus, and although today the term "Ladino" is very current in Guatemala, it is not so in El Salvador.

12 The science behind the frequency of seismic events is now well known. Around 160 million years ago, North America, South America, and Africa were amalgamated into a huge continent called Gondwana. Due to the lengthy drifting and dislocation process of tectonic plates, the different continents appeared. There are fifteen major tectonic plates in the world: seven are called primary plates, whereas the smaller ones are called secondary plates. When tectonic plates with a depth of approximately 100 kilometres move, they can provoke tremendous shocks that can trigger catastrophic effects. Central America is located on the Caribbean Plate, adjacent to the Cocos Plate, which forms the bed of the Pacific Ocean. The Cocos Plate is in constant subduction under the Caribbean Plate, thus creating a fault line under the sea floor that is 6 kilometres deep. When the plates slide, they liberate energy, causing telluric movements. In other words, there is an earthquake.

13 Comprehensive information regarding the seismic, volcanic, and landslide hazards in El Salvador can be found in the American Geological Society's large 2004 special issue entitled *Natural Hazards in El Salvador* (Rose et al. 2004).

14 During the colonial period, two modes of occupancy existed: individual property in the hands of Spanish *hacienderos* (estate owners) and property owned communally by Indigenous villages. *Haciendas* were large agricultural estates that hired local workers either permanently or on a seasonal basis to tend crops. Over the centuries, with the encroachment of *haciendas* on communal lands, the number of peasants employed by *hacienderos* grew considerably, as did competition for land between Spaniards, Ladinos, and Indios. Ladinos had very limited access to land, and most established themselves on the outskirts of large estates without having any property title. With the disintegration of Indigenous villages, the number of Ladinos grew, thereby estranging individuals from the customary obligations that are typically found in Indigenous villages. They became "free workers," generally employed by *hacienderos* as *colonos* (hired hands living in the domain), or *jornaleros* (dayworkers). The majority practised subsistence agriculture. Their communities were tolerated because they provided cheap and accessible manpower for the landowners.

15 At the beginning of the coffee boom, *finqueros* (*finca* owners) would establish themselves close to villages in order to better control workers. The latter would have a small plot of land near the *finca* on which to grow subsistence crops like corn and beans. The influence of the *finqueros* on the *campesinos* (peasants) persists in various ways in contemporary El Salvador. When I arrived in San Salvador, I rented for cheap a small room in a hotel, the owner of which was both a *finca* owner and a deputy at the national assembly. His workers all voted for him (indeed, he would say, "mis campesinos"), and in exchange he organized Christmas and Easter parties and made sure all the kids went to school. This form of patronage was not uncommon.

16 The legislative act of 26 February 1881 is very clear: "The existence of lands under the ownership of the *Comunidades* impedes agricultural development, obstructs the circulation of wealth, and weakens family bonds and the independence of the individual. Their existence is contrary to the economic and social principles that the Republic has accepted" (Browning 1971, 205).

17 The centre of the revolt was in an area where Indigenous identity remained strong, namely the towns of Izalco, Juayuá, Nahuizalco, and Tacuba, and where the *cacique* (traditional political leader) and *cofradias* (Indigenous religious orders) were still respected. "For the elite, then, the revolt combines their two worst nightmares, Indian rebellion and Communist revolution" (Paige 1998, 122). Jeffery Paige's account

uses bounded categories like "Indian" and "Communist" that have been nuanced in more recent work showing not only that La Matanza was an Indigenous revolt but also that small-scale Mestizo producers were part of the uprising (Gould and Lauria-Santiago 2008). Reacting with "paranoia," the elites allowed the Civil Guard, under the command of General Hernández Martínez, to squash the uprising in the most vicious manner. The violent crushing of civil discontent paved the way for the establishment of a political regime that would not hesitate to adopt brutal methods in the decades to follow (Anderson 1971). Martínez governed the country with a hand of steel from 1931 to 1944.

18 The amount of cultivated land increased from 43,018 hectares in 1960 to 122,255 hectares in 1965.

19 Major Roberto d'Aubuisson is considered to be the founder of the death squads. These were financed by rich oligarchs, such as Francisco Callejas Guerrero (ex-president of ANEP and president of Banco Credito Popular), Francisco José Guerrero (ex-president of the legislative assembly), and Eduardo Lemus O'Byrne (ex-president of ANEP). In 1979 ORDEN had 100,000 members, and its director was an ex-agent of the US Central Intelligence Agency who supported the armed forces. To differentiate between its units, the army gave them distinct names, such as the Fuerzas Armadas de Liberación Anticomunista – Guerra de Eliminación (FALANGE), the Brigada Anticomunista Salvadoreña (BACSA), the Organización para la Liberación del Comunismo (OLC), the Frente Anticomunista para la Liberación de Centroamérica (FALCA), and others (Peñate 1999).

20 Oscar Peñate (1999, 12) counts forty-six politico-military organizations of the left that joined the five organizations making up the FMLN: the Communist Party with its military branch called the Fuerzas Armadas de Liberación (PC-FAS), the Fuerzas Populares de Liberación Farabundo Martí (FLP), the Ejercito Revolucionario del Pueblo (ERP), the Fuerzas Armadas de la Resistencia Nacional (FARP), and the Partido Revolucionario de los Trabajadores Centroamericanos (PRTC).

21 To various degrees, foreign nations and international organizations were assisting the belligerent parties in forging a path toward peace. The United States was of course heavily involved, but so were the Socialist and Communist internationals, as well as the Grupo de Contadora (Colombia, Panama, Mexico, and Venezuela), the Grupo de Apoyo (Argentine, Peru, Brazil, and Uruguay), and of course the

United Nations. Needless to say, not all agreed on the way to achieve a peaceful resolution of the conflict. Furthermore, international events also had an impact. The end of the Cold War, the fall of the Berlin Wall, and the dismantling of the Soviet Union and the socialist bloc impacted the end of the war. The civil war caused 75,000 deaths.

22 An investigative report in the newspaper *El Faro* explains how an entire town near the Guatemalan border has come under the hands of the Cártel de Texis (Arauz, Martínez, and Lemus 2011).

CHAPTER ONE

1 The charter of the Red Cross movement, which guides the work of both the International Committee of the Red Cross and the International Federation of Red Cross and Red Crescent Societies, lays out the founding principles: humanity, impartiality, neutrality, independence, voluntary service, unity, and universality. The first four are shared by other humanitarian organizations, including the United Nations Office for the Coordination of Humanitarian Affairs, although these principles have been coming under increasing scrutiny.

2 Peter Walker (Walker and Purdin 2004), one of the original authors of the *Sphere Handbook*, has acknowledged the very technical nature of its standards. Although it has proved a useful tool for humanitarian practitioners in the field, the handbook does not truly provide a humanitarianism that integrates human rights (Benelli 2013).

3 From within the humanitarian enterprise, the main counter-argument is that any diversion from the principle of neutrality risks endangering the core purpose of humanitarian action, rendering it too political. From outside the humanitarian world, the critique may come from host governments that do not want external humanitarian actors to say anything about their domestic human rights record.

4 In defining the "modern gift to strangers," Godbout (1998, 65) seeks to distinguish it from other models of gift cycles embedded in strict moral codes, such as more obligatory and expected forms of giving at work, in mutual help networks, or in religious teachings. He rejects the idea that individuals give only when they follow strict and constraining codes of morality. And recent history has proven him right: there has been a huge explosion of gifting relations between strangers on social media. Nevertheless, morality can still be at play in these instances, even if the institutional moral discourse of humanitarianism is not binding. Many people today give to "social causes" and "humanitarian

crises" freely, and often anonymously, because they acknowledge that it is an "ethical" thing to do. Although critics may stress that this is an interested gift, because one may seek to feel good about oneself, there is no doubt that it is a significant phenomenon on which many humanitarian organizations financially depend.

5 In 2013 alone, private voluntary contributions to humanitarian causes amounted to US$5 billion, out of a total of US$17.9 billion given by bilateral and multilateral organizations (Global Humanitarian Assistance 2013).

6 Some recent publications have taken issue with this acceptance of the concept of moral economy (Palomera and Vetta 2016; Siméant 2015), arguing that by abandoning its original embeddeness in political economy, it loses its emancipatory potential and connection to structures of power. Indeed, E.P. Thompson (1993) – who popularized the term "moral economy" in his essay on nineteenth-century food riots in England – uses it to underscore that economic determinism alone cannot explain peasant revolts in that they also entailed moral motivations tied to feelings of injustice, namely regarding speculation on the price of food and the breach of a "moral contract" between capitalists and food producers. James C. Scott (1976) also stresses the importance of moral reasoning in the everyday lives of peasant groups. In both cases, the notion of moral economy is used to analyze the social relationships of peasant and, later, subaltern groups with the wider political-economic system of which they are part, insisting on the complementarity of moral and economic realms rather than their binary opposition. Fassin (2009) employs the term "moral economy" differently, drawing on a conceptual lineage originating in science research that ignores economic matters (e.g., questions about resources, production, labour, and consumption) and that emphasizes instead the prevalence of value-driven and affective configurations of a field of practice – in his case, the field of contemporary humanitarianism.

7 Mauss's (1925, 1954) interpretation led to many well-known rebukes in anthropological theory. Raymond Firth (1929) notes that Mauss was mystified by an Indigenous explanation, falling into a trap when he elevated the animist notion of *hau* as an explanatory principle for the return of the gift. Claude Lévi-Strauss (1971) writes that Mauss failed to see the underlying structure beneath the to-and-fro of giving and counter-giving transactions – the "total social facts" – he was analyzing, arguing instead that they revealed but one invariant: the obligation of exchange. Marshall Sahlins (1974) produced another famous

critique, comparing the gift to a form of "primitive" social contract à la Thomas Hobbes; but Sahlins takes individuals as his unit of analysis, whereas Mauss focuses on clearly recognized social groups. Later scholars considered the contrast between gift economies (based on morality and cycles of mutual indebtedness) and market economies (based on immediate monetary exchange) (David 1988; Testart 2013). However, Mauss's theory of the gift has not been completely abandoned. The Maussian gift allows one to move away from two dominant paradigms: methodological individualism, which leads to the *homo oeconomicus* of rational choice theory; and holism, where individual agency is stifled by the weight of tradition (Caillé 1996, 2000). The force of the "paradigm of the gift" is to insist that individuals seek to be recognized through the creation of social ties, a function the gift performs in myriad ways.

8 The Kula ring involved annual maritime expeditions during which various kinds of goods were exchanged between island populations. Some of these goods, such as food, were of a more utilitarian nature, and others held important symbolic significance. The latter were namely highly valued ornamental armbands and necklaces that were exchanged, and it was expected that they would not stay with the same person for too long. Trading partners would regularly participate in these transactions, meaning that each person held only a right of temporary possession over the object, as opposed to a right of ownership (Godelier 2002). Over time, these exchanges facilitated peaceful and friendly relationships between distant islanders and established reciprocal ties between trading partners. In this sense, the Kula ring not only facilitated complex economic transactions but also entailed important political matters, namely ensuring peace between social groups and prestige for those who held valuable ornaments. Mauss (1954) interprets the Kula as a system of giving and counter-giving that established alliances between groups. In terms of theoretical models, the gift appears as a base for social life and solidarity – although Mauss does not say this explicitly. Yet when one accepts a gift in order to maintain a social tie, it follows that the gift is a form of openness to the other, a will to establish a relation. In other words, the quest for sociability leads to giving, which leads to accepting, which leads to the obligation to reciprocate. Testart (2013), however, would call this a non-monetary exchange system.

9 An important feature of the potlatch system was its competitive nature. What can be confusing is that Mauss (1954) uses the term

"potlatch" to refer to other types of exchanges in different parts of the world – even though the concept is specific to the North American west coast and means "giving away" in Chinook. The potlatch was a remarkable ceremonial event attended by many Indigenous clans and lineages of the Pacific Northwest. A chief would invite neighbouring villages to days of feasting and dancing, during which he would display his power and wealth through the distribution – and destruction – of different types of goods, some very valuable, such as the copper blazons that conferred honour and mystical powers and that only the "nobles" could possess. A chief would lavishly bestow a tremendous amount of prized gifts on some of his guests, thereby showing how great, prestigious, generous, and powerful he was. At a later date, during another potlatch of his own, the recipient would reciprocate in kind with as many or more resources; if he did not do so, he would lose face. There was an element of competition – even of rivalry – for the more you gave away, the more prestige and honour you acquired vis-à-vis the receiver. The potlatch was a system that produced and maintained social hierarchies trough agonistic cycles of gift exchange.

10 Mauss followed in the footsteps of his uncle Émile Durkheim and was influenced by his vision of society as best understood in terms of its norms, rules, constraints, and obligations. In the Durkheimian tradition, society and morality tend to get fused as one analytical entity, and it becomes difficult to distinguish the two. Similar conclusions can be drawn from Mauss (1954), who stressed that in many Indigenous "gifting societies," there was an obligation to return a gift and that the transfers were reciprocal and could hierarchically connect individuals to larger segments of their society.

11 Bourdieu's (1977) notion of exchange is very different from Lévi-Strauss's (1971) – even if both thinkers rationalize. Lévi-Strauss conceives of exchange as a fundamental, universal, and unconscious mechanism rooted in the human mind. Exchange becomes a quasi-disincarnated truth, and there are hardly any exceptions to its rule. Bourdieu, in contrast, stresses the possibility of exceptions, arguing that exchange is first and foremost about the circulation of many various forms of capital: symbolic, social, cultural, and economic.

CHAPTER TWO

1 D.M. Dowling (2004, 282) reports that in 1999 it was estimated that around 1.6 million people (26 per cent of the population) lived in

adobe houses, with 70 per cent living in rural areas. After the 2001 earthquakes, out of all the affected houses in the country, 58 per cent were made of adobe, and of those, 70 per cent were completely destroyed – indicating that traditional adobe houses were prone to destruction (ibid., 285). However, it is worth indicating that not all adobe houses fell to the ground. Hundreds of houses that used reinforced adobe construction techniques withstood the earthquakes (ibid., 296).

2 I have placed the word "humanitarian" in quotation marks here because although some expert organizations such as the Red Cross did come to Lamaria, many of these individuals were not professionals from humanitarian agencies.

3 On a personal note, I should mention that it took me some time before I felt comfortable talking about these issues with the La Hermandad residents. I wished to establish a certain familiarity with them before asking them to tell me what had happened. Once people were accustomed to me, it was easier to broach the subject. However, various women I spoke to still suffered from psychological trauma, and although some psychological help for disaster victims had been offered in the aftermath of the earthquake, not all victims could be seen and certainly not over the long term. Hence I sometimes found myself in a delicate position.

4 As I was not present at that time, I condense in these lines the testimonies of dozens of people I met during my stay.

5 According to a survey led by the Institute of Public Opinion at the University of Central America in 2012, 47 per cent of the Salvadoran population identifies as Roman Catholic and 33 per cent as evangelical. The survey reported 17 per cent as having "no religion" (US Department of State 2012). Protestant, Pentecostal, and evangelical congregations appeared during the 1970s and 1980s with the arrival of American missionaries who had important funding and recruitment programs. The success of the Mormons and Baptists is a case in point. In the capital, the headquarters of the Baptist Church can bring together up to 15,000 faithful.

6 By "institutional humanitarianism," I mean the experts of the humanitarian world, those who make it their living. CARITAS (the social mission branch of the Catholic Church) is an international network that participates in the institutional logic of humanitarianism, and the Salvadoran Catholic Church was an important player during the crisis. However, in Lamaria neither the Catholic Church

nor its evangelical counterparts were experienced in responding to a humanitarian emergency.

7 These three NGOs are from the political "left," but they were not directly associated with the FMLN. There is an interesting historical context regarding the multiplication of NGOs in El Salvador after the signing of the peace accord in 1992. After the war, a number of ex-guerrilla members of the FMLN established themselves in the world of civil society, and some founded not-for-profit organizations like development NGOs. The directors of the three aforementioned organizations were sympathizers of the FMLN cause, and one was a well-known personality of the Communist Party. They were rather discreet and circumspect about their past when talking to me, a foreign anthropologist; nonetheless, I could still detect old grievances between various members of national NGOs. Although many civil society organizations presented a common front to the state in the disaster's aftermath, there was also a certain degree of mistrust between them.

8 After the war, the Salvadoran police corps was completely restructured and received training from foreign experts, including Canadian police forces. To avoid potential conflicts of interest, it was rare for a cadet to be hired by the police unit of his hometown. In Lamaria the majority of the police officers came from the western part of the country.

9 Many moral stances and features that I discuss in this chapter are present in Gamburd's account of aid in Sri Lanka after the 2004 tsunami. For example, the author mentions that people believed foreigners could afford to be generous because they had nothing to really gain from the disaster, contrary to Sri Lankan officials (Gamburd 2014, 161), a view that I heard from Don Rodolfo and others involved in Lamaria's humanitarian response structure. Another common issue is the disappointment that local aid officials can experience after months of delivering humanitarian aid. For instance, not unlike the sentiments of Sister Elena, one of Gamburd's informants, who was hired by the local government to participate in the distribution of aid to a refugee camp, lamented that "people [are] greedy and impatient ... and everyone is jealous ... [thinking], 'If someone across the street gets something, I want it too'" (ibid., 172–3).

10 Robbins (2009, 46) writes that "both reciprocity and recognition have a similar three-part rhythm: in both, something (the gift/recognition) must be given to the other, must be received by the other (who thereby acknowledges his/her worthiness as a subject), and must be matched

by a return from the other (who thereby recognizes the worthiness of the giver as a subject)."

CHAPTER THREE

1 I translate this expression from the pamphlet that was distributed by City Hall during the inauguration of the refurbished park. It says, "The symbolic value that a work of art holds is difficult to determine; the antique structures in the ... central park hold memories and indelible traditions that will last for centuries to come in the heart of the Lamarienses ... This work of art is a cultural heritage built by the people, for the people." To think that all the inhabitants of Lamaria felt those patrimonial sentiments would be pushing the statement too far!

2 See http://www.proesa.gob.sv/institution.

3 See http://www.fusai.org.sv.

4 See http://fundaungo.org.sv.

5 In Januray 2017 the United Nations humanitarian coordinator, Mourad Wahba, who had worked in Haiti for two years, said, "There are still about 55,000 people in camps and makeshift camps ... Many are still living in unsanitary conditions due to displacement caused by the earthquake. We have a very long way to go" (quoted in Cook 2017).

6 In the case of the Arab Spring and the Occupy movement, participation originated with citizen and activist groups seeking deep transformations in the very fabric of society. In the examples of Bolivia and Puerto Alegre, participation led to legislative measures that enhanced the active involvement of citizens in the governance of their cities (e.g., citizen groups vote on budgets, set priorities, and manage resources).

7 The World Bank (2013, 17) report summarizes the goals of community-driven development as follows: "Advocates of community development view it as a mechanism for enhancing sustainability, improving efficiency and effectiveness, scaling up poverty reduction programs, making development more inclusive, empowering poor people, building social capital, strengthening governance, and complementing market and public sector activities ... They argue that community-driven development in particular is able to achieve these results by aligning development priorities with community goals; enhancing

communication between aid agencies and beneficiaries; expanding the resources available to the poor (through microcredit, social funds, and occupational training); and strengthening the capacity of community-based organizations to represent and advocate for their communities. Community-driven development has the explicit objective of reversing power relations in a manner that creates agency and voice for poor people and gives them more control over development assistance."

8 Another way that community participation has been applied in development policy is through the notion of social capital. Social capital is a popular concept that has received a variety of nuanced definitions, but most would agree that it refers to a community's non-economic resources found in formal and informal networks based on relationships of trust (Coleman 1988; Putnam 1993). Social capital is composed of norms, institutions, and vertical and horizontal relations that characterize a group's interactions (Serageldin and Grootae 2000). Community participation is often used as a means to foster social capital. Although these two notions have their own intellectual pedigree, they are often packaged together in projects, including post-disaster reconstruction initiatives (Aldrich 2012; Chamlee-Wright 2007; Chamlee-Wright and Storr 2011).

9 Franz Fanon, an active supporter of the Algerian War of Independence (1954–62), in which he fought, published *The Wretched of the Earth* in 1961, where he advocates for the right of the people to rise against colonial rulers and oppressors. Fanon (1961) views participation as the equitable sharing of power with, and the redistribution of resources to, the poorest people. His is a very engaged approach to participation, compared with more watered-down versions found in donor-induced participation packaged in development projects.

10 Paolo Freire was a Brazilian educator famous for his book *Pedagogy of the Oppressed*, where he argues that education should "conscientize" poor and illiterate people. Freire (1968) argues that education should link knowledge to action and should help the oppressed to value their own life experiences and forms of knowledge – along with other forms of taught knowledge – so that they may become empowered. In a Freirian perspective, participation is ultimately a means for liberation, a praxis whereby people seek to actively change their societies both at a local level and beyond. Freire's work has had a tremendous impact on pedagogy and on community organizing and learning.

11 Robert Chambers (1983) developed the method of participatory rural appraisal, demonstrating how poor people can put their own needs and goals into the design of development projects. Many related methodologies appeared in the 1980s and 1990s, such as rapid rural appraisal, participatory action research, and participatory poverty assessments, which a growing number of NGOs put into practice.

12 A direct response to the valuable critiques in the edited volume *Participation? The New Tyranny* (Cooke and Kothari 2001) is the edited volume *Participation: From Tyranny to Transformation?* (Hickey and Mohan 2004). The latter argues that if participation were better connected to a sound understanding of people's rights and responsibilities and embedded in a rigorous analysis of their milieu's political economy, participation could lead to effective empowerment, as well as to sustainable development and governance. The point is to acknowledge the political complexities that inescapably arise when an outside party imposes community participation on a social group, however well intentioned and meticulous its initiative may be.

13 In the social sciences, this romanticization can be traced back to German sociologist Ferdinand Tönnies's (1887) distinction between the communitarian and the non-communitarian, or between the *gemeinschaft* (community) and *gesellschaft* (society). Regarding the first term, Western scholars entertained a nostalgia of enduring social ties based on territoriality, kinship relations, and the existence of tradition, all of which ensured the cohesion and shared identity of a social group generally considered small (Williams 1985).

14 Peter Lawther (2009, 155) outlines a number of advantages to community-driven reconstruction: "Being more cost effective, providing a potentially better product quality where technical and supervision skills are available, being more empowering, allowing for incremental re-construction thereby permitting occupancy before the house is fully completed, restoring confidence in those traumatized through the experience of disaster, providing local capacity building and employment, preserving of local cultural heritage through land use planning and vernacular housing style."

15 For the WFP (2001), food for work is not a payment for labour: "The World Food Program food ration is not a payment for work done. On the contrary it is a contribution that enables the participation for beneficiaries in activities that will benefit them and their communities. The food ration will be a key in the reconstruction process, offering the chance to re-define their own future ... WFP is using food as a tool to

enable tens of thousands of people to create assets, and to re-build their own communities and homes including the clearing of roads, the repairing of water systems, and the re-building of houses, small schools and bridges." A monthly family ration under a food-for-work system costs US$30 and contains 22 kilograms of corn, 22 kilograms of rice, 5 kilograms of beans, and 2.5 kilograms of vegetable oil (ibid.). The rations were established by the WFP, and food is preferably bought at the local and regional markets. In comparison, the monthly Red Cross food rations distributed during the emergency period in El Salvador amounted to 15 kilograms of flour, 10 kilograms of rice, 4 litres of vegetable oil, 12 kilograms of red beans, 1 kilogram of salt, and 5 kilograms of sugar, for a total of 47 kilograms per family (IFRC 2001).

16 Kenneth Werbin (2017) analyzes the concept of the list as a biopolitical instrument of population control, charting the deployment of lists as instruments of security in Nazi governmentality and eugenics, in the creation of big data with modern computer technologies, and in the contemporary establishment of juridico-legal no-fly lists and other security apparatuses.

17 Akin to the work of Raymond Williams in *Keywords* (1985) and Uwe Poerksen in *Plastic Words* (1995), French anthropologist Marc Abélès (1995) explains how concepts reproduce themselves in institutions to become strong operational categories that organize social processes, including beliefs and conduct. Institutional semantics are not neutral; they circulate representations of people's *devoir être* (i.e., the way they represent how they ought to be) that are not devoid of biases. One presupposes that, through participation, people will find meaningful levers for their individual and collective lives. At times, this may very well be the case; however, that does not make it an infallible rule. As these concepts gain currency in NGO practice, they transmit a "regime of value" (Appadurai 1986, 4).

18 The project leaders did not share their financial statements with me. However, I know that the cost per house amounted to US$4,500. Considering all the activities of the Red Cross in Lamaria, aside from housing reconstruction projects, such as refurbishing the offices of the local Red Cross and the Health Unit, rebuilding the school in Los Bálsamos, and finalizing the construction of the centre for the elderly managed by the nuns of the Missionary Sisters of Saint Peter Claver, the total amount would come close to US$1 million.

19 The country representative of MSF told me that the term *microondas* originated with him in an interview he did for a large newspaper on

the topic of post-disaster temporary housing. He was discussing the lengthy process of temporary shelter procurement and the lack of funding for permanent houses, indirectly critiquing the Salvadoran government. I do not deny him the paternity of the term, but it was so widespread that evidently the analogy came to the minds of many, not all of whom had read that newspaper article!

CHAPTER FOUR

1 When I told her that I enjoyed these kinds of stories, she laughed and said, "Le gustan las historias a la niña Alicia, que bueno!" (Alicia, she likes stories! That's cool!). And so the rumour went that this new girl from Canada liked to talk about things other than the project. "Niña," meaning girl, is a common way women salute each other, especially women from the rural areas. In the city the term is used only among people who know each other well, and I would never have called Doña Leonora, with whom I was staying, "niña." Using the term "niña" put everyone on equal footing – at the linguistic level at least. In La Hermandad the women called the men "Don," especially the masons and the supervisor, but the engineer was called by his profession, *ingeniero*, which created a hierarchical distance. I recounted the story about the *chumpe* to a friend from the capital who worked in a large telecommunications firm. She believed they existed and were the result of genetic manipulations.

2 The creation of the Gender and Disaster Network in 1997 marked an important development for gender and disaster studies as a field of research. There were already some networks that studied these matters, mainly in Latin America and South East Asia, but in the 1980s and early 1990s their influence remained mainly regional (Enarson 2004). A series of major disasters in the 1990s pushed forward the internationalization of various networks such as Radix, Desinventar, LA RED, and Provention that shared the objective of putting the multidisciplinary analysis of disasters at the forefront. Today, all major institutional players, from multilateral agencies to NGOs, have incorporated a gender perspective into their frameworks. In academia, too, gender and disaster have become a well-established field of research. Landmark books such as *The Gendered Terrain of Disaster: Through Women's Eyes* (Enarson and Morrow 1998), *Women, Gender and Disaster: Global Issues and Initiatives* (Enarson and Chakrabarti 2009), and *Women Confronting Disaster: From*

Vulnerability to Resilience (Enarson 2012) have had positive effects on policymaking.

CHAPTER FIVE

1 International organizations such as the United Nations Development Programme, United Nations Office for the Coordination of Humanitarian Affairs, International Labour Organization, and United Nations High Commissioner for Refugees follow the definition provided by the United Nations Economic and Social Council: "Mainstreaming a gender perspective is the process of assessing the implications for women and men of any planned action, including legislation, policies or programmes, in all areas and at all levels. It is a strategy for making women's as well as men's concerns and experiences an integral dimension of the design, implementation, monitoring and evaluation of policies and programmes in all political, economic and societal spheres so that women and men benefit equally and inequality is not perpetuated. The ultimate goal is to achieve gender equality" (ECOSOC 1997, 3).

2 Max Gluckman (1963) adopts a structural-functional approach to gossip, focusing on group behaviour (a systems approach), whereas Robert Paine (1967) analyzes gossip as a communication and information management device (an actor-centred approach) used by individuals to protect their own interests and attack others when open confrontation with them is too risky. These functions of gossip need not be mutually exclusive but can complement each other. For further discussion, see Merry (1984).

3 Various individuals working at City Hall confirmed this statement.

4 These were the words used by the WFP representative for the region. During the emergency, food aid was given without any expectation of contribution, but in the post-emergency period, a contribution through the creation of community assets was desired from the receiver.

CHAPTER SIX

1 Elisabeth Olivius (2013) writes these lines in the context of participatory technologies implemented in refugee camps in Bangladesh and Thailand. And there are similarities to La Hermandad. Her analysis considers the forms of participation sought by humanitarian organizations in two camps: one characterized by a lack of both community spirit and refugee involvement and one where the refugee population is

seen as overly politicized and taking too much control. She concludes that the desired forms of participation are generally those initiated by the humanitarian organization.

2 For instance, how to create trust through gift giving is a fertile field of research in studies about management practices, where the objective may be to create more humane working environments, but mistrust is generally something to be kept at bay or transformed (Mathews 2017; Raffnsøe 2015).

References

Aaltola, Mika. 2009. *Western Spectacle of Governance and the Emergence of Humanitarian World Politics*. New York: Palgrave MacMillan.

Abélès, Marc. 1995. "Pour une anthropologie des institutions." *L'Homme* 35, no. 135: 65–85.

Abu-Lughod, Lila. 2013. *Do Muslim Women Need Saving?* Cambridge, MA: Harvard University Press.

Adams, Vincanne. 2013. *Markets of Sorrow, Labors of Faith: New Orleans in the Wake of Katrina*. Durham, NC: Duke University Press.

Adams, Vincanne, Taslim Van Hattum, and Diana English. 2009. "Chronic Disaster Syndrome: Displacement, Disaster Capitalism, and the Eviction of the Poor from New Orleans." *American Ethnologist* 36, no. 4: 615–36.

Agamben, Giorgio. 1998. *Homo Sacer: Sovereign Power and Bare Life*. Stanford, CA: Stanford University Press.

Agier, Michel. 2002. "Between War and City: Toward an Urban Anthropology of Refugee Camps." *Ethnography* 3, no. 3: 317–41.

Aldrich, D.P. 2012. *Building Resilience: Social Capital in Post-Disaster Recovery*. Chicago: University of Chicago Press.

Allard, Olivier, Matthew Carey, and Rachel Renault. 2016. "De l'art de se méfier." *Tracés: Revue de sciences humaines*, no. 31: 7–20.

Álvarez, Antonio, and Joaquín Mauricio Chávez. 2001. *Tierra, conflicto y paz*. San Salvador: Asociación Centro de Paz.

Amit, Veret, and Nigel Rapport. 2002. *The Trouble with Community*. London: Pluto.

Anderson, Thomas. 1971. *Matanza*. Reprint, Connecticut: Curbstone, 1992.

Appadurai, Arjun, ed. 1986. *The Social Life of Things: Commodities in Cultural Perspective*. Cambridge, UK: Cambridge University Press.

Appelbaum, Richard, and William Robinson, eds. 2005. *Critical Globalization Studies*. New York: Routledge.

Arauz, Sergio, Óscar Martínez, and Efren Lemus. 2011. "El Cártel de Texis." *El Faro*, 16 May. http://elfaro.net/es/201105/noticias/4079.

Artiga-González, Álvaro. 2002. "La difícil democratización del régimen político salvadoreño." In Héctor Dada Hirezi, ed., *Más allá de las elecciones: Diez años después de los Acuerdos de Paz*, 15–77. San Salvador: FLACSO.

Asad, Talal. 2003. *Formations of the Secular: Christianity, Islam, Modernity*. Stanford, CA: Stanford University Press.

Barakat, S. 2003. *Housing Reconstruction after Conflict and Disaster*. London: Overseas Development Institute, Humanitarian Practice Network. http://odihpn.org/resources/housing-reconstruction-after-conflict-and-disaster.

Barenstein, Jennifer. 2005. *A Comparative Analysis of Six Housing Reconstruction Approaches in Post–Earthquake Gujarat*. Lugano, Switzerland: Dipartimento Ambiente Construzioni e Design, Sculoa Univeritaria Professionale della Svizzera Italiana. http://humanitarianlibrary.org/sites/default/files/2014/02/SUPSI.pdf.

– 2008. "From Gujarat to Tamil Nadu: Owner-Driven vs. Contractor-Driven Housing Reconstruction in India." Paper presented at the 4th International i-REC Conference, "Building Resilience: Achieving Effective Post-Disaster Reconstruction," Christchurch, New Zealand, 30 April to 2 May. http://www.irbnet.de/daten/iconda/CIB11511.pdf.

Barenstein, Jennifer, and Esther Leeman. 2012. *Post-Disaster Reconstruction and Change: Communities' Perspectives*. Boca Raton, FL: CRC Press.

Barnett, Clive. 2005. "Ways of Relating: Hospitality and the Acknowledgement of Otherness." *Progress in Human Geography* 29, no. 1: 5–21.

Barnett, Michael, and Janice Stein, eds. 2012. *Sacred Aid: Faith and Humanitarianism*. Oxford: Oxford University Press.

Barón Castro, Rodolfo. 1942. *La población de El Salvador: Estudio acerca de su desenvolvimiento desde la* época *prehispánica hasta nuestros días*. Madrid: Consejo superior de investigaciones cientifícas, Instituto Gonzalo Fernández de Oviedo.

Barrios, Roberto. 2014. "'Here, I'm not at ease': Anthropological Perspectives on Community Resilience." *Disasters* 38, no. 2: 329–50.

Benelli, Prisca. 2013. "Human Rights in Humanitarian Action and Development Cooperation and the Implications of Rights-Based

Approaches in the Field." Working paper. Advanced Training Program of Humanitarian Action, Harvard Humanitarian Initiative, Harvard University. http://www.atha.se/content/human-rights-humanitarian-action-and-development-cooperation-and-implications-rights-based.

Berlant, Lauren. 2011. *Cruel Optimism*. Durham, NC: Duke University Press.

Binford, Leigh. 2002. "Violence in El Salvador: A Rejoinder to Philippe Bourgois's 'The Power of Violence in War and Peace.'" *Ethnography* 3, no. 2: 201–19.

Blaikie, Piers, Terry Cannon, Ian Davis, and Ben Wisner. 1994. *At Risk: Natural Hazards, People's Vulnerability, and Disasters*. Reprint, New York: Routledge, 2004.

Boltanski, Luc. 1999. *Distant Suffering: Morality, Media and Politics*. Cambridge, UK: Cambridge University Press.

Bornstein, Erica. 2005. *The Spirit of Development: Protestant NGOs, Morality and Economics in Zimbabwe*. Stanford, CA: Stanford University Press.

– 2012. *Disquieting Gifts: Humanitarianism in New Delhi*. Stanford, CA: Stanford University Press.

Bornstein, Erica, and Peter Redfield, eds. 2011. *Forces of Compassion: Humanitarianism between Ethics and Politics*. Santa Fe, NM: SAR Press.

Bourdieu, Pierre. 1977. *Outline of a Theory of Practice*. Cambridge, UK: Cambridge University Press.

– 1996. "Marginalia: Some Additional Notes on the Gift." In Alan Schrift, ed., *The Logic of the Gift*, 231–41. London: Routledge.

Bourgois, Philippe. 2001. "The Power of Violence in War and Peace: Post–Cold War Lessons from El Salvador." *Ethnography* 2, no. 1: 5–34.

Bradshaw, Sarah. 2002. "Exploring the Gender Dimensions of Reconstruction Processes Post–Hurricane Mitch." *Journal of International Development* 14, no. 6: 871–9.

Bricmont, Jean. 2006. *Humanitarian Imperialism: Using Human Rights to Sell War*. New York: Monthly Review Press.

Brown, Oli, and Alec Crawford. 2006. *Addressing Land Ownership after Natural Disasters*. Winnipeg: International Institute for Sustainable Development.

Browne, Katherine E., and B. Lynne Milgram, eds. 2009. *Economics and Morality: Anthropological Approaches*. New York: Altamira.

Browning, David. 1971. *El Salvador: Landscape and Society*. Oxford: Clarendon.

Button, Gregory, and Anthony Oliver-Smith. 2008. "Disaster Displacement and Employment." In Nandini Gunewardena and Mark Schuller, eds, *Capitalizing on Catastrophe*, 123–46. New York: Altamira.

Cahill, Kevin, ed. 2003. *Traditions, Values and Humanitarian Action*. New York: Centre for International Health and Cooperation and Fordham University Press.

Caillé, Alain. 1996. "Ni holisme ni individualisme méthodologiques: Marcel Mauss et le pradigme du don." *Revue européenne des sciences sociales* 34, no. 105: 181–224.

– 2000. *Anthropologie du don: le tiers paradigme*. Paris: Desclée de Brouwer.

Canada Revenue Agency. n.d. "Gifting and Receipting." http://www.cra-arc.gc.ca/chrts-gvng/chrts/prtng/gftng-rcptng-eng.html.

Cañas, Antonio, and Héctor Dada. 1999. "Political Transition and Institutionalization in El Salvador." In Cynthia J. Arnson, ed., *Comparative Peace Processes in Latin America*, 69–95. Stanford, CA: Stanford University Press.

Cannon, Terry. 2000. "Vulnerability Analysis and Disasters." In D.J. Parker, ed., *Floods*, vol. 1, 45–55. London: Routledge.

Carey, Matthew. 2017. *Mistrust: An Ethnographic Theory*. Chicago: University of Chicago Press.

Cernea, Michael M., ed. 1985. *Putting People First: Sociological Variables in Rural Development*. London: World Bank and Oxford University Press. http://documents.worldbank.org/curated/en/161691468765016390/pdf/multi-page.pdf.

Certeau, Michel de. 1984. *The Practice of Everyday Life*. Trans. Steven Rendall. Berkeley: University of California Press.

Chambers, Robert. 1983. *Rural Development: Putting the Last First*. New York: Routledge.

Chamlee-Wright, Emily. 2007. "The Long Road Back: Signal Noise in the Post-Katrina Context." *Independent Review* 12, no. 2: 235–59.

Chamlee-Wright, Emily, and Virgile Henry Storr. 2011. "Social Capital as Collective Narratives and Post-Disaster Community Recovery." *Sociological Review* 59, no. 2: 266–82.

Ching, Erik. 2004. "Patronage and Politics under General Maximiliano Hernández Martínez, 1931–1939: The Local Roots of Military Authoritarianism in El Salvador." In Aldo Lauria-Santiago and Leigh Binford, eds, *Landscapes of Struggle: Politics, Society and Community in El Salvador*, 50–70. Pittsburgh: University of Pittsburgh Press.

– 2014. *Authoritarian El Salvador: Politics and the Origins of the Military Regimes, 1880–1940*. Notre Dame, IN: University of Notre Dame Press.

Chomsky, Noam. 1999. *The New Military Humanism: Lessons from Kosovo*. London: Pluto.

Chouliaraki, Lilie. 2013. *The Ironic Spectator: Solidarity in the Age of Post-Humanitarianism*. Cambridge, UK: Polity.

Cleaver, Francis. 2001. "Institutions, Agency and the Limitations of Participatory Approaches to Development." In Bill Cooke and Uma Kothari, eds, *Participation? The New Tyranny*, 36–55. London: Zed Books.

Coleman, James. 1988. "Social Capital in the Creation of Human Capital." *American Journal of Sociology* 94: S95-S120.

Cook, Jesselyn. 2017. "7 Years after Haiti's Earthquake, Millions Still Need Aid." *Huffington Post*, 12 January. http://www.huffingtonpost.com/entry/haiti-earthquake-anniversary_us_5875108de4b02b5f858b3f9c.

Cooke, Bill, and Uma Kothari, eds. 2001. *Participation? The New Tyranny*. London: Zed Books.

Cornwall, Andrea. 2007. "Myths to Live By? Female Solidarity and Female Autonomy Reconsidered." *Development and Change* 38, no. 1: 149–68.

– 2008. "Unpacking 'Participation': Models, Meanings and Practices." *Community Development Journal* 43, no. 3: 269–83.

Coutin, Susan. 2007. *Nations of Emigrants: Shifting Boundaries of Citizenship in El Salvador and the United States*. Ithaca, NY: Cornell University Press.

Cuny, Fred. 1983. *Disasters and Development*. Oxford: Oxford University Press.

Cupples, Julie. 2007. "Gender and Hurricane Mitch: Reconstructing Subjectivities after Disaster." *Disasters: The Journal of Disaster Studies, Policy and Management* 31, no. 2: 155–75.

Daniel, Valentine E., and John Knudsen. 1995. *Mistrusting Refugees*. Berkeley: University of California Press.

Darcy, James. 2004. "Human Rights and Humanitarian Action: A Review of the Issues." Background paper prepared for the workshop "Human Rights and Humanitarian Action," Overseas Development Institute, London.

Daugherty, Arron. 2016. "El Salvador Most Violent Country in the Western Hemisphere." *InSight Crime*, 4 January. http://www.insightcrime.org/news-briefs/el-salvador-is-most-violent-nation-in-western-hemisphere.

David, Cheal. 1988. *The Gift Economy*. London and New York: Routledge.

Davidson, Colin H., Cassidy Johnson, Gonzalo Lizarralde, Nese Dikman, and Alicia Sliwinski. 2007. "Truths and Myths about Community Participation in Post-Disaster Housing Projects." *Habitat International* 31, no. 1: 100–15.

Davis, Ian. 1981. *Shelter after Disaster*. Oxford: Oxford Polytechnic Press.

DeChaine, Daniel Robert. 2005. "Framing Humanitarian Action: Doctors Without Borders." In *Global Humanitarianism: NGOs and the Crafting of Community*, 67–104. New York: Rowan and Littlefield.

del Castillo, Graciana. 2008. *Rebuilding War-Torn States: The Challenge of Post-Conflict Economic Reconstruction*. Oxford: Oxford University Press.

Demerath, Loren, and Andrey V. Korotayev. 2015. "The Importance of Gossip across Societies: Correlations with Institutionalization." *Cross-Cultural Research* 49, no. 3: 297–314.

Dekens, Julie. 2007. *Local Knowledge for Disaster Preparedness: A Literature Review*. Kathmandu, Nepal: International Centre for Integrated Mountain Development. http://www.ndma.gov.pk/Publications/Local%20Knowledge%20for%20Disaster%20Preparedness%20a%20Literature%20Review.pdf.

Donini, Antonio, ed. 2012. *The Golden Fleece: The Manipulation and Independence of Humanitarian Action*. Sterling, VA: Kumarian.

Dowling, D.M. 2004. "Adobe Housing in El Salvador: Earthquake Performance and Seismic Improvement." In William I. Rose, Julian J. Bommer, Dina L. López, Michael J. Carr, and Jon J. Major, eds, *Natural Hazards in El Salvador*, 281–300. Boulder, CO: Geological Society of America.

Duffield, Mark, 2007. *Development, Security and Unending War: Governing the World of Peoples*. Cambridge, UK: Polity.

Durkheim, Émile. 1895. *The Rules of Sociological Method*. Reprint, New York: Free Press, 1982.

Dynes, Russell R., E.L. Quarantelli, and Gary A. Kreps. 1972. *A Perspective on Disaster Planning*. Columbus: Disaster Research Centre, Ohio State University.

Eade, Deborah, and Tony Vaux, eds. 2007. *Development and Humanitarianism: Practical Issues*. Sterling, VA: Kumarian.

Economic and Social Council of the United Nations (ECOSOC). 1997. "Coordination of the Policies and Activities of the Specialized Agencies and Other Bodies of the United Nations System." Agreed

Conclusions 1997/2. http://www.un.org/womenwatch/osagi/pdf/ECOSOCAC1997.2.PDF.

Enarson, Elaine. 1998. "Through Women's Eyes: A Gendered Research Agenda for Disaster Social Science." *Disasters* 22, no. 2: 157–73.

– 2000. *Gender and Natural Disasters*. Geneva: Recovery and Reconstruction Department.

– 2004. "International Perspectives on Gender and Disaster: Differences and Possibilities." *International Journal of Sociology and Social Policy* 24, nos 10–11: 49–93.

– 2012. *Women Confronting Disaster: From Vulnerability to Resilience.* Boulder, CO: Lynne Rienner.

Enarson, Elaine, and P.G. Dhar Chakrabarti, eds. 2009. *Women, Gender and Disaster: Global Issues and Initiatives*. London: Sage.

Enarson, Elaine, and Betty Hearn Morrow, eds. 1998. *The Gendered Terrain of Disaster: Through Women's Eyes*. Westport, CT: Greenwood.

Ensor, Marisa Olivo. 2009. "Gender Matters in Post-Disaster Reconstruction." In Marisa Olivo Ensor, ed., *The Legacy of Hurricane Mitch*, 129–55. Tucson: University of Arizona Press.

Escobar, Arturo. 1995. *Encountering Development: The Making and Unmaking of the Third World.* Princeton, NJ: Princeton University Press.

Esnard, Ann-Margaret, and Alka Sapat. 2014. *Displaced by Disaster: Recovery and Resilience in a Globalizing World.* London and New York: Routledge.

Fabian, Johannes. 1983. *Time and the Other: How Anthropology Makes Its Object*. New York: Columbia University Press.

Fallahi, A. 2007. "Lessons Learned from the Housing Reconstruction Following the Bam Earthquake in Iran." *Australian Journal of Emergency Management* 22, no. 1: 26–35.

Fanon, Franz. 1961. *The Wretched of the Earth*. Reprint, New York: Grove, 2005.

Fassin, Didier. 2009. "Les économies morales revisitées." *Annales: Histoire, Sciences Sociales* 6: 1237–66.

– 2011a. "A Contribution to the Critique of Moral Reason." *Anthropological Theory* 11, no. 4: 481–91.

– 2011b. *Humanitarian Reason: A Moral History of the Present.* Berkeley: University of California Press.

– 2011c. "Noli me tangere: The Moral Untouchability of Humanitarianism." In Erica Bornstein and Peter Redfield, eds, *Forces of Compassion:*

Humanitarianism between Ethics and Politics, 35–52. Santa Fe, NM: SAR Press.

– 2014. *Moral Anthropology: A Critical Reader*. London and New York: Routledge.

Fassin, Didier, and Mariella Pandolfi, eds. 2010. *Contemporary States of Emergency: The Politics of Military and Humanitarian Interventions*. London: Zone Books.

Faubion, James. 2011. "From the Ethical to the Thimical (and Back): Groundwork for an Anthropology of Ethics." In Michael Lambek, ed., *Ordinary Ethics: Anthropology, Language and Action*, 84–104. New York: Fordham University Press.

Feldman, Ilana. 2011. "The Humanitarian Circuit: Relief Work, Development Assistance, and CARE in Gaza, 1955–67." In Erica Bornstein and Peter Redfield, eds, *Forces of Compassion: Humanitarianism between Ethics and Politics*, 203–26. Santa Fe, NM: SAR Press.

Feldman, Ilana, and Miriam Ticktin, eds. 2010. *In the Name of Humanity: The Government of Threat and Care*. Durham, NC: Duke University Press.

Felten-Biermann, C. 2006. "Gender and Natural Disaster: Sexualized Violence and the Tsunami." *Development* 49, no. 3: 82–6.

Ferguson, James. 1994. *The Anti-Politics Machine*. Minneapolis: University of Minnesota Press.

Firth, Raymond. 1929. *Primitive Economics of the New Zealand Maori*. London: George Routledge and Sons.

Fordham, Maureen. 2000. "Working across Barriers: How Are Disaster-Impacted Communities Divided and with What Effects on Women and Children?" Paper presented at the conference "Reaching Women and Children in Disasters," Florida International University, Miami, 4–6 June.

Forsythe, David. 2013. "On Contested Concepts: Humanitarianism, Human Rights, and the Notion of Neutrality." *Journal of Human Rights* 12, no. 1: 59–68.

Forte, Maximilian, ed. 2014. *Good Intentions: Norms and Practices of Imperial Humanitarianism*. Montreal: Alert.

Foucault, Michel. 1978. *The History of Sexuality. Vol. 1, An Introduction*. New York: Vintage.

– 1990. *History of Sexuality*. Vol. 1, *An Introduction*. New York: Vintage.

– 1991. "Governmentality." In G. Burchell, C. Gordon, and P. Miller, eds, *The Foucault Effect: Studies in Governmentality*, 87–104. Chicago: University of Chicago Press.

Fowler, William, Jr. 1988. "La población nativa de El Salvador al momento de la conquista española." *Mesoamerica* 9, no. 15: 79–116.

Fraser, Heather. 2005. "Four Different Approaches to Community Participation." *Community Development Journal* 40, no. 3: 286–300.

Freire, Paolo. 1968. *Pedagogy of the Oppressed*. Reprint, New York: Continuum, 2007.

Gabiam, Nell. 2012. "When 'Humanitarianism' Becomes 'Development': The Politics of International Aid in Syria's Palestinian Refugee Camps." *American Anthropologist* 114, no. 1: 95–107.

Gambetta, D., ed. 1988. *Trust: Making and Breaking Cooperative Relations*. Oxford: Basil Blackwell.

Gamburd, Michele Ruth. 2014. *The Golden Wave: Culture and Politics after Sri Lanka's Tsunami Disaster*. Bloomington: Indiana University Press.

Garber, Megan. 2014. "'Gift' Is Not a Verb." *The Atlantic*, 12 December. http://www.theatlantic.com/entertainment/archive/2014/12/gifting-is-not-a-verb/383676.

Giraud, Claude. 2007. *De l'espoir: Sociologie d'une catégorie de l'action*. Paris: L'Harmattan.

Global Humanitarian Assistance. 2013. *Global Humanitarian Assistance Report 2013*. http://www.globalhumanitarianassistance.org/wp-content/uploads/2013/07/GHA-Report-2013.pdf.

Gluckman, Max. 1963. "Gossip and Scandal." *Current Anthropology* 4, no. 3: 307–16.

Godbout, Jacques. 1998. *The World of the Gift*. Montreal and Kingston: McGill-Queen's University Press.

Godelier, Maurice. 2002. "Some Things You Give, Some Things You Sell, but Some Things You Must Keep for Yourselves: What Mauss Did Not Say about Sacred Objects." In Edith Wyschogrod, Jean-Joseph Goux, and Eric Boynton, eds, *The Enigma of Gift and Sacrifice*, 19–37. New York: Fordham University Press.

Gould, Jeffrey, and Aldo Lauria-Santiago. 2008. *To Rise in Darkness: Revolution, Repression, and Memory in El Salvador, 1920–1932*. Durham, NC: Duke University Press.

Graeber, David. 2001. *Toward an Anthropological Theory of Value: The False Coin of Our Own Dreams*. New York: Palgrave.

Gregory, Christopher. 1982. *Gifts and Commodity*. London: Academic.

Grenier, Yvon. 1999. *The Emergence of Insurgency in El Salvador*. Pittsburgh: University of Pittsburgh Press.

Gujit, Irene, and Meera Kaul Shah, eds. 1998. *The Myth of Community: Gender Issues in Participatory Development*. London: Intermediate Technology.

Gunewardena, Nandini. 2008a. "Human Security versus Neoliberal Approaches to Disaster Recovery." In Nandini Gunewardena and Mark Schuller, eds, *Capitalizing on Catastrophe*, 3–27. New York: Altamira.

– 2008b. "Peddling Paradise, Rebuilding Serendib: The 100-Meter Refugees versus the Tourism Industry in Post-Tsunami Sri-Lanka." In Nandini Gunewardena and Mark Schuller, eds, *Capitalizing on Catastrophe*, 69–92. New York: Altamira.

Gupta, Akil, and James Ferguson. 1992. "Beyond 'Culture': Space, Identity, and the Politics of Difference." *Cultural Anthropology* 7, no. 1: 6–23.

Hardin, Russell. 2006. *Trust*. Cambridge, UK: Polity.

Harrell-Bond, Barbara. 1986. *Imposing Aid: Emergency Relief to Refugees*. Oxford: Oxford University Press.

– 2002. "Can Humanitarian Work with Refugees Be Humane?" *Human Rights Quarterly* 24, no. 1: 51–85.

Hénaff, Marcel. 2010. *The Price of Truth: Gift, Money and Philosophy*. Stanford, CA: Stanford University Press.

Herskovits, Melville. 1937. *Life in a Haitian Valley*. New York: Knopf.

Hewitt, Kenneth, ed. 1983. *Interpretations of Calamity from the Viewpoint of Human Ecology*. Boston: Allen and Unwin.

Hickey, Samuel, and Giles Mohan. 2004. *Participation: From Tyranny to Transformation? Exploring New Approaches to Participation in Development*. London: Zed Books.

Hilhorst, Dorothea, and Bram Jansen. 2010. "Humanitarian Space as Arena: A Perspective on the Everyday Politics of Aid." *Development and Change* 41, no. 6: 1117–39.

Hirshman, Albert. 1984. *Getting Ahead Collectively: Grassroots Experience in Latin America*. New York: Pergamon.

Hollenbach, Pia. 2013. "Dynamics of Multi-Local Gifts: Practices of Humanitarian Giving in Post-Tsunami Sri Lanka." *Development in Practice* 23, no. 3: 319–31.

Hopgood, Stephen, and Leslie Vinjamuri. 2012. "Faith in Markets." In Michael Barnett and Janice Stein, eds, *Sacred Aid: Faith and Humanitarianism*, 37–64. Oxford: Oxford University Press.

Hyndman, Jennifer. 2008. "Feminism, Conflict and Disasters in Post-Tsunami Sri Lanka." *Gender, Technology and Development* 12, no. 1: 101–21.

– 2011. *Dual Disasters: Humanitarian Aid after the 2004 Tsunami.* Sterling, VA: Kumarian.

Hynes, Tricia. 2003. *The Issue of 'Trust' or 'Mistrust' in Research with Refugees: Choices, Caveats and Considerations for Researchers.* Geneva: UNHCR Evaluation and Policy Analysis Unit. http://www.unhcr.org/3fcb5cee1.pdf.

International Committee of the Red Cross (ICRC). 2015. *Sustainable Development at the ICRC: Annual Report 2014.* Geneva: ICRC. https://www.icrc.org/en/document/sustainable-development-icrc-annual-report-2014.

International Federation of Red Cross and Red Crescent Societies (IFRC). 1994. *The Code of Conduct for the International Red Cross and Red Crescent Movement and NGOs in Disaster Relief.* Geneva: IFRC and ICRC. http://media.ifrc.org/ifrc/who-we-are/the-movement/code-of-conduct.

– 2004. *World Disasters Report 2004.* Geneva: IFRC. http://www.ifrc.org/Global/Publications/disasters/WDR/58000-WDR2004-LR.pdf.

Jauhola, Marjaana. 2010. "Building Back Better? Negotiating Normative Boundaries of Gender Mainstreaming and Post-Tsunami Reconstruction in Nanggroe Aceh Darussalam, Indonesia." *Review of International Studies* 36, no. 1: 29–50.

Jenkins, Pam, and Brenda Phillips. 2008. "Battered Women, Catastrophe, and the Context of Safety after Hurricane Katrina." *NWSA Journal* 20, no. 3: 49–68.

Joseph, Miranda. 2002. *Against the Romance of Community.* Minneapolis: University of Minnesota Press.

Juhn, Tricia. 1998. *Negotiating Peace in El Salvador: Civil-Military Relations and the Conspiracy to End the War.* New York: Palgrave Macmillan.

Kapferer, Jean-Noël. 1990. *Rumors: Uses, Interpretations and Images* New Brunswick, NJ: Transaction.

– 1992. "How Rumors Are Born." *Society* 29, no. 5: 53–60.

Keane, Webb. 2010. "Minds, Surfaces and Reasons in the Anthropology of Ethics." In Michael Lambek, ed. *Ordinary Ethics: Anthropology, Language and Action,* 64–83. New York: Fordham University Press.

Kennedy, David. 2004. *The Dark Side of Virtue: Reassessing International Humanitarianism.* Princeton, NJ: Princeton University Press.

Klein, Naomi. 2007. *The Shock Doctrine.* New York: Picador.

Klose, Fabian, ed. 2016. *The Emergence of Humanitarian Intervention: Ideas and Practice from the Nineteenth Century to the Present.* Cambridge, UK: Cambridge University Press.

Kluckhohn, Clyde. 1944. *Navaho Witchcraft*. Boston: Beacon.

Kopytoff, Igor. 1986. "The Cultural Biography of Things: Commoditization as Process." In Arjun Appadurai, ed., *The Social Life of Things: Commodities in Cultural Perspective*, 64–94. Cambridge, UK: Cambridge University Press.

Korf, Benedikt. 2007. "Antinomies of Generosity: Moral Geographies and Post-Tsunami Aid in Southeast Asia." *Geoforum* 38, no. 2: 366–78.

Korf, Benedikt, Shalul Hasbullah, Pia Hollenbach, and Bart Klem. 2010. "The Gift of Disaster: The Commodification of Good Intentions in Post-Tsunami Sri Lanka." *Disasters* 34, no. S1: S60–S77.

Kyamusugulwa, Patrick Milabyo. 2013. "Participatory Development and Reconstruction: A Literature Review." *Third World Quarterly* 43, no. 7: 1265–78.

Laidlaw, James. 2014. *The Subject of Virtue: An Anthropology of Ethics and Freedom*. Cambridge, UK: Cambridge University Press.

Lambek, Michael, ed. 2010. *Ordinary Ethics: Anthropology, Language and Action*. New York: Fordham University Press.

Lardé y Larín, Jorge. 1978. *El Salvador: Inundaciones, incendios, erupciones y terremotos*. Reprint, San Salvador: Consejo nacional para la Cultura y el Arte, 2002.

Large, William R., ed. 2005. *An Enduring Partnership for Development: Central America and the IDB since 1990*. Washington, DC: Inter-American Development Bank.

Latouche, Serge. 2000. *La planète uniforme*. Paris: Climats.

Lauria-Santiago, Aldo, and Leigh Binford. 2004. "Local History, Politics and the State in El Salvador." In Aldo Lauria-Santiago and Leigh Binford, eds, *Landscapes of Struggle: Politics, Society and Community in El Salvador*, 1–12. Pittsburgh: University of Pittsburgh Press.

Lavell, Allen. 1999. "The Impact of Disasters on Development Gains: Clarity or Controversy." Paper presented at the IDNDR Program Forum, Geneva, 5–9 July.

Lavell, Allen, and Andrew Maskrey. 2013. *The Future of Disaster Risk Management: Draft Synthesis Document, Meeting Notes, Background Papers and Additional Materials from a Scoping Meeting for GAR 2015*. San Jose, Costa Rica: FLACSO and UNISDR. http://www.la-red.org/public/2013/2013-08-14_UNISDR_FLACSO_GARscoping_Document_LaRed.pdf.

Lawther, Peter. 2009. "Community Involvement in Post Disaster Re-construction: Case Study of the British Red Cross Maldives

Recovery Program." *International Journal of Strategic Property Management* 13, no. 2: 153–69.

Lefebvre, Henri. 1992. *The Production of Space*. London: Blackwell.

Lévi-Strauss, Claude. 1971. *Mythologiques*. Vol. 4, *The Naked Man*. Reprint, Chicago: University of Chicago Press, 1990.

Levitt, Jeremy. 2009. *Hurricane Katrina: America's Unnatural Disaster*. Lincoln: University of Nebraska Press.

Lizarralde, Gonzalo, and Mark Massyn. 2008. "Unexpected Negative Outcomes of Community Participation in Low-Cost Housing Projects in South Africa." *Habitat International* 32, no. 1: 1–14.

Luft, Rachel. 2010. "Racialized Disaster Patriarchy: An Intersectional Model for Understanding Disaster Ten Years after Hurricane Katrina." *Feminist Formations* 28, no. 2: 1–26.

Luhmann, Niklas. 1979. *Trust and Power*. New York: John Wiley and Sons.

Macías, Ricardo Córdova. 1993. *El Salvador: Las negociaciones de paz y los retos de la postguerra*. San Salvador: Instituto de Estudios LatinoAmericanos.

Maldonado, René, Sandra Patricia Gonzáles Cerna, Luis Adalberto Aquino, Xiomara Hurtado de García, and Morena Orantes de Palacios. 2009. *International Remittances in El Salvador*. Mexico: Centre for Latin American Monetary Studies and Inter-American Development Bank.

Malinowski, Bronisław. 1922. *Argonauts of the Western Pacific*. Reprint, London: Routledge, 1978.

Malkki, Liisa. 1996. *Purity and Exile: Violence, Memory and National Cosmology among Hutu Refugees in Tanzania*. Chicago: University of Chicago Press.

– 2015. *The Need to Help: The Domestic Arts of International Humanitarianism*. Durham, NC: Duke University Press.

Marable, Manning, and Kristen Clarke, eds. 2008. *Seeking Higher Ground: The Hurricane Katrina Crisis, Race, and Public Policy Reader*. New York: Palgrave Macmillan.

Martínez, Luis Ernesto Romano. 1996. "Implicaciones sociales de los terremotos en San Salvador (1524–1919)." In Virginia García Acosta, ed., *Historia y desastres en América Latina*, vol. 1, 46–66. Puerto Limón, Costa Rica: LA RED and CIESAS. http://www.desenredando.org/public/libros/1996/hydv1/HistoriaYDesastresVol_I-1.0.0.pdf.

Maskrey, Andrew, ed. 1993. *Los desastres no son naturales*. Puerto Limón, Costa Rica: LA RED and ITDG. http://www.desastres.hn/docum/crid/Febrero2006/CD-2/pdf/spa/doc4081/doc4081-contenido.pdf.

Mathews, Martin. 2017. "Gift Giving, Reciprocity and the Creation of Trust." *Journal of Trust Research* 7, no. 1: 90–106.

Mauss, Marcel. 1925. "Essai sur le don: Forme et raison de l'échange dans les sociétés archaïques." *L'Année Sociologique*. https://monoskop.org/images/b/ba/Mauss_Marcell_Essai_sur_le_don_Forme_et_raison_de_lechange_dans_les_societes_archaiques.pdf.

– 1954. *The Gift: The Form and Reason for Exchange in Archaic Societies*. Reprint, London and New York: Norton, 2000.

McMichael, Philip. 2008. *Development and Social Change*. Thousand Oaks, CA: Pine Forge.

Mercer, Jessica, Ilan Kelman, Lorin Taranis, and Sandie Suchet-Pearson. 2010. "Framework for Integrating Indigenous and Scientific Knowledge for Disaster Risk Reduction." *Disasters* 34, no. 1: 214–39.

Merry, Sally Engle. 1984. "Rethinking Gossip and Scandal." In Daniel B. Klein, ed., *Reputation: Studies in the Voluntary Elicitation of Good Conduct*, 47–74. Ann Arbor: University of Michigan Press.

Miyazaki, Hirokazu. 2015. "Hope in the Gift – Hope in Sleep." In Sune Liisberg, Esther Oluffa Pedersen, and Anne Line Dalsgård, eds, *Anthropology and Philosophy: Dialogues on Trust and Hope*, 209–23. New York: Berghahn Books.

Mohanty, Chandra. 2003. *Feminism without Borders: Decolonizing Theory, Practicing Solidarity*. Durham, NC: Duke University Press.

Montes, Segundo. 1979. *El compadrazgo: Una estructura de poder en El Salvador*. San Salvador: UCA Editores.

Montgomery, Tommie Sue. 1995. *Revolution in El Salvador: From Civil Strife to Civil Peace*. Boulder, CO: Westview.

Montoya, Ainhoa. 2015. "The Turn of the Offended: Clientelism in the Wake of El Salvador's 2009 Elections." *Social Analysis* 59, no. 4: 101–18.

Moser, Caroline, and Annalise Moser. 2005. "Gender Mainstreaming since Beijing." *Gender and Development* 13, no. 2: 11–21.

Mosse, David. 2003. "The Making and Marketing of Participatory Development." In P. Quarles van Ufford and A.K. Giri, eds, *A Moral Critique of Development: In Search of Global Responsibilities*, 43–75. London and New York: Routledge.

Oliver-Smith, Anthony. 1995. "Peru's Five Hundred Year Earthquake: Vulnerability to Hazard in Historical Context." In Ann Varley, ed., *Disasters, Development and Environment*, 31–48. London: John Wiley and Sons.

– 2004. "Theorizing Vulnerability in a Globalized World: A Political Ecology Perspective." In Greg Bankoff, Georg Frerks, and Dorothea

Hillhorst, eds, *Mapping Vulnerability: Disasters, Development, and People*, 10–24. London and Sterling, VA: Earthscan.

Oliver-Smith, Anthony, and Suzanna Hoffman, eds. 1999. *The Angry Earth: Disaster in Anthropological Perspective*. New York: Routledge.

– 2001. *Catastrophe and Culture: The Anthropology of Disaster*. Santa Fe, NM: SAR Press.

Olivius, Elisabeth. 2013. "(Un)Governable Subjects: The Limits of Refugee Participation in the Promotion of Gender Equality in Humanitarian Aid." *Journal of Refugee Studies* 27, no. 1: 42–61.

Ong, Aihwa, and Stephen J. Collier, eds. 2004. *Global Assemblages: Technologies, Politics and Ethics as Anthropological Problems*. Oxford: Wiley-Blackwell.

Orbinski, James. 2009. *An Imperfect Offering: Humanitarian Action for the 21st Century*. New York: Bloomsbury.

Paige, Jeffery. 1993. "Coffee and Power in El Salvador." *Latin American Research Review* 28, no. 3: 7–40.

– 1998. *Coffee and Power: Revolution and the Rise of Democracy in Central America*. Cambridge, MA: Harvard University Press.

Paine, Robert. 1967. "What Is Gossip About? An Alternative Hypothesis." *Man* 2, no. 2: 278–85.

Palomera, Jaime, and Theodora Vetta. 2016. "Moral Economy: Rethinking a Radical Concept." *Anthropological Theory* 16, no. 4: 413–32.

Pandolfi, Mariella. 2003. "Contract of Mutual (In)Difference: Government and the Humanitarian Apparatus in Contemporary Albania and Kosovo." *Indiana Journal of Global Legal Studies* 10, no. 1: 369–81.

Parry, Jonathan, and Maurice Bloch, eds. 1989. *Money and the Morality of Exchange*. Cambridge, UK: Cambridge University Press.

Peñate, Oscar, ed. 1999. *El Salvador: Sociología General*. San Salvador: Editorial Nuevo Enfoque.

Petryna, Adriana. 2002. *Life Exposed: Biological Citizens after Chernobyl*. Princeton, NJ: Princeton University Press.

Phillips, Brenda D., and Maureen Fordham. 2010. "Introduction." In Brenda D. Phillips, Deborah S.K. Thomas, Alice Fothergill, and Lynn Blinn-Pike, eds, *Social Vulnerability to Disasters*, 1–26. Boca Raton, FL: CRC Press.

Phillips, Brenda D., Deborah S.K. Thomas, Alice Fothergill, and Lynn Blinn-Pike, eds. 2010. *Social Vulnerability to Disasters*. Boca Raton, FL: CRC Press.

Poerksen, Uwe. 1995. *Plastic Words: The Tyranny of Modular Language*. University Park: Pennsylvania State University Press.

Polanyi, Karl. 1944. *The Great Transformation*. Boston: Beacon.

Programa de la Naciones Unidas para el Desarollo (PNUD). 2001. *Informe sobre desarollo humano El Salvador 2001*. San Salvador: PNUD.

– 2013. *Informe sobre desarollo humano El Salvador 2013*. San Salvador: PNUD.

Putnam, Robert D. 1993. "The Prosperous Community." *American Prospect* 4, no. 13. http://prospect.org/article/prosperous-community-social-capital-and-public-life.

– 2000. *Bowling Alone: The Collapse and Revival of American Community*. New York: Simon and Schuster.

Raffnsøe, Sverre. 2015. "Empowering Trust in the New." In Sune Liisberg, Esther Oluffa Pedersen, and Anne Line Dalsgård, eds, *Anthropology and Philosophy: Dialogues on Trust and Hope*, 187–208. New York: Berghahn Books.

Razack, Sherene. 2007. "Stealing the Pain of Others: Reflections on Canadian Humanitarian Responses." *Review of Education, Pedagogy and Cultural Studies* 29, no. 4: 375–94.

Redfield, Peter. 2011. "The Impossible Problem of Neutrality." In Erica Bornstein and Peter Redfield, eds, *Forces of Compassion: Humanitarianism between Ethics and Politics*, 53–70. Santa Fe, NM: SAR Press.

– 2013. *Life in Crisis: The Ethical Journey of Doctors Without Borders*. Berkeley: University of California Press.

Rieff, David. 2002. *A Bed for the Night: Humanitarianism in Crisis*. New York: Simon and Schuster.

Robbins, Joel. 2007. "Between Reproduction and Freedom: Morality, Value, and Radical Cultural Change." *Ethnos* 72, no. 3: 293–314.

– 2009. "Rethinking Gifts and Commodities: Reciprocity, Recognition and the Morality of Exchange." In Katherine E. Browne and B. Lynne Milgram, eds, *Economics and Morality: Anthropological Approaches*, 43–58. New York: Altamira.

– 2013a. "Beyond the Suffering Subject: Toward an Anthropology of the Good." *Journal of the Royal Anthropological Institute* 19, no. 3: 447–62.

– 2013b. "Monism, Pluralism, and the Structure of Value Relations: A Dumontian Contribution to the Contemporary Study of Value." *HAU: Journal of Ethnographic Theory* 3, no. 1: 99–115.

Romano, Luis, and Carlos Acevedo. 2001. *Economía, desastre y desarrollo sostenible*. San Salvador: FLACSO.

Rorty, Richard. 1993. "Human Rights, Rationality and Sentimentality." In Stephen Shute and Susan Hurley, eds, *On Human Rights: The Oxford Amnesty Lectures 1993*, 111–34. New York: Basic Books.

Rose, William I., Julian J. Bommer, Dina L. López, Michael J. Carr, and Jon J. Major, eds. 2004. *Natural Hazards in El Salvador*. Boulder, CO: Geological Society of America.

Rose, Niklas. 1996. "'The Death of the Social'? Re-figuring the Territory of Government." *Economy and Society* 25, no. 3: 327–56.

Rufin, Jean-Christophe. 1986. *Le piège humanitaire*. Paris: Jean-Claude Lattès.

Sachs, Wolfgang. 1992. *The Development Dictionary: A Guide to Knowledge and Power*. London: Zed Books.

Sahlins, Marshall. 1974. *Stone Age Economics*. New York: Routledge.

Samuels, Annemarie. 2013. "Aceh Thanks the World: The Possibilities of the Gift in a Post-Disaster Society." *Anthropology Today* 29, no. 4: 8–11.

Scheper-Hughes, Nancy. 2000. "The Global Traffic of Human Organs." *Current Anthropology* 41, no. 2: 191–224.

Schiocchet, Leonardo. 2014. "Suspicion and the Economy of Trust among Palestinian Refugees in Lebanon." *Cambridge Anthropology* 32, no. 2: 112–27.

Schuller, Mark. 2015. *Humanitarian Aftershocks in Haiti*. New Brunswick, NJ: Rutgers University Press.

Scott, James C. 1976. *The Moral Economy of the Peasant: Rebellion and Subsistence in South East Asia*. New Haven, CT: Yale University Press.

Sen, Armatya, and Martha Nussbaum. 1993. *The Quality of Life*. Oxford: Oxford University Press.

Sen, Gita. 2005. "Neolibs, Neocons and Gender Justice: Lessons from Global Negotiations." Working paper. United Nations Research Institute for Social Development, Geneva. https://www.econstor.eu/bitstream/10419/148800/1/862966787.pdf.

Serageldin, Ismail, and Christiaan Grootae. 2000. "Defining Social Capital: An Integrating View." In Partha Dasgupta and Ismail Serageldin, eds, *Social Capital: A Multifacted Perspective*, 40–58. Washington, DC: World Bank. http://documents.worldbank.org/curated/en/663341468174869302/pdf/multi-page.pdf.

Shaw, Rajib, Anshu Sharma, and Yukiko Takeuchi, eds. 2009. *Indigenous Knowledge and Disaster Risk Reduction: From Practice to Policy*. New York: Nova Science.

Sheets, Payson. 1999. "The Effect of Explosive Volcanism on Ancient Egalitarian, Ranked and Stratified Societies in Middle America." In

Anthony Oliver-Smith and Suzanna Hoffman, eds, *The Angry Earth: Disaster in Anthropological Perspective*, 37–58. New York: Routledge.

Shipton, Parker. 2007. *The Nature of Entrustment: Intimacy, Exchange and the Sacred in Africa*. New Haven, CT: Yale University Press.

Shore, Chris, and Susan Wright, eds. 1997. *The Anthropology of Policy: Critical Perspectives on Governance and Power*. New York: Routledge.

Silber, Irina Carlota. 2011. *Everyday Revolutionaries: Gender, Violence and Disillusionment in Postwar El Salvador*. Piscataway, NJ: Rutgers University Press.

Silk, J. 2004. "Caring at a Distance: Gift Theory, Aid Chains and Social Movements." *Social and Cultural Geography* 5, no. 2: 229–51.

Siméant, Johanna. 2015. "Three Bodies of Moral Economy: The Diffusion of a Concept." *Journal of Global Ethics* 11, no. 2: 147–62.

Simmel, Georg. 1950. *The Sociology of Georg Simmel*. New York: Free Press.

Singer, Peter. 2009. *The Life You Can Save*. New York: Random House.

Slim, Hugo. 1997. "Relief Agencies and Moral Standing in War: Principles of Humanity, Impartiality, Neutrality and Solidarity." *Development in Practice* 7, no. 4: 342–52.

– 2015. *Humanitarian Ethics: A Guide to the Morality of Aid in War and Disasters*. Oxford: Oxford University Press.

Sliwinski, Alicia. 2010. "The Politics of Participation: Involving Communities in Post-Disaster Reconstruction." In Gonzalo Lizarralde, Cassidy Johnson, and Colin Davidson, eds, *Rebuilding after Disasters: From Emergency to Sustainability*, 177–92. Abingdon, UK: Spon.

– 2016. "The Value of Promising Spaces: Hope and Everyday Utopia in a Salvadoran Town." *History and Anthropology* 27, no. 4: 430–46.

Sphere Project. 1997. *Humanitarian Charter*. http://www.spherehandbook.org/en/the-humanitarian-charter.

– 2011. *The Sphere Handbook: Humanitarian Charter and Minimum Standards in Humanitarian Response*. http://www.spherehandbook.org.

Stewart, Pamela J., and Andrew Strathern. 2004. *Witchcraft, Sorcery, Rumors and Gossip*. Cambridge, UK: Cambridge University Press.

Stirrat, Jock. 2006. "Competitive Humanitarianism: Relief and the Tsunami in Sri Lanka." *Anthropology Today* 22, no. 5: 11–16.

Stirrat, R.L., and Heiko Henkel. 1997. "The Development Gift: The Problem of Reciprocity in the NGO World." *Annals of the American Academy of Political and Social Science* 554: 66–80.

Stonich, Susan. 2008. "International Tourism and Disaster Capitalism." In Nandidi Gunewardena and Mark Schuller, eds, *Capitalizing on*

Catastrophe: Neoliberal Strategies in Disaster Reconstruction, 47–68. New York: Altamira.

Syed, Jawad. 2010. "Reconstructing Gender Empowerment." *Women's Studies International Forum* 33, no. 3: 283–94.

Tanner, Thomas, and Leo Horn-Phathanothai. 2014. *Climate Change and Development*. London and New York: Routledge.

Terry, Fiona. 2002. *Condemned to Repeat? The Paradoxes of Humanitarian Action*. Ithaca, NY: Cornell University Press.

– 2011. "The International Committee of the Red Cross in Afghanistan: Reasserting the Neutrality of Humanitarian Action." *International Review of the Red Cross* 93, no. 881: 173–88.

Testart, Alain. 2013. "What Is a Gift?" Trans. Susan Emanuel and Lorraine Perlman. *HAU: Journal of Ethnographic Theory* 3, no. 1: 249–61.

Thompson, E.P. 1993. "The Moral Economy Reviewed." In *Customs in Common: Studies in Traditional Popular Culture*, 259–351. New York: New Press.

Ticktin, Miriam. 2014. "Transnational Humanitarianism." *Annual Review of Anthropology* 43: 273–89.

Tönnies, Ferdinand. 1887. *Community and Society*. Trans. and ed. Charles P. Loomis. Mineola, NY: Dover, 2011.

United Nations Children's Fund (UNICEF). 2005. *The State of the World's Children: Childhood under Threat*. New York: UNICEF.

United Nations Development Programme (UNDP). 2014. *Human Development Report 2014: Sustaining Human Progress: Reducing Vulnerabilities and Building Resilience*. Geneva: UNDP.

United Nations International Strategy for Disaster Reduction (UNISDR). n.d. "Terminology." http://www.unisdr.org/we/inform/terminology.

US Department of State. 2012. *El Salvador 2012 International Religious Freedom Report*. Washington, DC: Bureau of Democracy, Human Rights and Labour, US Department of State. http://www.state.gov/documents/organization/208690.pdf.

Vargas, Oscar. 2001. *Diagnostico de situación del municipio de Armenia después de los terremotos de 2001*. San Salvador: Fundación Dr Guillermo Manuel Ungo (FUNDAUNGO).

Vasquez Lezama, Paula. 2010. "Compassionate Militarization: The Management of a Natural Disaster in Venezuela." In Didier Fassin and Mariella Pandolfi, eds, *Contemporary States of Emergency: The Politics of Military and Humanitarian Interventions*, 197–216. London: Zone Books.

Walker, Peter, and Susan Purdin. 2004. "Birthing Sphere." *Disasters* 28, no. 2: 100–11.

Weiss, Thomas. 2012. *Humanitarian Intervention*. Cambridge, UK: Polity.

– 2013. *Humanitarian Business*. Cambridge, UK: Polity.

Werbin, Kenneth. 2017. *The List Serves: Population Control and Power*. Amsterdam: Institute of Network Cultures.

White, Alistair. 1973. *El Salvador*. Reprint, San Salvador: UCA Editores, 1996.

White, Gilbert. 1974. *Natural Hazards: Local, National, Global*. Oxford: Oxford University Press.

Wilches-Chaux, Gustavo. 1993. "La vulnerabilidad global." In Andrew Maskrey, ed., *Los desastres no son naturales*, 9–49. Puerto Limón, Costa Rica: LA RED and ITDG. http://www.la-red.org/public/libros/1993/ldnsn/html/cap2.htm.

Williams, Raymond. 1985. *Keywords*. Oxford: Oxford University Press.

Wisner, Ben. 2001. "Risk and the Neoliberal State: Why Post-Mitch Lessons Didn't Reduce El Salvador's Earthquake Losses." *Disasters* 25, no. 3: 251–68.

Wisner, Ben, Phil O'Keefe, and Ken Westgate. 1977. "Global Systems and Local Disasters: The Untapped Power of Peoples' Science." *Disasters* 1, no. 1: 47–57.

Wolf, Eric. 1957. "Closed Corporate Peasant Communities in Mesoamerica and Central Java." *Southwestern Journal of Anthropology* 13, no. 1: 1–18.

World Bank. 2011. *Migration and Remittances Factbook 2011*. 2nd ed. Washington, DC: World Bank. http://siteresources.worldbank.org/INTLAC/Resources/Factbook2011-Ebook.pdf.

– 2013. *Localizing Development: Does Participation Work?* Washington, DC: World Bank. https://openknowledge.worldbank.org/bitstream/handle/10986/11859/9780821382561.pdf?sequence=1&isAllowed=y.

World Food Programme (WFP). 2001. *Assistance to Earthquake Victims: EMOP 10022.0 El Salvador 2001*. San Salvador: World Food Programme.

Zigon, Jerrett. 2008. *Morality: An Anthropological Perspective*. London: Berg.

– 2009. "Within a Range of Possibilities: Morality and Ethics in Social Life." *Ethnos* 74, no. 2: 251–76.

– 2014. "Attunement and Fidelity: Two Ontological Conditions for Morally Being-in-the-World." *Ethos* 24, no. 1: 16–30.

Index